One Student at a Time

Leading the Global Education Movement

One Student at a Time

Leading the Global Education Movement

Fernando M. Reimers

With contributions from

Nour Abu Ragheb . Joel Adriance . Wilson Aiwuyor .
Shatha AlHashmi . Zohal Atif . Suman Barua .
Sergio Cárdenas Denham . Mariali Cardenas Casanueva .
Manuel Cardoso . Mariam Chughtai . Gilda Colin . Peter Cooper .
Mariana Clucellas . Bettina Dembek . David Edwards . Nelly ElZayat .
Erin Esparza . Armando Estrada Zubía . Ana Florez . Soujanya Ganig
Luis E. Garcia de Brigard . Eugenia Garduño .
Emanuel Garza Fishburn . Juliana Guaqueta Ospina .
Ghazal S. Gulati . Anne Elizabeth Hand . Ming Jin . Kevin Kalra .
Zahra Kassam . Myra M. Khan . Susan Kippels . José La Rosa .
Annika Lawrence . Sandra Licón . Michael Lisman .
Mingyan "Ophelia" Ma . Janhvi Maheshwari-Kanoria . Tara Mahtafar .
Luis Felipe Martínez-Gómez . Nicholas Moffa .
Jomphong Mongkhonvanit . Eliana Carvalho Mukherjee .
Lily Neyestani-Hailu . Maria Elena Ortega-Hesles .
Ana Gabriela Pessoa . Teresa Cozetti Pontual Pereira . Kevin Roberts .
Haneen Sakakini . Shajia Sarfraz . Colleen Silva-Hayden .
Juan de Dios Simón . Daniel Tapia-Quintana . Maya Thiagarajan .
Ernesto Treviño . Leanne Trujillo . Pam Vachatimanont .
Ethan Van Drunen . Razia Velji . Jamie Vinson .
Austin Volz . Elyse Katherine Watkins

ISBN-10: 1973827972
ISBN-13: 978-1973827979

Library of Congress Control Number: 2017911578
CreateSpace Independent Publishing Platform
North Charleston, South Carolina

"Whether you opened this book looking for practical guidance on how to address some of the most critical issues in education or in search of powerful and inspiring tales of impact, you're in luck. The stories of wisdom, passion, and determination that Dr. Reimers has assembled here in this volume make me both grateful for the work Harvard Graduate School of Education alumni are doing and hopeful for the world they are building—one student at a time."

James E. Ryan, Dean of the Faculty and Charles William Eliot Professor, Harvard Graduate School of Education.

"The essays in this book challenge us to re-think leadership in a global society characterized by fluidity, increased insecurity and inequality. At a time when authoritarian, nativist, exclusivist, and arrogant leaders emerge by exploiting fear, misogyny and xenophobia, this book emphasizes the need for trust and cooperation amongst countries and individuals. Cooperation without which humanity will not be able to materialize the goal of sustainable societies. It highlights the case for cultivating a generation of global citizens who know how to include rather than exclude, respect rather than reject, listen rather than pontificate. Fernando Reimers and his colleagues show us how we can preserve, sustain, and deepen the values of democracy, liberalism, and human rights through a global education movement...one that encourages citizens and leaders to challenge taboos, remain curious enough to learn, and demonstrate strength through humility. We CAN deny the trappings — the hubris — of arbitrary power; this passionate collection proves it. A testament to the great human potential and the possibilities of our times, these are inspiring voices that provoke us to remain optimistic!"

George Papandreou, former Prime Minister and former Minister of Education of Greece.

"This is a highly readable and useful study of the challenges and opportunities that those advancing education for all around the globe face. A must read for all education leaders interested in freedom and justice.

Arne Duncan, Former US Secretary of Education.

"The book is an excellent example of how to assess the impact of an educational program through the work of its graduates, a valuable reading for those who work in higher education. The book presents an ambitious graduate program that aims to influence the improvement of educational systems around the world cultivating the leadership capacities of the students. The description of the challenges that these leaders take on as they transform education around the world as teachers, project leaders and policy makers, provides the reader with an engaging and informative outlook into the program's effectiveness."

Cecilia Maria Velez White, President, Universidad de Bogota Jorge Tadeo Lozano and former Minister of Education of Colombia.

"Preparing today's young people for the challenges of the 21st century-rapid change, unpredictability, globalization, new technologies, and political conflict-will require very different forms of education than those that marked the 19th and the 20th centuries. There is an enormous need throughout the world for a new generation of educational innovators with the values, passion, professional training, and experience to lead this process of global and national change, while still realizing it must take root one student at a time. In this important book we hear from many such young entrepreneurs about their own learnings in leading educational change."

Dr. Charles MacCormack, President Emeritus, Save the Children.

"This work both inspires and challenges those of us working in education to reevaluate our role as global, political change-makers. It situates the global roles of education within context of the profound work of Professor Fernando Reimers and the work his students are doing all over the world in a powerfully vulnerable and reflective way. It is an incredible collection of leadership and policy lessons offered through the biographies of some incredible leaders in the field who are having a profound impact across the globe."

Earl Martin Phalen, Founder and CEO of the George and Veronica Phalen Leadership Academies.

"The collective wisdom of this book is a great inspiration and a rich source of advice for every leader, not only in education. It gives us practical insights into the key leadership competences needed in a world of continuous learning and adaptation. This vibrant global education network is the best place to stand and a great lever to move the world!"

Dr. Antonella Mei-Pochtler, Senior Partner & Managing Director, The Boston Consulting Group.

"Fernando Reimers takes the title for this book from his wife, who taught him that "the deepest way to educate is one student at a time." As the long-serving director of the Harvard's Graduate School of Education's master's program in International Education Policy, Reimers has been one of the leaders of a global education movement, which his students are taking forward, one educator at a time. In this volume, sixty former students share hard-fought, universal lessons for educators across the globe. One of my favorites is that we must balance patience with setbacks and at the same time balance process with impatience for results. Reimers' larger lesson concerns the role of higher education to prepare global citizens as defenders of democracy. This is Reimers' most personal volume to date as he encourages us all to discover our common humanity through this work."

Kathleen McCartney, President of Smith College.

"For any who doubt that international education can be transformative or worth the investment, be prepared to be converted. And for all of us who need new talking points, read this book."

Allan Goodman, President, Institute for International Education.

"Universalizing education and making it a force for peace and sustainability calls upon the knowledge of a constellation of leaders – in schools, universities, civil society, the private sector, governments and international organizations. This book provides fascinating insight into the trajectories of graduates from Harvard's Graduate School of Education International Education Policy Program. Each one of them is driven by a passionate commitment to leave no one behind and advance educational opportunities for all children and youth across the world. In their own voice, they reflect on the challenges of innovation and reform, of pushing the boundaries of teaching and learning in their societies. They belong to a global education movement that must be supported to fulfill a fundamental human right and the most powerful development catalyst at a time of complex change and accelerating globalization, one that more than ever requires the nurturing of global citizens."

Irina Bokova, Director-General of UNESCO.

"This vivid collection of experiences from the educational frontline is a vital reminder of the compelling leadership contribution of those who power and shape the impact of education in communities across the world. Read it and catch an urgent vision of how we might build a more connected and progressive global educational system with incalculable benefit for society."

Dame Julia Cleverdon Co- Founder of Step up To Serve in the UK.

"*One student at a time* epitomizes the calling of true educators who see the urgency of getting education to those who need it most. Responses to the multifarious contexts of education addressed in this book are highly insightful and pragmatic - whether it be schooling, organizational transformation, program development, policy or governance. The anecdotes and cases make for excellent reading — coming from a confluence of brilliant minds and inspired hearts catalyzed by an outstanding professor who has impacted many through his amazing care and scholarship."

TAN Oon Seng, Professor and Director, National Institute of Education, Singapore.

"This book is a testament to the power of intentional efforts to cultivate educational leadership — leadership with the values, mindsets, skills, and understandings to effect transformation, leadership that is both locally rooted and globally informed. Read it to gain insight into global education but even more so into what it will take to develop a growing cadre of people who will reshape education across the world so that today's children can shape a better future for themselves and all of us."

Wendy Kopp, CEO & Co-founder, Teach For All.

"Education gives people the freedom to live the life of their choosing. But the complex machinery that has to be put in place in each country to give all people the education they deserve does not develop spontaneously. It is not a natural consequence of development. It is the cause of development. And in some countries we see that machinery developing, and in others we don't. Why? Simple. Some societies decide to do it, and others don't. And when that happens, it is a process shaped by people. They are the designers, engineers, architects and operators of that machinery. Fernando Reimers shares with us the journeys and travails of such designers, architects engineers and operators. Those are the leaders that shape education of the world. Learning about the journeys of those leaders is critical for two reasons. First, because we need examples and inspiration about how to better shape educational systems. And second because we need, urgently, more people like them."

Jaime Saavedra Chanduvi, Education Sector Manager, World Bank and former Minister of Education of Peru.

"Imagine asking educational leaders from countries all over the world to describe what their goals are, how much impact do they think they have had, what challenges have they faced, and what lessons have they drawn from these experiences. Some lead schools, others lead government or international institutions, some have created their own non-profit or for-profit organizations. All have in common that they are graduates of the Harvard Graduate School of Education where they studied from the professor who invited them to write the chapters for this shared edited book. Their insights, their thoughtfulness, their extreme challenges in some cases, their successes, the sweep of their vision, and the tenderness of the humility evident in many, makes this a gripping book, a motivator of action, and a guide toward a cosmopolitan educational transformation everywhere."

Jorge I. Domínguez. Professor of Government, Harvard University.

"Moved by a speech by St. Theresa, the patron saint of Kolkata's poor, a high school student from the USA asked what he could do to assist. She responded "find your own Kolkata." This volume of essays by education leaders demonstrates the infinite variety of education Kolkatas in the global north and south. It is a must read for anyone interested to help children and youth, especially those without opportunity, get the education and training they need to succeed in the 21st century. Professor Reimers, challenges the reader to reflect seriously on how education can foster democracy and a more peaceful world."

Dzingai Mutumbuka, former minister of education of Zimbabwe, former ADEA Chair and former education sector manager at the World Bank.

"An invaluable source of insights into the practical challenges of improving education programs and systems across a range of cultural and political contexts, this book offers intimate testimonies to how cooperative education can dramatically change a person's life and in so doing, better the lives of countless others. It stands as a unique and thrilling proof that persons working together can accomplish much more than individuals alone."

Noel McGinn, Professor Emeritus, Harvard Graduate School of Education.

To my sons Tomas and Pablo,

Who inspire me as they live lives of purpose

Contents

Acknowledgements

This book examines how graduates of the International Education Policy Program at the Harvard Graduate School of Education advance educational opportunity around the world, and how they overcome the challenges of leading change in educational institutions. I owe much gratitude first to those who made and make this program possible, and then to those who helped me write the book itself.

The International Education Policy Program at Harvard exists, first and foremost, because a group of dedicated and talented professionals each year trust us to help them develop the necessary skills to advance the expansion of relevant educational opportunities to all of the world's children and youth. I thank them most sincerely for their commitment to this work and for trusting us to educate them.

My colleagues at the Harvard Graduate School of Education who teach these students, those who have taught in the program in the past, and my colleagues in the administration of the school who provide all the necessary support to make this program possible, have my deepest gratitude. I am also indebted to my colleagues in the field of international education who welcome these students as their junior colleagues upon graduation. Many of these colleagues contribute to the education of these students in numerous ways, as mentors, attending student conferences, providing internships, or simply offering guidance on ways to strengthen the program. Supporting the students who graduate from the International Education Policy Program takes this large community bound together in our shared understanding that education is a human right, and that achieving this right requires preparing professionals who work every day to educate all children well.

It is the legacy of those who preceded us in advancing international education at Harvard that makes the work we do possible and I count my blessings in being able to build on that legacy.

There are so many individuals I would have to mention in expressing my gratitude for their support, that it is best that I say simply that I know full well that it takes a village to educate these leaders of global education, and that I thank everyone at the Harvard Graduate School of Education, and our friends and colleagues around the University and beyond, for their contributions to this shared labor of love.

I am also deeply appreciative to those colleagues who helped with the study presented in this book and with the writing. First, I thank the graduates of the International Education Policy Program who took the time to respond to the survey I administered about their work, impact and challenges, and to those among them who, in addition, wrote the essays presented in the book. I am also grateful to Benjamin Alford and to Ana Teresa del Toro for their valuable research assistance analyzing the content of the essays, to Kristin Foster for her excellent help editing and preparing the manuscript for publication and to Paulo Costa for the design of the book cover. I greatly appreciate the generosity of those colleagues who took the time to read the manuscript and write endorsements.

At home I thank my sons Tomas and Pablo who, since its inception, embraced the International Education Policy Program as it grew into my life. Their respect for my students, and for their work, their curiosity and advice about issues big and small pertaining to leading the program provided valuable sustenance over the last twenty years. I will always be grateful for their help, as they grew up and until they went to college, on a wide range of subjects, from assisting during the many receptions we hosted for students and colleagues at home, to discussing with me the feedback my students provided in course evaluations. I treasure memories of many insights that I drew from conversations with each of them. I remember Tomas, who just graduated from college, one early morning while he was in the second grade walking into my home office curious about what I was writing, a paper examining the literacy experiences of low income students in school based on a student survey. As I explained the study to him he said with brilliant simplicity 'and if some of these students are not very good readers, how do you know how they understood the questions in your questionnaire?'. More recently, as I was writing this book, Pablo, now a rising junior in college, offered insightful ideas on whether the impact of graduates who taught directly was comparable to the impact of those influencing policy. I have been incredibly fortunate that both of them attended Harvard College, providing me with the joy of their frequent company over the last few years. I have enjoyed that they have both been at home the last few weeks of writing this book, as Tomas is packing to move to New York City, and appreciated the humor in the family joke of counting how many minutes in a conversation until dad brings up this book. Just as students educate their teachers, children educate their parents and I have been immensely fortunate to have both wonderful and generous students as well as two sons who have made me a better person, teacher and father, and given me much purpose and happiness.

My biggest gratitude, as always, is to my wife and colleague, Eleonora Villegas-Reimers. She is the person who helped me understand, when we first met — and over the thirty-four years I have been in love with her — that we have the greatest impact in education one student at a time. She is also the most helpful supporter of projects big and small in which I have embarked myself and both of us, including this one. For her patience during the long days when I would get up at 4.30am in the morning and stay up late working on this book, and speak about little else until the book was finished, I am most grateful. I don't know how to thank her for her love these past 34 years other than to hope for a long life together.

Fernando Reimers
Cambridge, Massachusetts July 2017

Leading the expansion of relevant educational opportunities around the world

by Fernando M. Reimers

Introduction

I have long thought that education, the intentional creation of opportunities for others to gain knowledge and skills that expand their freedoms, is a wonderful privilege and a great invention. While I have learned to provide a rational justification for the importance of education, I know that I feel its importance in my heart. This may be because I realized early in life how lucky I was to be able to study, or because I was fortunate to have parents who valued learning and supported my education. Maybe it was because I had good teachers. Or it could be because at some point in my schooling I realized my parents were sacrificing so I could have more education than they themselves had.

I was 12 years old when I began to understand how transformative education could be. My mother, who was a very active participant of the parent teacher association of the school I attended in Caracas, persuaded the principal that he should invest in a few typewriters, so that the students in the school would learn some useful skills to help them get jobs. My mother was a secretary, so it made sense to her that learning to type would give us some advantages in the job market. The school I attended ended in the ninth grade; it did not offer the full twelve grades of instruction required to finish high school. I suppose many of the students in my school, and in my neighborhood, ended their studies in the ninth grade, at which point they got a job. Many of us understood it was a privilege to complete nine grades of schooling, as there were plenty of children our ages already working, some helping in the local businesses which flanked the streets in my neighborhood. Others packed groceries in the local markets, carrying bags for customers to receive tips. Still others, probably not living in the neighborhood, shined shoes or sold newspapers on the street. So, at the age of 12, I considered myself lucky to be in school.

I did not feel so lucky when my mother signed me up to join typing lessons alongside a group of nine girls in an afterschool class. As the instigator of the idea of offering such lessons, my mother may have thought her own son would have to be in the first group of students to learn these valuable skills. Needless to say, I did not see eye to eye with my mother on the value of spending my afterschool time in that way. I found the exercise of learning to type without looking at the keyboard boring. Being the only boy among nine girls in a typing class did not exactly conform to the gendered norms that ruled our pre-adolescent lives. But my mother was a force to be reckoned with. She had worked hard to instill in us the notion that we should live according to our conscience and not by social expectations and I knew that it would be futile to bring up the views of my peers. Also, it was not as if I had much choice over the matter, as twelve year olds in Venezuela in those days typically followed their parents' designs for them without quibble.

So over several months, which felt like an eternity, I spent an hour a couple of afternoons a week with the nine girls in the small cafeteria of the school, where we laid our typewriters on a long table, sat in long benches on both sides, and typed away page after page "A," "S," "D," "F," with the left hand, and then "N," "L," "K," "J," with the right, each letter with a different finger. And then we moved to type the keys on the upper row on the keyboard, and then the lower row. We had to type without looking at the keyboard until, as a result of repeated and monotonous practice, those keys had become to our brains an extension of our fingers, their location known the way we know how to keep our balance on a bike. Then we were tested for speed and taught to type fast. Progressively, it felt as if our eyes could see the typebars print the letters on a blank sheet of paper on direct command by our thoughts.

My mother had personally negotiated with the vendor the purchase of these typewriters on behalf of the school, persuading the store to provide the school with a significant discount over the retail price. For my pains, enduring the sarcastic questions of my classmates about whether I was looking forward to becoming a secretary, my Christmas present that year was… a typewriter. An Olivetti Lettera portable manual typewriter, with a shiny plastic gray frame in its own suitcase. It was identical to those ten typewriters on which I had learned to type, which we took out of their cases two afternoons a week, to practice for an hour until we had memorized the location of each key. My mother explained she had been able to purchase it at the same discount that the vendor had extended to the school for the ten typewriters. Given that my Christmas gift was normally a book – _one_ book – I understood immediately how vested my mother was in my typing skills as I could figure out that the cost of this typewriter was significantly greater than the cost of a book. So I began then to type and, in a way, I have not stopped since. Learning that skill shaped the course of the rest of my life in ways I could not have foreseen then.

I first typed letters to my grandparents and my cousins who lived in Spain, from where my parents had immigrated to Venezuela. I wrote several letters a week to my relatives and became a regular in the local post office. Since it took a couple of weeks for the letters to travel from Venezuela to Spain, and the same amount of time for the reply letters to return, I often had several letters "out" and received letters in reply not to the last letter, but to ones written a few letters back. I kept a log of the content of my letters to my various correspondents, the most consistent of which were my grandfather and one cousin, and asked them to reference the date of my correspondence in their reply, so I could know which of my several letters they were referencing.

I did enjoy corresponding with my family, especially because we did not own a telephone (international phone call costs would have been prohibitively expensive anyway) and I became the carrier of news from the family abroad to my parents and younger brother, and the carrier of home news to my relatives. However, as a means of communication, the long delay in the feedback loop made correspondence with Spain less than satisfying. I explored new genres unsuccessfully. I attempted to write a children's story but found no audience for it at home or school. I tried typing poetry, but found penmanship more suitable for this. In these explorations one day, I wrote a short essay and asked my teacher if she could post it on the bulletin board in the classroom, so that my classmates could read it. Since this was a very small school, the principal visited each classroom often. He remarked on my first essay, and a week later on my second essay. The principal then asked me whether I would want to publish a newspaper. He took me to a small room where he kept a mimeograph. He explained to me how to type in the stencils, and gave me ten stencils. For the entire school year, every week, I met him for fifteen minutes as he ran fifty copies of my newspaper, which I would then sell so we could pay for the cost of the stencils and the ink. I learned valuable things in these fifteen minutes of attention from my principal. He suggested I might increase demand for the newspaper if I had other students write in it too, so I became an editor as well as a scribe for those classmates interested in writing a story. This may have also propped up demand for the typing classes.

These conversations with the principal opened doors I could not have imagined. He invited me to enter into a national competition organized by the Ministry of Education on the occasion of the 500th anniversary of the birth of Nicolas Copernicus. The terms of the competition were to explain the significance of his contributions to Astronomy. Even though my knowledge of both Astronomy and Copernicus was pretty much non-existent at the time, my principal explained that since I knew how to type, and had experience writing by now, I could write an essay. He also pointed out that I enjoyed reading as I had read most of the books available in the school library, two bookcases about six feet tall located in his office. So I read everything I could about Copernicus. There was not much in our small school library and there was no public library anywhere near my home (it was only when I transferred to another school, at the end of high school, that I first visited a public library). There were books in my home but none about Copernicus. So I enlisted my friends and fellow writers in the school newspaper in finding everything they could on Copernicus, and together we put together a modest dossier of newspaper clippings about the man and the model of the universe he had formulated. The occasion of the 500th anniversary of his birth helped, as newspapers published several accounts of his life and contributions. Armed with that dossier of newspaper clippings and with a lot of cross-referencing in an encyclopedia in the school, I was able to metaphorically transport myself to Poland five centuries earlier and imagine how his discovery of a heliocentric solar system would have been received in his times. I found the use of the encyclopedia particularly helpful, as it drove me to make connections across topics, allowing me to imagine what the implications of those relationships might have been. I felt like a Sherlock Holmes of sorts, one of my favorite books at the time, drawing timelines of seemingly random historical facts, hypothesizing connections between them, and then searching further in the encyclopedia for ways to test those hypotheses. That project became the center of my attention for several months, and typing my final essay gave me more pleasure than anything I had written up to that point. I mailed my essay to the Ministry of Education to the address provided by the principal. Some months later I received a notification from the Ministry informing me that I had won the contest, a full scholarship to finish high school studies in Poland, courtesy of the Polish government.

My mother would have none of my travelling to Poland at the age of 14 to finish my high school in Polish, so I had to call the Ministry of Education and explain, somewhat sheepishly, that I would not be able to accept the award. It was kind of embarrassing, especially as I had to first explain this to the principal and then make the call to the Ministry from the principal's office, with him and his secretary present, obviously disappointed. I had a hard time following my mother's reasoning in making me turn down the scholarship, given how much she valued education. I did, however, receive an alternative prize directly from the hands of the Minister of Education of Venezuela: a diploma and a cassette recorder. More importantly the awards were given at a special ceremony in the planetarium of a big park, after a show which explained the highlights of Copernicus's contribution. My principal was so proud that he packed my entire class, and a few other classes, in a school bus and brought us all to the event. At the event, I sat next to another student from another school who proudly told me he had won the first prize: a scholarship to study in Poland! I didn't have the heart to tell him he should have thanked my mother! But, even though I could not receive the prize I had won, the entire affair felt pretty good for a consolation second prize. I still keep a picture of the Minister of Education shaking my hand, giving me a diploma, next to my principal whose smile would make you think he had won the prize himself. My classmates enjoyed the visit to the planetarium and the recorder helped me enhance the newspaper operation, as I now could record interviews. I also began to record one hour tapes with family news, in which I interviewed my parents and my brother and then mailed to my grandparents.

When the principal then invited me during my last year in the school to apply to another national competition, this time to write an essay about Antonio Jose de Sucre, one of the leaders of the Independence

Movement in Venezuela, it was an easy decision for me. I now knew how to research a topic with relatively limited access to bibliographic sources, how to write an essay, how to type it and how to mail it. I even knew how to politely decline the award should it not meet with my mother's approval. Plus my typing skills had improved considerably as a result of hundreds of letters and many newspapers published every week over many months. I also had developed a taste for historical research, my version of Sherlock Holmes cracking cases of the distant past. I had learned to enjoy establishing and imagining relationships between historical developments in various fields of human activity and across places. I won that contest too. This time I could receive the prize, a voucher to purchase books of my choosing at a bookstore specializing in academic books, for an amount about twice the cost of the typewriter, which funded my first scholarly library, an eclectic collection consisting of about fifty books in history, literature, philosophy and science assembled with the help of the knowledgeable bookstore owner.

I suppose it was the fact that it had given my school principal some pleasure to see me win those prizes, or maybe that he had enjoyed watching me launch the school newspaper, that caused him to call my parents to a meeting to discuss my educational future. Before that meeting I would have been uncertain about what the next steps would be after completing the ninth grade in that school. The outcome of that conversation was that at the end of that school year, upon completion of the ninth grade, I transferred to a very good school far away from my home. It was a school with a very good reputation, particularly in preparing people who wanted to study law, which my principal had suggested I should do.

I would travel about two hours each way to school every day, taking two different buses and then walking 20 minutes from the last bus stop to the school as it was off the public transportation route. The intended plan that I would finish high school there and then go to law school made sense to me, even though I did not know any lawyers or have access to anyone who had gone to college: Neither of my parents had attended college and I don't think anyone in the apartment building where I lived did either. But I knew that law school was what people who got involved in politics did, and my principal had told me several times, during those conversations when we printed the 50 newspaper copies, that I would be a good politician. I think he meant it as a compliment!

The school was amazing. The curriculum of the school was, as were many of the faculty, very progressive. The school had originally been established by Spanish political refugees who had left Spain during Franco's dictatorship. The founder had taught in the *Instituto Escuela* in Madrid, a progressive institution committed to a liberal arts education and to the promotion of critical thinking. He had modeled the *Instituto Escuela* in Caracas after it. In time, he transferred the school to one of the teachers, and eventually they moved from the original location in an older part of the city to a new development in the suburbs.

It was to that new location that I travelled every day. The school sat atop a mountain in one of Caracas' most exclusive residential neighborhoods. The daughters of the President of the country, and of several members of the cabinet, attended that school. Many of the children, those who did not live within walking distance, were driven to school, some by their parents, others by chauffeurs, some came on the school bus. Since my home was very far away from the school bus route, I relied on public transportation. The school had extraordinary athletic fields and facilities, a track, basketball courts, volleyball courts and a soccer field. The library took up the equivalent of six or eight of the classrooms in my previous school and had a full-time librarian. The teachers were outstanding, and some of them taught in university part-time. One of them was a published poet. Another made us read the daily newspapers and debate the news in class. Another was fascinated by politics and talked about recent political developments, particularly those concerning the transition to democracy which had taken place the year I was born, as if they were the outcome of the actions of his friends and neighbors – they probably were! Many of them assigned us research papers and it was for that purpose that I first visited the national library. It was a wonderful school in many ways. Even the long commute was a blessing, as it helped me learn to read in moving vehicles, which has served me well throughout life. So I read many of the books in the school library on my journey to and from school, and I learned about my city, as I looked out the window during that two-hour journey travelling through Caracas.

One of the books I read during my long commute was "The Revolution of Intelligence" by Luis Alberto Machado, a short text published in 1975, my junior year in high school.[1] The thesis of the book was simple: people are not born smart; they become smart as a result of education. I loved that thesis, perhaps because I found it reaffirming given my own insecurities about whether I belonged in that school. My first term I had failed most subjects and the principal called my father in to discuss the matter. This was deeply embarrassing as I had thought, given the amount of time I spent studying and my academic performance in my previous school, that I was a good student. The notion that effort and opportunity, and not genes or social origin, were what caused people to be smart was, in some ways, liberating. I clearly benefited from the power of that idea as my academic performance improved and I graduated as valedictorian of my class.

I did not, however, go to law school, which caused some of my teachers consternation. Two events led to my change of heart. It was not that I had any doubts about my ability to go to college or to study law. All students at the *Instituto Escuela* went to college and I benefited from that ethos. The school had a wonderful counseling department where dedicated professionals met with us to help us decide on what we wanted to study. For a student like me, the counseling department was particularly helpful. It enabled me to provide an answer to my father's good question about how much college was going to cost when I first announced that I was planning to attend.

One of the causes of my change of heart was the publication by Luis Alberto Machado, and the discussions it was generating. In several interviews about the book Machado argued that if people become smart as a result of opportunity, it is an obligation of a democratic state to create such opportunities, a thesis he would subsequently develop in another book.[2] I found that thesis captivating. Perhaps it resonated so strongly because I read it as I was studying history and sociology. Or

---

[1] Luis Alberto Machado. *La Revolución de la Inteligencia*. Barcelona: Seix Barral. 1975.

[2] Luis Alberto Machado. *El Derecho a Ser Inteligente*. Barcelona: Seix Barral. 1978.

perhaps it echoed the stark inequities I witnessed as I travelled through the city, passing by slums in the mountains on my way to one of Caracas' most elite institutions. Or perhaps it reflected the influence of some of my teachers, including my literature teacher whose strong commitment to social justice resonated in her poetry as much as in her classes. Perhaps it was my history teacher that made me feel that the fledgling democratic experiment was the result of what ordinary people did. Maybe it was my photography teacher who encouraged me to do a series of photos of working children in my neighborhood for a school exhibit. Whatever the reason, the book fueled my desire to enable people from all backgrounds to develop their talent.

The second reason was more private, and not one that I am particularly proud of. I did not share it with anyone at the time. The day after it had been announced that I would be receiving the graduation award as valedictorian, as we were lining up to walk into our classrooms, one of my classmates asked me what my plans were upon graduation. I told him I was going to law school. "Do you know what that means?" he asked "Do you know what a lawyer does, or how to get a job as a lawyer?" I did not respond. It was obvious that I didn't. "Look around," he said, "all of us have relatives who practice law. My father owns the law firm his father established. So-and-so's father is a partner in a law firm, so is so-and-so." He explained that they were all going to work with their relatives and would, in time, be partners in those firms their families owned. He explained in a way that sounded as if he was trying to be helpful, that my best bet if I wanted to become a lawyer would be to work for him or another of my classmates, for the alternative would be to work as a clerk in a lower court for most of my life, in hopes of one day moving up through the ranks.

I was not certain what he was trying to accomplish offering avuncular advice, but I could not understand why my career prospects would have more to do with the family ties or the wealth of my classmates than with my skills and effort. But, since his grandfather was a prominent lawyer and politician who had served several times as a member of the cabinet and his father was a prominent lawyer, I assumed my classmate knew what he was talking about. So, without consulting with anyone else, I changed my mind and decided I would not be going to law school. I went to the counseling department and asked them to help me figure out what I could study that would help me advance educational opportunities for all. I did not have much time, as I would have to take a college entrance examination soon. My counselors were not pleased, and it took me several meetings to get them to understand that I was not asking for permission but for help in carrying out a decision I had already made. I was going to follow my conscience even if it disappointed everyone in that school.

Once I had a plan, I notified my parents that I was going to study psychology, which was the science that would help me figure out how to make everybody smart. That is what I did, enrolling at the Universidad Central de Venezuela, the oldest public university in the country. I was lucky that tuition was free, and the education I received was wonderful. Incidentally, Luis Alberto Machado was appointed Secretary for the Development of Human Intelligence in 1979, as I was in college, and advanced many programs to foster the cognitive development of the population. This reaffirmed my emerging understanding that ideas can, in time, change the world.

Since the day I made the decision that I would work to create the conditions necessary to help people develop their talent, this is what I have strived to do. Over the last twenty years, I have done this primarily as a faculty member at the Harvard Graduate School of Education. While this is not exactly the path I had charted that day in high school when I changed my mind about going to law school, or even the path I had imagined when I graduated college, it has been an enjoyable and fulfilling journey.

One of the things I have done over the last twenty years is to help graduate students prepare to advance educational opportunities for all children around the world. Soon after arriving at the Harvard Graduate School of Education, I led the design of a master's program in international education policy. Each year, the program recruits students who are committed to empowering learners to not only become architects of their own lives but also to become contributing members of their communities. It gives me great joy to work with these graduate students and, especially, to follow their careers after they graduate. I stay in touch with many of my former students, and make a point each year to reach out to about 100 graduates, in my travels or by correspondence (yes, those typing lessons still serve me well), or now by Skype or phone. In these conversations I ask them what they do and what they find challenging, and I welcome their advice about how we can better prepare those who are following in their footsteps.

I draw satisfaction from being able to do this work at Harvard, the institution where I pursued graduate studies in education. This school opened for me opportunities I could not have imagined when I was learning to type or reading books during my long commutes to high school. Working to help advance the Harvard Graduate School of Education's mission feels as if I am paying back what I have received, in a way that is both a great pleasure and a great privilege.

Becoming a Harvard professor in 1998 was not the path I imagined when I arrived at this school as a graduate student in 1983. At that time, I had just finished a short stint as a faculty member at the Universidad Central de Venezuela, upon completion of my undergraduate studies. I was teaching experimental psychology and doing research on ways to stimulate the creativity of preschool children. I saw very few connections between the teaching and research in that school and the large and exciting programs to foster intelligence that the Minister for the Development of Human Intelligence was advancing. I could not understand why we weren't all part of that ambitious national program. Additionally, as I began to teach experimental psychology, one of my former professors recommended me for a part-time consulting position with a firm that was helping a state government understand how to better align the curriculum of a technical institute with workplace needs. I began to discover that the links between experimental research and creating opportunities for all students to develop their talent could be tenuous, and realized I was more interested in helping to improve the functioning of education institutes so people could get jobs. I concluded that the path between experimental research and creating opportunities for all students to develop their talents was too long and fraught with challenges, and that universities were far too removed from real problems for my taste. So, I thought that completing a doctorate in administration, planning and social policy would give me the necessary preparation to achieve my goal: to become Secretary of Education of Venezuela so that I could help advance the conditions that provided all children opportunities to develop their talents. As with my earlier plan to become a lawyer, I did not really know, at the time, the path to becoming a Secretary of Education.

One of the many transformational opportunities Harvard provided me came in the form of a fellow student, also from Venezuela, who I met on my first day in the University. She laughed when I told her my plans to become Secretary of Education. I, in turn, was puzzled by her desire to become a teacher, since this is exactly what she was doing in Venezuela prior to graduate school. As we walked along the Charles River or down Brattle Street, we engaged in long conversations and animated discussions about the best way to provide students opportunities to develop their talents. I would argue that the best path to large-scale impact was to become Secretary of Education, and she would argue that it was to teach "one student at a time." We continue those conversations to this day, as Eleonora and I got married 31 years ago.

I quickly put in place a plan B after realizing that Harvard graduates were not typically invited to become Ministers of Education immediately upon receiving their diplomas, and that I lacked the experience, the knowledge, and the social or political capital to become a Minister. After graduation, I pursued a career advising ministers of education in a number of countries around the world. I was an education specialist at the World Bank, thinking that this was not only a good way to serve my goal of expanding educational opportunity, but also a good route to eventually become Secretary of Education. So when the chairman of the department from which I had graduated at Harvard called me, while I was busily negotiating large national programs to educate low-income children with the governments of Mexico and Peru, to suggest that I apply to a faculty search to rebuild the international education program at Harvard, I was not immediately receptive to the idea. I did, nevertheless, apply. By the time I received an offer of appointment, I had convinced myself, with Eleonora's help, that the best way for me to expand educational opportunity for all was by educating others.

I settled into my office in Gutman Library in the first days of January 1998. As this was the winter break, there were few students and faculty around and I wondered whether I had made a big mistake trading the activity and buzz of the World Bank for the dark and empty hallways of Gutman Library in early January.

Students and colleagues eventually arrived, and soon after, I was busy working with some colleagues designing a new master's program to prepare people for leadership careers in the field of international education. What was then just a concept turned into a wonderful two decades and a total of almost one thousand graduates of this program today. Those students have given me many joys and I consider them all part of my extended family.

During these years, I have also managed to stay active advising governments and working to expand educational opportunity, albeit in different ways than I would have had I become Secretary of Education.

In many ways, I have held on to the strong convictions I had as a teenager taking the bus from my home, up the mountain, past the slums, into an elite and privileged school. I remain convinced that education can transform people's lives and help them decide what life they want to live, and I know that it is an obligation of a democratic state to provide opportunities for all to be educated. However, as I have grown and evolved, so too has my perspective on education.

A silent global revolution which transformed humanity

When I committed myself to working on expanding educational opportunity, I only knew the three schools I had attended myself. In the years since, I have visited and studied thousands of schools; worked with several dozen governments, international development agencies, foundations and other organizations involved in expanding educational opportunity; studied many different education programs and met thousands of educators from many different countries. I have also learned much from my graduate students, most of whom arrive at Harvard with some professional experience and many of whom I remain in touch with after they graduate. These opportunities have persuaded me that education is a most wonderful human invention that has caused one of the most remarkable silent revolutions in the shared history of humanity. This revolution has provided most members of our species with a shared experience in these wonderful institutions we have invented to pass on to the young what we consider good: schools.

I now know, as my wife had explained when we first met in 1983, that indeed the deepest way to educate is one student at a time, and for any

13

of us involved in supporting schools, at whatever level we do this, it is essential that we keep that personal experience of each learner at the core of what we do. Most of my former students do not go on to become teachers, but instead work to support what teachers and students do. Yet I know that they are all working to help educate children, youth and adults, one student at a time.

What I find most remarkable about this silent revolution which has transformed humanity is that most of this transformation has taken place over a relatively short period in human history. Public schools to educate all children were invented less than two centuries ago, and for most of the world, universal public education is an aspiration which resulted from including education as one of the human rights in the declaration adopted by the United Nations in 1948. That was only seventy years ago!

It is telling that this global education revolution resulted from a compact designed to create the conditions for global peace and sustainability. This is a tall ethical goal for public education, to educate all children so we can have peace in the world. The institution established to advance Human Rights, the United Nations, adopted at the General Assembly of 2015 a compact that builds upon those rights, the Sustainable Development Goals, which outline an ambitious and hopeful vision of the conditions necessary to have peace and sustainability in the world. Education is not only one of those goals, but it is also a means necessary to achieve all others.

I am now, however, more convinced than ever that this silent revolution was not meant to happen organically. It was not inevitable but the result of deliberate choices made by individuals who believed that freedom and equality would only be advanced by providing all people with opportunities to develop skills. Those people lead these institutions all over the world. They do this from multiple roles: some of them teach, others administer schools, others provide support for schools and for teachers, others work for governments, some work for the public sector, and some work for the private sector. Some work in institutions in their countries of origin, while others work for international development organizations. This is a remarkable net of organizations which form the institution of education, and just as remarkable are the results they have achieved. They provide educational opportunities to more than one billion people between the ages of 5 and 17 every year.[3] Those who do this kind of work are the leaders of a global movement to educate humanity, for the goals of achieving peace and sustainability. I am immensely grateful that some of the leaders of this Global Education Movement have been my students.

The Global Education Movement to educate all children and its fragility

Public education is a remarkable human invention that in a relatively short period in human history has provided the majority of the younger members of our species with a shared experience through an institution invented to pass on the values and knowledge which older generations consider important, and also to equip them with the skills and dispositions to break with tradition to improve the world. The following chart illustrates how the percentage of the world population with some basic education increased over the last two centuries.

---

[3] There are 263 million children and youth in this age group out of school, and providing them opportunities to study should be a priority. However, it is still remarkable that over 1.2 billion are in school. Sources:
http://www.indexmundi.com/world/age_structure.html and
http://www.unesco.org/new/en/education/themes/leading-the-international-agenda/education-for-all/single-view/news/263_million_children_and_youth_are_out_of_school_from_primar/

Share of the world population older than 15 years with at least basic education

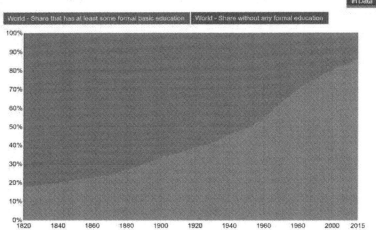

Source: Global education (OECD ♦ IIASA)
OurWorldInData.org/primary-education-and-schools/ ♦ CC BY-SA

Most of that significant educational expansion, which took place as the population grew considerably,[4] benefited from the perception among progressive policy elites and civic, government, and business leaders that the various alternative purposes served by education converged and that there were limited tradeoffs between them. Undergirding such consensus were the liberal values of freedom and equality. With the creation of the first democratic republics in the eighteenth century, the world began to democratize fairly rapidly, spreading these liberal values; additionally, the adoption of the Universal Declaration of Human Rights and the creation of a new post World War II order further intensified the widespread acceptance of these core values. The chart illustrates how the increase in the percentage of the population with some basic education accelerates after 1960s, arguably the results of

---

[4] In 1950, the world's population was 2.5 billion, and the percentage of the population with some basic education was 49%. In 2015, the world population was 7.4 billion, and the percentage of the population with some basic education 86%. This means education systems expanded access even as the number of youth increased significantly. Sources for world population https://ourworldindata.org/world-population-growth/ and for percentage of the population with some schooling https://ourworldindata.org/primary-education-and-schools/.

successful efforts of UN institutions the previous decade in working with governments to advance the right to education. Such expansion in access to education produced a remarkable achievement, the universalization of basic literacy, as shown in chart 2. Note how the percentage of the population that is illiterate declines precipitously after 1950.

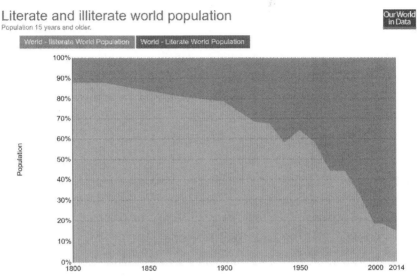

Literate and illiterate world population
Population 15 years and older.

This perceived convergence of education purposes since December 10, 1948 saw that alternative education goals were complementary and that there were limited tradeoffs between them. It saw the same skills that helped people become productive as also helping them to engage as citizens. It saw advancing human rights as also advancing economic freedoms. The underlying assumption was that economic, political, social, and cultural development converged. Policies that fostered economic development fueled cultural values that were supportive of economic progress; this in turn fostered more social inclusion and political development. There were multiple reinforcing loops connecting the many facets of development. It was also assumed that globalization would be mutually reinforcing with these processes, and it was expected that, globally, the world would be moving towards convergence in an ongoing cycle towards greater freedom, equality, and happiness.

For example, as evidence of this perceived convergence of purpose, during the most significant period of educational expansion in Latin America in the 1950s and 1960s, UNESCO played a key role advocating for such expansion in regional meetings that brought together ministers of education and of finance making the case for universal education as a human right as well as an economic investment.[5] The theory of human capital, the notion that economic development could be planned and that countries could leapfrog stages of economic development by making strategic investments in human capital and infrastructure, played as important a role in the expansion of education as the notion that education was a fundamental human right, foundational to many other rights and freedoms, and helpful to advance democratic culture.

A more recent example of the perception that various goals were complementary is that in 2000, when the Organization for Economic Cooperation and Development launched the Programme for the International Student Assessment (PISA), it anchored the assessment of the basic literacies in language, mathematics and sciences as those levels necessary to participate in knowledge economies and democratic societies. For instance, the definition of literacy that the PISA studies are aligned to is: "Reading literacy is understanding, using, and reflecting on written texts, in order to achieve one's goals, to develop one's knowledge and potential, and to participate in society."[6]

The trajectory of the global educational expansion was certainly not linear; events such as economic circumstances and wars influenced the priority that public education could receive. In addition, interruptions and discontinuities took place as a result of conflict over education

---

[5] Reimers, F. *Deuda Extena y Financiamiento de la Educacion. Su Impacto en Latinoamerica.* Santiago, UNESCO-OREALC. 1990.
[6] OECD *Measuring Student Knowledge and Skills. A New Framework for Assessment.* Paris, 1999, page 19.
https://www.oecd.org/edu/school/programmeforinternationalstuden tassessmentpisa/33693997.pdf.

goals, and of conflicting views on the priority of education relative to other societal investments. I have elsewhere discussed how the history of public education in Latin America can be construed as the history of the competition between two political projects, a conservative project that saw social relations between groups as fixed and a liberal project interested in advancing the freedoms and opportunities of subdominant groups.[7]

Such discontinuities notwithstanding, the overarching picture remains that the expansion of public education has, over the last seven decades, benefited from consensus on the benefits of education to serve many different goals, assuming limited tradeoffs between them. The political philosophy of Liberalism was the foundation of such consensus.

As liberalism, which has provided the foundation for much of the work of governments and of the global institutions created after World War II, is increasingly challenged by populist and nationalist movements, it is necessary to reexamine the question of what it means to educate citizens in our times.

Historical roots of the cosmopolitan purposes of public education

The idea that all persons should be educated is relatively recent. It is primarily a product of the Enlightenment and of liberal political thought. As part of the ideology of liberalism, public education's goals were to promote freedom and equality and to educate citizens for a liberal political order.

The Enlightenment was a cosmopolitan project, founded on the basic idea that all people had the same rights. The promotion of the institutions to advance such equality of rights was one that engaged people across borders. In this sense, the idea of fraternity included in the motto of the French revolution (*Liberté, égalité et fraternité*, which translates as Freedom, equality and solidarity) referred not only to solidarity among fellow citizens within the same national jurisdiction,

---

[7] Reimers, F. Social Progress in Latin America. Victor Bulmer-Thomas and John Coatsworth (Eds.) *Cambridge Economic History of Latin America*. Vol II. Pp. 427-480. Cambridge University Press. 2006.

but to solidarity across national borders to advance freedom and equality. The expansion of three institutions which resulted from the Enlightenment, democracy, the public school and the modern research university, benefited from global cooperation and from a fundamental understanding that such transnational solidarity was essential to advancing a global project to expand freedom and equality.

The establishment of the first independent and democratic republics benefitted from such solidarity across nations. It was for this reason, for instance, that Francisco de Miranda, born in Caracas and one of the intellectual architects of the independence movement in South America, served in the revolutionary wars of the United States, France, and South America. Similarly, Alexander Hamilton, born in Charlestown on the island of Nevis, would join the independence movement of the United States and would go on to be one of the founding fathers of the American democratic experiment. It was that same commitment to a global project of advancement of liberal values that drove Frenchman Marie-Joseph Paul Yves Roch Gilbert du Motier, best known as the Marquis de Lafayette, to serve in the American War of Independence as well as in the French Revolution.

Similarly, the establishment of public education, understood by the founders of the first democratic republics to be essential to the well-functioning of democracy, benefited from global cooperation. For example, on a visit to seek assistance from the British, Simon Bolivar (one of the leaders of Independence in South America) was introduced by Francisco de Miranda, who lived in London at the time, to Joseph Lancaster, the creator of the monitorial system of instruction, which allowed extending education to low-income students. Bolivar would eventually persuade Lancaster to move to Caracas and establish the first teacher training institution. Similarly, Venezuelan-born Andres Bello, serving as the first rector of the University of Chile, created a contest inviting faculty to design approaches to educating citizens in the newly independent republic. Argentinean Domingo Faustino Sarmiento, a faculty member at the University of Chile, submitted and won the contest with his thesis "Popular Education," an approach that drew on his conversations with Horace and Mary Peabody Mann, who led the movement for public education in Massachusetts.

Scientific research and the modern research university, the third institution advanced by the Enlightenment, are also at heart cosmopolitan enterprises. When some of the signatories of the United States Declaration of Independence chartered the American Academy of Arts and Sciences in 1780, the oldest scientific academy in the United States, they tasked it not only with the promotion of scientific inquiry to advance the public good, but with the promotion of exchanges among scientists, no matter their country of residency. The same year, John Adams wrote the Massachusetts constitution, whose first article speaks eloquently about the public purposes of our universities — at the beginning about who needed to be educated and why, and at the end about virtues they needed to learn. Three decades later, the creation of the University of Berlin sparked a veritable global movement of renewal of higher education institutions around the world along similar lines as Adams had imagined for the American Academy and for our public universities, away from institutions devoted to the transmission of religious dogma, into institutions committed to the advancement of scientific research, the promotion of critical thinking, and the education of the public. This cosmopolitan aspiration of the Enlightenment is eloquently captured in this quote from Johann Wolfgang von Goethe: *"He who speaks only one language sees the world with only one eye."*

The institutions which were built on ideas from the Enlightenment were imperfect, as there were inherent contradictions in that they "limited" the ideals/ideas of freedom, equality and brotherhood (and even citizenship rights) to certain groups, excluding women and some racial groups, while "allowing" slavery, exploitation, colonialism/domination, and sexism to be the norm in these "enlightened" societies that affirmed that "all men are created equal... and endowed with certain inalienable rights." Yet, the liberal values that were foundational to the creation of these institutions provided the basis to over time untangle and correct these contradictions, thus making possible the progress we have made globally in the advancement of universal human rights. In this sense, the institutions of democracy are always a work in progress, advancing towards the achievement of the aspirations of freedom and equality, and the institutions of public education and of the modern university are also a work in progress, advancing as a result of continuous challenges to live up to their promise to advance freedom and equality. It is as a result of those challenges that democracy progresses towards recognizing the rights of groups previously denied those rights, such as women or racial minorities, and that public schools and universities also progress, expanding access to students from all walks of life and backgrounds.

It was thus a result of the cosmopolitan aspirations of those who led the establishment of the institutions of democracy, public education and modern universities, that solidarity and cooperation across national borders fueled their global expansion. Created to advance the values of liberty, equality and solidarity, the development of these institutions benefited from a form of solidarity that transcended national boundaries, from global solidarity or global citizenship.

The Global Expansion in public education, for example, benefited from the consolidation of the new independent and democratic nation states, from the expansion of liberalism in the 1800s, and again after World War II as a result of the creation of a global architecture to promote the liberal ideas of freedom and equality around the world.

Under liberalism, it was assumed that public education could serve democratic political and economic goals with limited tradeoffs between them. Additional goals such as advancing human rights and modernization were also seen as convergent with political and economic goals. For this reason, most governments advancing education as part of liberalism saw limited tradeoffs between the goals of education, and the same was true of the international organizations created to advance global security after World War II.

The challenges to liberalism from communism and fascism presented alternative goals for public education, questioning the notion that individuals could be free to choose which education to pursue, and emphasizing political and economic goals, as well as downplaying human rights and modernization. Those challenges helped those who valued freedom and equality to think with greater moral clarity about the need to align education institutions to the institutions of democracy. Harvard president James Bryan Conant, for example, understood that admitting only white Protestant males from privileged backgrounds to study at Harvard was more aligned with the ideology of racial superiority advanced by Hitler than with the values on which the American democratic experiment was founded. As a result of this understanding, he initiated reforms designed to create a more inclusive admissions process at Harvard. He opened admission to students from different social backgrounds and created financial aid programs; later he extended similar reforms for colleges across the country.

The construction of the post-war order, which began with the establishment of the United Nations and the approval of the Universal Declaration of Human Rights, brought into focus the moral purpose of educating all persons. Article 26 of the Declaration of Human Rights emphasizes that the point of educating all is to educate each in the rights of every person and in the institutions which have been created to advance them. The declaration is, therefore, a seminal document in the advancement of global citizenship, and Article 26 calls for education for global citizenship, a cause that UN institutions have advanced episodically throughout their history.

The challenges to aligning education systems with a cosmopolitan vision of freedom and equality

The tensions between the Soviet block and the liberal world during the Cold War, however, impeded the development of a global consensus with respect to advancing a global citizenship agenda. This is perhaps the reason why the tacit operational education consensus of many of the international development institutions created after World War II evolved into getting all children in schools rather than focusing more intentionally on what they should learn in school, or how their learning should align with a liberal vision of freedom and equality, as had been intended in the UN Charter. Consensus on those topics was as difficult to reach in international institutions as it was in societies in which there is much political contestation. This is, perhaps, the reason the PISA studies so far have focused on domains such as literacy, mathematics and science, and not on domains like civics or global citizenship; it is perhaps the reason multilateral and bilateral banks have seldom addressed questions of curriculum content and seldom funded education operations designed to promote democratization, and the reason organizations like UNESCO have found it difficult to advance human rights education around the world, even though they were

23

created to do this.[8] It should be noted that the OECD has been working for the last several years to add a dimension of global competence to the PISA assessments, but reaching consensus among the governments participating in these discussions on the merits and approaches to doing this has proved challenging. It remains to be seen whether the dimensions of global competency, which will be eventually incorporated into the assessment, will include civic dimensions or merely dimensions relevant for economic competitiveness. In spite of these challenges, the United Nations institutions have made efforts to advance global citizenship, most recently as part of the Sustainable Development Goals agenda, which for the first time in 2015 included a focus on educating for global citizenship.

Given the difficulties in reaching explicit consensus on the value of aligning education goals with a liberal cosmopolitan vision of freedom and equality, many nations as well as international organizations focused instead on particular competencies as goals for the public education system, without attempting an integrated view of how those competencies would align with a democratic vision advancing the values of freedom and equality. Speaking about "skills for a knowledge economy" was less contentious, in international fora, than speaking about "skills for a democratic society."

It is arguably for this reason that the curriculum frameworks in most countries focus on the basic literacies of language, mathematics and science, but to a significantly lesser extent on civics. Increasingly, curriculum frameworks are expanding to include other competencies, not only to other cognitive domains, but also to social and emotional domains.[9] Governments and educators now are also interested in character, self-regulation, self-awareness, grit, tolerance and leadership.

---

[8] For example, UNESCO has conducted studies of the way in which textbooks can foster human rights and tolerance among people along various dimensions of diversity, but has been unable to focus attention, at the ministerial meetings they convene every two years, for example, on specific cases where governments have used textbooks to develop animus against people from other nations or cases where intolerant groups have influenced the history curriculum.

[9] Reimers, F. and Chung, C. (Eds) *Teaching and Learning for the Twenty First Century*. Cambridge: Harvard Education Press. 2016.

But, for the most part, those interests are not framed as part of a vision of how the integration of those capacities will enable people to individually and collectively advance social or economic goals. This is a difficult conversation to have in settings where there is no consensus about which economic strategy to pursue to integrate the country in a global economy, a conversation which will become more difficult as the values of liberalism are increasingly contested.

In spite of the challenges to developing clear and coherent visions for the purposes of public education, however, the dominance of liberalism as the organizing principle of the post war order, particularly given the support of countries with large economies also committed to liberalism, fueled a set of education purposes more or less aligned with the ideals of freedom and equality, even if those were not spelled out explicitly. The fall of the Berlin Wall, the collapse of the Soviet Union and the acceleration of globalization in the last two decades made these education aims of liberalism the dominant tacit consensus in most of the world. As explained earlier, the undergirding rationale of such consensus was that there were limited tradeoffs between alternative education purposes: that the same skills that helped people become productive also helped them engage as citizens, and that advancing human rights was also advancing freedoms.

The challenges to the tacit liberal values that undergird global educational expansion

Such tacit consensus on the reason why nations advance public education and cooperate with others in this enterprise is increasingly challenged by an emerging populist ideology.

Populism posits that ordinary people are exploited by elites and challenges the notion of representative democracy with direct action by the masses. Since direct action by large numbers is impractical, too often populism results in autocratic rule by a leader, communicating directly with the masses, unobstructed by either intermediary institutions or the checks and balances of democratic government. Some recent populist leaders include Jean-Marie Le Pen in France, Pim Fortuyn in the Netherlands, Hugo Chavez in Venezuela, Evo Morales in Bolivia, Alberto Fujimori in Peru, and more recently Narendra Modi in India, Andrzej Duda in Poland, and Donald Trump in the United States.

25

Historically populism has at times led to the breakdown of democracy and to fascism, characterized by a complete power grab based on extreme nationalism and racial superiority ideologies, as illustrated by the breakdown of the Weimar republic in Germany and the rise of Hitler to power in the 1930s, or the creation of the one party dictatorship by Benito Mussolini in Italy in the 1920s. More recently, other populist leaders have used democratic structures to bring about autocratic regimes, as is the case with Vladimir Putin in Russia, Robert Mugabe in Zimbabwe, Recep Erdogan in Turkey or Hugo Chavez and his appointed successor Nicolas Maduro in Venezuela.

Modern populists exploit the following ideas. The first is that globalization and liberal policies do not benefit all, and that there are important groups of the population who are left behind without hope of seeing their conditions improve. Populists attribute this to elites who are not accountable to those groups, and to a model of development that fails to envision a role for the groups who are left behind. Populists also exploit cultural divides and deep differences in values and worldviews among the population. In India, since the arrival of Mr. Modi to the office of prime minister, intolerance has become virulent and mobs now attack and kill Muslims over their religious and cultural practices, such as eating beef. These trends in India are a real threat to religious minorities, especially as the country does not seem to have a viable opposition party to provide an alternative view and counter the possible rise of fascism and Hindutva ideologies.

In the recent presidential election in the United States, the populist base of President Trump draws on older Jeffersonian and Jacksonian ideas to challenge the political establishment which advances the progressive views of the Hamiltonians and Wilsonians which have dominated since World War II. The Hamiltonians advance the idea of the United States playing a leadership role in creating a global liberal order to contain the Soviet Union and advance US interests. The Wilsonians also advance a global liberal order in terms of values that would reduce global conflict and violence. They promote human rights, democratic governance and the rule of law. The Jeffersonians, on the other hand, believe that minimizing the global role of the United States would reduce costs and risks. Jacksonian populist nationalists, in contrast, focus on both restoring the dignity of American citizens who felt "left behind" and delinking from cosmopolitan enlightenment ideals and the global liberal order.[10]

These populist views are a challenge to the ideas of a universal project to advance freedom, equality, and human rights. They are a challenge to the project of globalization, they may be a challenge to the idea of representative democracy, and they have implications for public education and for the global project of advancing education for all.

The educational implications of populism

It is consistent with populist views to advocate more power to local groups to define the goals of education, and fewer roles for government and for inter-governmental institutions. Replacing global and national politics with local politics, of course, does not mean greater consensus. Instead, it may mean more conflict, perhaps with fewer rules of arbitration. The divisions between cosmopolitans and populists exist in local communities. One question is how will these differences be resolved? Will the rule of law and expertise continue to play a role? We should expect less trust in public education institutions, resulting from less trust in governments, in experts and in elites. It is also possible that we will witness a renewed emphasis on identity politics and culture wars in education.

There are four interrelated risks we can expect to emerge from these challenges to the liberal values of freedom and equality as organizing principles of public education.

The first is a risk to the idea of human rights, which may undermine support for public education and for global citizenship education. If nationalism is the new organizing force, the notion of in-group and out-group is defined by citizenship and not by membership in humanity, a challenge to the cosmopolitan foundation of the liberal values of the Enlightenment. Since one of the consequences of globalization has been migration, non-citizens will be the first target for exclusion. This may undermine consensus on the importance of public education.

---

[10] Walter Russell Mead "The Jacksonian Revolt. American Populism and the Liberal Order" *Foreign Affairs*. March/April 2017.

If cultural wars define the politics of education, we should expect to see an increase in the ongoing battles over the rights of cultural and ethnic minorities, like the right to see them represented in the curriculum or the right to access various levels of education. In the United States, for example, there are individuals and groups lobbying schools for changes in the curriculum, which reduce the emphasis on global topics and content. Conservative groups have long engaged in battles over the curriculum and textbooks in schools. These battles have intensified since the last presidential campaign as reported to me by a number of teachers and school leaders working in global citizenship education efforts. In New Jersey, for example, the director of English and social studies of the Rumson Fair-Haven regional high school was recently challenged in a petition organized by a parent over the inclusion of two books in the history curriculum (Ariel Dorfman's *Death and the Maiden* and Bernard MacLaverty's *Cal*), and for globally-oriented texts such as Chimimanda Ngozi Adichie's *Americanah*.[11] The efforts to ban books such as these from the curriculum continues by advocates who self-identify as having been mentored by national advocates of similar efforts. One example is Dr. Sandra Stotsky, one of the expert witnesses who testified in the court case involving the Mexican American Studies Program in the Tucson Unified School District; Dr. Stotsky's position has been promoted by the *Breitbart*'s website.[12] An expression of the challenges to the rights of minority groups to access education, at the time of this writing the civil rights division of the US Department of Justice was preparing to investigate and sue universities over affirmative action admissions policies deemed to discriminate against white applicants.[13]

---

[11] Jack Shea, personal communication, May 2017.

[12] This is a far right news website which the New York Times has characterized as disseminating news that are ideologically driven, racist, misogynist and xenophobic

[13] Charlie Savage, Justice Dept. to Take On Affirmative Action in College Admissions. The New York Times. August 1, 2017. https://www.nytimes.com/2017/08/01/us/politics/trump-affirmative-action-universities.html

A second risk concerns our ability to address global challenges. The prospects for international collaboration in addressing shared global challenges diminish as the world moves towards national populism, and the goals of education move away from preparing students to understand global interconnectedness and globalization. Climate change, for instance, can only be addressed if leaders and people of different nations collaborate in addressing it. Without the capacity to collaborate with people from different cultures the prospects that we will be able to effectively address challenges like this diminish considerably.

A third risk is a breakdown of the institutions that were created to protect freedom, democracy, the rule of law, public education, and basic human rights. This is the risk that populism might evolve into fascism. There are early warnings of this risk in schools. The sharp increase in intolerance in America has been clearly expressed in and around schools and universities, in the form of more explicit expression of anti-Semitism, white supremacy, Islamophobia and hatred towards people of color and immigrants.[14]

A fourth risk follows from the previous ones and it is that lack of trust in institutions, elites and governments, will make the challenge of resolving these conflicts greater.

Can the institutions created to advance a liberal world order save it?

Individuals or institutions interested in a global liberal order should consider a new focus on education for democratic citizenship, including global citizenship. This means supporting educators so that schools can advance human rights, educate about shared global challenges, educate for engaged citizenship, focus on dispositions and values as much as skills and attend to the conditions that make it possible for schools to

---

[14] Southern Poverty Law Center. After Election Day. The Trump Effect. The Impact of the 2016 Presidential Election on Our Nation's Schools. 2016. See also Hate Map. https://www.splcenter.org/hate-map Accessed May 5, 2017.

be effective in achieving these goals. This is the case for global citizenship education. Education was always meant to be cosmopolitan, global education, but this notion was implicit because the expansion of public education was part of a project that was global and widely supported. This project is now contested, and for this reason the ethical foundations of education need to be pursued intentionally with greater resolve and effectiveness than ever.

For educational institutions to advance progress, greater freedoms, and justice, it is necessary that education leaders take responsibility for this task. This is the task of the Global Education Movement, a movement that was not meant to happen. It was a movement that leaders intentionally made happen. If we are to educate and support leaders of the global education movement, we should learn from those who do this work, learn what challenges they face and discern how to support their leadership.

Studying leadership in the global education movement

To shed some light on the work of leaders of the global education movement and examine how best to support leaders like them, I studied the careers of the graduates of the International Education Policy Program, the program I designed twenty years ago and currently direct at Harvard. I invited all graduates to fill out a survey with a series of questions about their work and careers. I was able to obtain contact information for the majority of the 922 program's alumni. Of those, 208 answered the survey. I personally invited 90 of those graduates to write a short reflection addressing four questions:

1) What are your goals and what work do you do?
2) What impact does your work have?
3) What challenges do you face in this work?
4) What lessons have you learned in doing this work?

Sixty-two of those 90 graduates agreed to write; the rest explained they could not do it at this time. One of the essays written had to be withdrawn because the UN agency in which this graduate works did not provide clearance for him to share the views in the essay publicly because they thought it might jeopardize the work of that agency in that country. This book presents the essays written by these graduates as well

30

as the analysis of the survey results and essays. In this introductory chapter, I highlight some of the key themes addressed in their essays, and supplement this information with quantitative information from the survey. My motivation to undertake this project is three-fold.

First, I was genuinely curious to spend some time thinking through what work my graduates do and what challenges they face. Over the years, I have engaged them in conversations over these topics as a way to learn how best to serve them. I do this in meetings I hold with graduates when I travel, and in one-to-one communications with many of them. In these ways I try to reach about a hundred graduates each year. As a result of following the careers of my graduates I had learned that some of them followed paths I had not expected. Not all of them, for example, would go on to work for governments or for international organizations, which was one of the initial hypotheses on which we based the design of the program. So I thought that examining their work and professional challenges more systematically would enhance my reflection, and provide them also a valuable opportunity for reflection and learning from one another. I expected that this study would help me re-examine some of the hypotheses on which I base my teaching and the direction of the program.

Second, I do think that leading this global education movement is hard and difficult work that requires expert knowledge. I am concerned by the trend in the world that devalues expertise and institutions, including universities, and I think it is necessary that we codify the expertise that undergirds professional educational practice. This expert knowledge is available to some who do this work; they have earned it as a result of experience and study. But it is private knowledge, shared often only in the context of workplaces or with close friends. I thought it would be valuable to make some of this knowledge visible to others, as a way to invite others to do the same, and to stimulate dialogue on the challenges of this valuable form of global education leadership. I have elsewhere explained why I think knowledge relevant to improve educational policy and practice needs more fluid and multiple forms of interaction between researchers and practitioners.[15] There are multiple reasons why the

---

[15] Fernando Reimers. 2017. *Empowering All Students at Scale.* Middletown, DE. Create Space.

knowledge of practitioners about how to advance educational opportunity is not often shared, including the bureaucratic norms of organizations that prevent such public reflection and sharing. As an example, one of the leaders I invited to write an essay for this book, a senior education specialist in a UN agency, sought the necessary approval from the office of Human Resources in headquarters as is necessary when staff in that agency publish, such approval was denied, in spite of the fact that the essay had received support from the director of the country office where this leader works, and in spite of two rounds of revisions which addressed the concerns raised. I did not see anything sensitive topic brought up in the essay, but obviously those whose approval was critical saw things differently. I believe processes of this sort have the effect of discouraging education leaders working in those organization from taking the time to reflect on their practice and sharing those reflections publicly.

My third motivation to write this book is to test an approach I think would benefit many educational institutions: to take the time to follow our graduates and to learn from them. Most of the goals we care about in education are long-term. Unfortunately, we have few instruments that provide ready access to the long-term outcomes of our work for guidance. As we displace metrics on long-term outcomes with metrics of short-term results (grades, graduation rates, satisfaction of students) we run the risk of displacing also the most meaningful goals and of losing sight of what really matters. This is not to suggest that grades, progression in school, graduation rates or transition to college are unimportant. Clearly they are valuable mileposts to guide the work of students as well as educators, but they are not outcomes in and of themselves; they are important because they make other outcomes possible as they empower students to live fulfilling lives and make a positive difference in the world. Since it is those long term outcomes that most matter, we should spend greater efforts seeking feedback on how we do in achieving them. There are, obviously, challenges to systematically obtaining information on the long-term educational consequences of our education programs or of our teaching, so we should start with what is feasible. Taking the time to talk to one hundred former students a year is within reach of most educators, particularly given the availability of modern communication technologies. The value of such feedback is irreplaceable. Inviting students to write a reflection and taking the time to think those through takes a little more doing, but is also within reach. I hope that this book will help me test whether there is value, not just to me but to others, in doing this. If there is value, I may do more of this work in the future. Sometimes we find inspiration in simple ideas, as I did when I read the book "The Revolution of Intelligence," and perhaps the ideas in this book will inspire others.

What do these education leaders do?

Among those who responded to the survey, 90% of them are working in the field of education. Three fourths of them are women. They are cosmopolitans who see themselves as global citizens. All of them speak English and at least another language, 39% speak at least two languages in addition to English and 18% speak three or more languages other than English. When asked whether they consider themselves global citizens 77% indicate that they do to a great extent and 22% do to some extent. When asked whether they agreed with the statement that they consider themselves more of a global citizen than a citizen of the country where they were born, 33% indicated that they agreed to a great extent, and 48% to some extent. Two thirds of them (68%) know what the UN Sustainable Development Goals are, and an additional 25% are familiar with them. All of them are interested in advancing educational opportunities, 91% say they are very interested and 8% are interested in this goal. Most of them report that their work advances educational opportunities (47% very much so and 27% to some extent) and the United Nations Sustainable Development Goals (29% to a great extent and 43% to some extent).

These graduates describe their work as consisting of expanding access to education (14%), improving quality (21%), enhancing the relevance of education (13%), achieving impact on a large scale (13%), influencing policy (11%) and influencing practice (16%).

They work in a variety of roles: 11% of them teach, 7% work in school administration, 3% in system administration, 12% are researchers, 9% work in an organization they created, 10% in an organization providing services to schools in a single country, 10% in an international organization providing services to schools or governments, 13% in international development organizations, 5% in international consulting companies, and 4% in foundations.

A third of these leaders have created at least one education organization (one in five have created one and 11% two or more). Two thirds of them have created at least one educational program that has reached some scale (one in five have created one program, and almost half have created two or more programs).

Their essays provide nuance to the variety of roles from which these leaders advance educational opportunity. Most speak with great clarity about their professional purposes as advancing broader goals of social progress, economic development and justice. For some of them, those goals are tied to aspects of their identity and biography that helped them discover the transformative power of education. These excerpts from the essays illustrate the ethical foundation that animates the work of these leaders:

"When I first started teaching, I taught because I wanted to create a more just and equitable world."

"After teaching in a low income school in Bogotá, Colombia's capital, I decided that education in Colombia needed to be addressed urgently, and that it should be addressed by adequately prepared leaders with personal and professional motivation to advance educational opportunity for all children in the country."

"I believe in the principle that education needs to prepare people to become good citizens and part of an effective workforce. Increasing educational relevancy to social and economic demands has been central to my career in education."

"My belief in education as the fundamental engine, both for individual development and for the social, economic and civic development of our larger communities prompted me to leave a long career in business."

At the core of what these leaders do is support learning for students and teaching. A few do this directly by teaching, while others work in schools creating programs for teacher professional development or developing curriculum. These include schools and programs that serve primarily marginalized children, as well as international schools that serve children from privileged families. In these roles these leaders advance progressive ideas of what learning and teaching should be to empower students. One of them, for instance, leads programs that provide children who live in urban slums in Delhi and Mumbai in India with opportunities to not only engage in project-based learning and sports, but also to learn English and computer skills, experiences which elude most children of similar backgrounds. Another created space in the curriculum for Palestinian children to discuss their reactions to the effects of occupation. Those who teach often extend their influence by creating learning communities and supporting other forms of professional development for other teachers. Some of them influence educational administration and school culture so they can best support teachers and effective learning. The director of an elite international school in the Himalayas leads a fund that provides scholarships for refugee children to enroll in the school, as well as three centers that extend the impact of the school to the outside world. The first center provides outdoor education for local government officials; the second center brings social entrepreneurs and students together with the goal of imagining creative solutions to challenging social issues and the third center provides professional development for teachers and principals on project-based education focused on local development.

Those leaders who teach and work in schools often take on other assignments which expand their influence. For instance, the director of a proprietary English curriculum school in Myanmar serving privileged children volunteered to create a teacher training institute for a trust serving monastic schools, helping them shift from an exclusive focus on access, to a focus on quality and relevancy of what was taught in the sixty schools they supported. He was able to engage many of the students and parents as volunteers to support the monastic schools, to create space for dialogue among board members who included members of the military leadership as well as leaders of the opposition party of Aung San Su Kyi, and to influence national policy on the inclusion of students with special needs.

A teacher in Singapore's United World College wrote a book on parenting, leads professional development programs for teachers in her school and serves as a consultant for other schools. The director of curriculum of a private international school in Beijing translated two of my books on global citizenship education and assisted with their publication in China.

Some of these leaders develop products and programs for schools and non-formal environments. These include programs to support early literacy for marginalized children, programs to help youth gain job or entrepreneurial skills, and technologies to support the acquisition of basic literacies. Additionally, they include programs that provide college graduates with online opportunities to gain skills valued by employers, prepare college graduates for international graduate studies, or prepare government administrators with skills to foster government innovation.

Some of these leaders have created educational organizations ranging from organizations that directly educate students, to those that offer services to existing schools or provide supplementary education services to students. These include, for example, organizations of volunteers to teach English to students in public schools, organizations that place recent college graduates in high poverty schools, part of the Teach for All network and organizations that develop citizenship education curriculum and that offer professional development to help transform school culture. Other organizations include those that support effective engagement of low-income parents with schools, universities serving low-income students, organizations to support other education organizations, and preschools or education consulting companies.

Those who have created organizations often build on this experience to participate in other roles which augment their influence, for example as members of government councils or public-private collaborations focused on the improvement of education. For example, the creation of a citizenship education organization in Mexico provided the founders credibility, which resulted in their inclusion in a regional council to foster civility and the rule of law in the state of Nuevo León; these leaders were eventually invited to participate in the design of the national civic education curriculum in Mexico. One of the co-founders of this civic education organization went on to create a network of business leaders in the Mexican states of Nuevo León and Coahuila, with the aim of strengthening corporate social responsibility in those states. The founder of an education services organization was invited to become a trustee and acting director of the Crown Price Foundation in

Jordan, which focuses on youth empowerment. The founder of a technical education institute in Thailand was invited to chair the Federation of Colleges of Technology and Vocational Education of Thailand under the Patronage of HRH Princess Maha Chakri Sirindhorn. The founder of a range of education organizations in Colombia was appointed as Deputy Secretary of Education for the country.

These leaders also work in higher education institutions, either preparing teachers, or in research and development on behalf of the improvement of K-12 education. One of them is the associate director of a newly established school of education in Pakistan with the mission of preparing innovative education leaders for that nation. Another works in a university in Colombia, designing approaches for the assessment of teacher quality and developing approaches to improve quality in networks of schools serving low-income children. Another is a teacher educator. Two of them work as Director and Deputy of a regional Latin American center that supports the professional development of education staff and the development of educational research and instructional materials to support adult education. One works to help universities develop assessment systems of higher cognitive skills and collaboration. Another leads a technical and vocational institute serving low-income students in Thailand. One conducts research to support K-12 education policy and programming in Chile. Another strengthens the administration of a university serving low-income students in Mexico, and another promotes religious tolerance and pluralism through an institute of higher education.

A number of these leaders work or have worked for government, often in senior positions. These include a deputy secretary of education in Colombia, a director of curricular development of the national Ministry of Education in Brazil in charge of leading the implementation of a new common curriculum core from early childhood to high school, a director in the national Ministry of Education in Guatemala, in charge of a range of education programs to serve indigenous children and youth including alternative educational programs with linguistic and cultural relevance. As Director of the Digital Inclusion and Literacy Program of the Mexican government, one of these leaders oversaw the procurement process for the acquisition of 960,000 tablets and their distribution to 32,000 public primary schools in the country. Another leader is developing a new pre-service teacher education program that will be implemented nationwide in public teacher education institutes in Peru. Another leader plays a similar role in Argentina.

Many of these leaders work for multilateral international development institutions, such as the United Nations, UNESCO, UNICEF, The World Bank Group, regional institutions such as the Inter-American Development Bank and bilateral development assistance agencies such as the United States Agency for International Development. Their work in these agencies is varied and involves working in partnership with national governments in policy dialogue and in the design and implementation of programs of technical assistance. One of these leaders developed the first UN guide for business investment in education as part of the UN Secretary General Ban Ki Moon's Global Education First Initiative to overcome the global learning crisis, to then mobilize the business community to collaborate on an international scale targeting children and youth who are often ignored due to a lack of resources or major crises. One of the leaders works for the Global Partnership for Education, working with governments in the design of national plans and implementation strategies; several of them work for UNESCO, providing technical assistance to governments to align their education programs with the broader development agenda reflected in the Sustainable Development Goals. Two of them manage large programs of assistance at the United States Agency of International Development.

Working in close coordination with international development organizations and with governments are leaders who work for consulting companies, who often implement donor-funded programs. A number of leaders in this book reflect on that kind of work, including some of them working to strengthen the capacity of ministries of education to support early literacy instruction, education in conflict and emergency settings, or increasing the capacity of school districts in the United States to support students with disabilities.

Other leaders work for global non-profits that advance their own programs, such as Education International, a global federation of over 400 teacher unions; Room to Read, a large organization supporting literacy in several countries in Africa and Asia; the World Federation of United Nations, supporting the implementation of global citizenship education programs, or LASPAU, an organization working to strengthen higher education institutions in Latin America. Some of them work in foundations that directly implement programs or fund them. As a senior education advisor to the Qatar Foundation, one of these leaders has generated a range of innovative education programs, including an experimental school focused on 21st century competencies and a virtual school.

In these various roles to advance educational opportunity, these leaders report that they are happy, satisfied and effective. When asked to what extent they are happy, 66% answered 'very happy' and 33% said 'rather happy'.[16] When asked how satisfied they were with their professional work, 38% of respondents are 'extremely satisfied' and 52% are 'moderately satisfied'. When asked how effective they were 26% said 'very effective' and 60% 'effective'.

What impact do they have?

The impact of these leaders ranges from direct impact on the students some of them teach in classrooms or through the programs they develop and implement, to the more indirect impact on the students who are influenced by the policies and programs these leaders develop. Many of them have impact at several of these levels, directly influencing some students, while also indirectly influencing a larger number. For most of them, their impact is indirect and mediated by other individuals and institutions which they affect. All of these leaders have clear theories of how their work influences the systems in which they work, and many think about ways to have an impact that is sustained beyond the time when they are in the leadership roles that allow them the opportunity to have such influence.

---

[16] These figures for happiness compare well with figures for the population of college graduates. Data from the World Values Survey on happiness are, for college graduates in the United States, 34% very happy and 54% rather happy.
Source: http://www.worldvaluessurvey.org/WVSOnline.jsp

For example, the director of curricula of the Ministry of Education in Brazil, describes her impact in this way:

"Over the last year, my work in the Ministry of Education has indirectly influenced the 47.8 million students enrolled in public (82%) and private (8%) Basic Education, nationally. More immediately and directly, my work has affected the four million primary school students in schools that are implementing the program Novo Mais Educação - NME (literally, New More Education) and the three million high school students in schools that are implementing the program Ensino Médio Inovador – ProEMI (literally, Innovative High School)."

This kind of indirect impact in large numbers of children is reported by those who work for national ministries of education or for international development agencies collaborating with them. For instance, redesigning the program of initial teacher preparation that will be rolled out to all public teacher education institutes in Peru will, over time, influence all teachers in the country, and consequently all students as well. Similar large scope of impact is reported by those working to serve particular groups of children, for instance the director general in the Ministry of Education in Guatemala is developing innovative and culturally relevant programs to serve indigenous students. Those working for international development agencies have impact of a similar scale.

The deputy secretary general of Education International, the international federation of teacher unions says:

"Assuming that our influence is spread evenly across our members' organizations and their individual members, one might approximate that on average each member teaches around forty students per year (this could vary between 20-150) - 32 million multiplied by 40 equals 1.28 billion students."

The Vice President for Innovation at Pearson speaks about her impact as follows:

"Over the last year, I believe we have reached close to 1 million students. Over the course of a decade, I believe we have reached over 50 million students. However, my hope is to reach 1 billion learners!"

Others have more limited impact through programs that directly serve students, although the scale is still significant. For example, a program to empower youth to become social entrepreneurs directly supports 1,500 young entrepreneurs in 90 countries, who impact the lives of 1.7 million people each year.

Still others report impact at a smaller scale, in the thousands or hundreds, often mentioning multiple levels of impact. For instance, through the development of programs of citizenship education one of these leaders has directly reached 300 teachers and 10,000 students and parents per year, while contributing to developing the national civic education curriculum in Mexico, which will eventually impact all students in the country.

In the survey, these leaders were asked to estimate the number of students they impacted directly and indirectly. Two thirds were able to provide estimates of direct impact over the preceding year, ranging from 25, for those who teach, to 8,000,000 for national system level leaders. Of those, 19 report impact on over 100,000 students and ten report an impact on over one million students. These reports suggest that the quantitative impact of these leaders grows not linearly, but exponentially, as they move into positions where they can have greater influence. Clearly, these estimates of impact should be interpreted cautiously because it is not possible to establish whether the reported impact across respondents is essentially the same process. For instance, the impact reported by a director of curriculum who transforms the intended curriculum and which reaches a sizeable percentage of the student population is arguably a different phenomenon than the impact reported by a teacher as a result of her daily interactions with her students.

In addition to their quantitative impact, these leaders also describe their impact in ways clearly focused on the quality and relevancy of the education to which the students they affect have access. It is noteworthy how many of these leaders speak about this impact in ways that explicitly relate to the advancement of broader social purposes.

For many of these leaders, their careers and impact are supported by professional networks. When asked whether fellow graduates of the International Education Policy program had helped them hear about professional opportunities, 73% replied 'yes'. In addition, 60% indicated that fellow graduates had helped them solve professional challenges. They interact with fellow graduates often, on average 70 times a year, ranging from 5 times a year to daily contact. A number of these graduates are on various social platforms which enable frequent interaction with fellow graduates. The importance of professional networks is also highlighted as graduates are asked which factors have limited their professional advancement. Lack of networks is the most often mentioned (by 29% of them), followed by gender (which 23% of these leaders mention). One in ten leaders mention race and social origin as factors that have hindered their professional advancement.

What are the challenges they face?

Leading is not for the faint of heart. These leaders describe a wide range of professional challenges, from the challenges underlying the education problems they are trying to address, to the challenges of mobilizing and empowering others to collaborate in order to address them.

The education challenges they describe involve inadequate organization, capacity, funding or alignment and coordination among the various agencies and actors. For example, commenting on the lack of global early educational opportunities, one of the leaders describes the low levels of financial resources available to fund high-quality educators, compounded by the lacking business skills of those running these centers, which are too small to have the necessary resources to provide high quality professional development, curriculum, or the support of technology. The fragmentation of the ownership of such centers limits the opportunity to implement solutions at scale, for instance, like common technological platforms. He described also how the lack of coordination between the health and education communities limits the opportunities for young children's healthy development, and how the lack of attention by leaders in the business community to this sector perpetuates the neglect of this critical level of educational opportunity.

Challenges are complex and capacity is limited…

Leaders share that the challenges ahead in expanding opportunities in education for all at the international level are complex: they require innovation, strong alignment between different moving pieces, a high degree of coordination between complex processes, and high levels of resources, among other elements.

A significant challenge is the need for greater institutional capacity, an issue many of these leaders are directly addressing. Several of them mentioned the temptation to short-cut such limitations by working through parallel structures, but explained why this would be counterproductive to the goal of building the capacity for sustainable delivery of high quality education programs. Along with the design of a new high school curriculum in Brazil, for example, the director of curriculum for the Ministry is developing plans to fund and support the development of internal capacity in cities and states to implement a new curriculum. A UNESCO consultant on a teacher education program in Myanmar describes this challenge as follows:

"There remains a great need to strengthen capacity within the MoE in Myanmar to take on evidence-based reforms and to build understanding of the fundamentals of teacher education and curriculum development at all levels, making up for years of limited exposure to new strategies and techniques."

It's a system...

Two challenges a number of these leaders describe are the need for greater alignment among various education programs or components of the same program, as well as the long time that education programs take to produce results. These leaders see education as the result of a system, and work to align the various components of the system. This work requires communication and negotiation with stakeholders internal to their organizations and across organizations, making such alignment difficult to sustain over the long period of time necessary for these efforts to produce results.

"I also need to create space for our projects to respond to unforeseen circumstances they will encounter in the future. When I write an intervention, it may be for 3, 5, or even 7 years in the future... So I need to work with our contracting office to make sure they are comfortable and understand what USAID is buying while at the same allowing our future intervention the room to grow and react to the world it will be living in."

The leader of an effort to revamp initial teacher education in Peru explained how this program is part of a broader initiative involving the improvement of the overall quality of the teaching career, which includes higher salaries and more opportunities for in-service professional development. The deputy director of the international federation of teachers unions describes the challenge of systemic coherence as follows:

"My challenge at the moment was to help move us to a systems approach within a world that sees education as a simplistic result of a few inputs, and build partnerships across sectors with a view to a whole-child, whole-school approach."

Describing how improving quality and relevance of education is more challenging as well as more interesting than increasing access, an education advisor for USAID explained that this is because it is harder to obtain political buy-in because multiple components need to be brought into alignment:

"Working on quality and relevance is often more complex and difficult politically than access issues, but once established quickly grow to scale. Certainly we all know that improving reading is not as simple as creating a new set of textbooks for teachers to use -- it is showing the government the current reading levels and offering policy solutions for improvement, establishing national standards and benchmarks, creating new materials and teaching pedagogies, proving the concept, training in-service teachers, incorporating new pedagogies and materials into pre-service curriculum, training administrators, finding time in the school schedule, working with the teacher unions, assessing progress, and mobilizing the parents and communities. Each step has its own ministry staff and department(s), proponents and opponents, competing priorities and varying levels of interest. Add in elections, coups, deaths and the need for broad participation and incremental progress becomes piecemeal to great victories. I still believe that once these collective challenges are overcome, there is the possibility of making systematic impact on a large scale, especially if the improved materials and practices are integrated into the regional and national education systems."

It takes time...

Leaders work to provide these reforms with the necessary support over time to "stay the course," which requires luck, patience, and persistence:

"In my tenure with UNESCO Yangon, I worked with four different Ministers of Education, requiring constant consultation and orientation as well as patience in allowing for new structures to be put in place; there is no shortcut to reform."

Many leaders address the challenges of managing the discontinuities likely to result over time in support for education projects and policies, and explained that such discontinuities induce a short-term bias in the way many people approach leading change:

"Most funders and institutions in our country who invest in education projects expect to see impact right away which is hard when the system requires major cultural renovations. This is also an issue with government institutions and ministries of education where, in general, there is short attention for initiatives related to education innovation and its impact in the long run. Administrations only last a few years, which barely provides the time to get to understand the system and perhaps attempt a few quick fixes."

"Working closely with ministries of education is complex and involves balancing political timelines with activity timelines, not to mention competing demands and priorities within the ministry. Changes in ministry staff can lead to unexpected delays, or demands in activity implementation, and may result in a complete re-design of a capacity building approach or intervention. These unexpected changes, which are largely out of the control of project implementers, have direct implications on our ability to effectively partner with students, teachers, schools, and ministries. "

"The technical proposals or academic analysis provide evidence and data, but it is necessary to understand the political agendas of people in Congress, senior government officials and other elected officials. We often plan the technical part very well, we enjoy seminars with hard and heavy data, but political timing is not always the timing of technical processes. Another challenge is dealing with promises and good intentions

without budgets. If a budget is not there in our annual operational plan, anybody can say anything but it will be hard to deliver that promise."

Even if there is political stability and transitions favor educational progress and the work the leaders are pushing forth, these leaders see bureaucracy and state administration as slowing down the change process and often placing unnecessary roadblocks to progress:

"In this type of work, we are so far removed from the student, and similarly from the timeline when our work will begin to have an effect, that it is difficult to assess how many students we could affect through the system. There is also the fear that our work could be erased should there be a new administration. This distance between what we do on a daily basis and our purpose can be dangerous for losing a shared vision, but it also allows us to handle a different set of challenges that comes with policy and central government level work."

Related to this issue is the question of sustainability of education policies and other initiatives, and of how to ensure that initiatives extend even beyond a cycle of initial program implementation and generate lasting change for students and their families. Leaders share a variety of struggles around how to help cultivate more lasting change in their projects and programs:

"In addition to adapting to unexpected changes, a continuous challenge I face is ensuring that program interventions are sustained and continued by local actors after projects officially end. This challenge is particularly difficult given the short life span of most projects (typically no more than five years) and the fact that building trust and buy-in among local stakeholders takes time. The ability to sustain program interventions is further complicated by the withdrawal of program resources at the close of a project, which highlights the importance of investing in capacity development of local actors and introducing cost-effective approaches to educational reform."

"The challenge of political discontinuity is closely related to another great challenge: motivating the civil servants who are the heart of these bureaucracies and are the only ones who can ensure the continuity of policies. This challenge is exacerbated by the apathy that sets in once these civil servants have endured many changes in leadership. Influencing, motivating and building their capacity is the biggest challenge that people who are nominated to positions in government face, if they want their reforms to have long-term impact.

It's all about the people...

Many of the leaders in this book share challenges about initiating change, especially around motivating others to embrace change and do things differently from "the way they have done them before." Leaders share that it is sometimes difficult to motivate individuals, teams and organizations to push for different solutions or to aspire to generate change, as there are too many built-in forces working to maintain the status quo:

"The main leadership challenges I have faced are related to managing resistance to change, identifying variables that can be modified in the system and that really strengthen it, and empowering the main actors of that system to discover ways in which they can expand the impact of their work by their own means and in collaboration with others."

"Creating a culture that supports change in this state of affairs is a difficult task. It is challenging to state these purposes and to discuss them with key stakeholders. As a result, it becomes very difficult to know why the system must change, the causes of the challenges, and to eventually define how it would change. For that reason, collaborative leadership is relevant to guarantee a plural and holistic perspective/approach to undertake a change and generate positive impact."

"One of the most significant challenges to creating meaningful, long-term change is that education systems are built to reinforce the status quo. Unless innovations or policy changes ultimately affect the quality of teaching and learning that takes place in classrooms, there will not be meaningful improvement in student outcomes. It is difficult for even the most ambitious, capable system leaders to adopt effective, evidenced-based innovations that effectively improve teaching and learning at scale. They can face a myriad of barriers ranging from lack of capacity at the local level (whether it be talent or resources) to effectively adopt new practices, garnering political capital and trust to implement changes that affect teacher practice or contracts, or having sufficient time to pilot, refine and scale an innovation. Even when leaders can overcome these barriers, they find it difficult to scale innovation system-wide, and in many cases inertia or continuous resistance forces systems to revert to old practices."

Many of the leadership challenges refer to the challenge of motivating others to embrace change, and to achieve coordination of efforts among a range of stakeholders with a bearing on the problems these leaders are trying to tackle. Leaders share struggles of ensuring that all stakeholders are on the same page and in agreement about new initiatives, whether these are at the school, system, or policy level:

"One of the most difficult leadership challenges I have faced during my time at the Inter-American Development Bank has been attempting to generate consensus around how best to organize and streamline efforts to improve access to education and education quality throughout Latin America and the Caribbean. While it is clear that the vast majority of people who work in international education policy are deeply engaged in the work in order to improve the educational opportunities of children and learners, I have learned that the intelligent, passionate people in the field frequently disagree about how best to do so."

In this process of achieving and maintaining consensus among key stakeholders, communications was often mentioned as a significant challenge, as described by the director of curriculum in the Ministry of Education in Brazil:

"The first and probably biggest challenge is communication, both internal, within the Ministry, and external to each of the stakeholders of the process. It has been my experience in the almost 10 years I have worked in public education that communication is always an important challenge. In large, complex systems there are many stakeholders to take into account and communication usually needs to be customized to each one. Most governments focus their communication staff solely on the press and not on this internal and external communication to stakeholders."

Mindsets matter...

One challenge brought up by several of these leaders is the challenge of prevailing mindsets, views about education that limit the consideration of improvement options. Some spoke about the lack of appreciation for the complexity of teaching and learning:

"Yet, I often find that not only the outside world but teachers themselves often fail to recognize the tremendous complexity of the teaching profession."

One view many of these leaders described was the low priority that education received from governments or development agencies, so they see their role as advocating for the importance of education. The director of education in the Ministry in Guatemala referred to the related challenges of insufficient funding and low priority given by many in Guatemala to the education of the children of the poor. A leader working with refugees explains:

"The challenge was to have the staff in the large NGOs whether in the field or in the HQ change their perspective and view refugees as humans."

Relatedly, a researcher at a university in Colombia explained:

"Among these challenges is a deep sense of inequity and anger ingrained in Colombian society. Inequity has led to segregation of opportunities that destroys the will of low-income students to work hard as well as their hopes of having a good future."

Several leaders referred to the low value in which the teaching profession was held in their societies as a constraint to mobilizing the resources or adopting the programs necessary to support higher levels of quality in schools.

A mindset that impedes change is the acceptance of the status quo as the "natural" way things ought to be. This can include pride in the history of an institution and acceptance of prevailing norms and practices (for instance, giving more attention or resources to certain students). Many of these leaders describe parents as exerting an influence on schools that is vested in the status quo and impedes change.

The representations that parents and teachers have of what good education looks like configure a culture of education that can impede the adoption of new practices. The leader of an organization teaching children in the slums of Delhi and Mumbai referred to the challenge that most teachers and staff had not been exposed to or experienced high quality education. The director of a youth leadership development program spoke about the need to change mindsets with respect to the roles that young people could and should play in society and about the approaches to teaching and learning that are effective.

Another mindset that undermines long-term efforts of educational change is one that seeks evidence of results caused by specific interventions, which replace the focus on the performance of a system overall or for a longer period of time:

"Education funding is understandably accompanied by demands for results that are in some cases attributable to specific interventions. However, the process of building and strengthening education systems requires an understanding that the desired impacts will be achieved only if there is a sustained long-term engagement, unlike in other sectors such as agriculture where returns for investment may be visible within a one or two-year period."

A mindset mentioned by one leader as detrimental was a 'savior mentality' on the part of leaders, a limiting view because it can blind us to the resources that exist in the very communities we seek to serve, and can impede listening to the voices of community members. Several of the leaders highlighted the importance of an asset-based approach that appreciates the agency of underserved students and their parents, and that builds on that agency, rather than imposes on them solutions based on somebody else's definition of their needs.

Trust is key...

Aligning the competing interests of the various stakeholders affected by educational change is difficult, especially so in contexts in which there is low trust, a theme mentioned by several of these leaders.

"In one of my roles, I was tasked with leading partners, including governments, to execute donor-funded programs. The politics involved in such a multi-party initiative were many, and oftentimes, priorities were not aligned. There were differences in what groups would benefit, in how and when activities could be implemented, and with who we could work to design and implement activities. While most parties had the best intentions for learners, they had different visions for what "best" meant, and how to get there. Most parties also had additional needs and interests to take care of..."

Describing the lack of trust between the public and private sector, one of these leaders said:

"But what has surprised me most has been the lack of conversation between these two worlds. Mutual suspicion, skepticism and contempt has created and amplified a useless schism that has held back the advancement of educational opportunity around the world."

Fear nothing… but fear itself…

These challenges, and the scale and complexity of the systems these leaders are trying to influence, can lead to fear. The former deputy secretary of education of Colombia describes this as follows:

"I was quickly overwhelmed by the paradoxical feeling of having the tools and formal authority to implement real change, while at the same time being paralyzed by a feeling of helplessness resulting from the sheer magnitude of the school system, depth of bureaucracy and consequence of the stakes. There was an irony in knowing that every decision I made would greatly affect the futures of many children and being petrified about making those very decisions at the same time. I immediately understood the reason why the prevalent view of the public sector is one of inefficiency, paralysis and impossibility. It is humans, after all, who run the public sector — humans who are prone to fear, who are risk averse and who have a survival instinct. Humans who are only so strong and are suddenly tasked with altering the course of a gigantic organism."

Leaders also face challenges in building and finding their voice and making themselves heard, both as professionals as well as when they work in cultures that are different from their own and when they belong to subdominant groups in the societies where they are working. Several highlighted how necessary it is for education and development institutions to intentionally become more diverse to have a wider range of voices and perspectives participate in advancing educational opportunities. Leaders share struggles about how to build the confidence necessary to participate actively as well as how to best manage their roles when working in other countries:

"While the work is rewarding, there are leadership challenges associated with being a professional expatriate in the UAE, including the hierarchical structures. There have been challenges for me moving into a very hierarchical system where titles and positions may, at times, provide individuals with complete authority; this is in contrast to countries like the United States where, in general, workplaces are more horizontal. This sometimes makes it not only more difficult for me to have my voice heard, but

also to encourage team members to speak up and share their opinions. Secondly, while I have a multicultural background and had studied Arabic before moving to the UAE, I still encounter unique cultural differences that can challenge my work in the education sector."

"Being a woman in a patriarchal society imposes a challenge in many dimensions. At the beginning, it is difficult to be heard and you must work harder to gain trust and respect and make your ideas count."

"While I know I have the training, and experience to take command of what I do, I do not always have the confidence that should match these skills. This stems from needing to figure out many work challenges in silo through my own research, and by trial and error as a last resort. In attempts to avoid failure, I sometimes overly seek consensus rather than backing my opinions, even when I know they are strongly evidence-based. As I advance in my career, I am working to break this habit because I know others look to depend on me for advice. I remember to use the very strategies from the youth development programs that I designed for others: encouraging myself to learn from failure rather than shying away from it, setting realistic goals, and using my own management style instead of imitating others."

The challenges identified in these essays were included in the form of questions in the survey administered to the 208 leaders, who were asked to indicate which of these they had experienced. The following table reports the percentage of respondents who strongly agreed that these were challenges. The challenges experienced by the greatest number or leaders include the length of time it takes to produce results, the need for a high degree of coordination between complex processes, politics — organizational or national — and limited institutional capacity to execute reforms.

Table 1. Challenges you have experienced leading educational change	%	Count
It takes a long time to produce results	52%	109
A high degree of coordination between complex processes is needed	47%	98
Organizational politics undermine the work	47%	98
There is too limited institutional capacity to execute	43%	90
National politics interfere	42%	88
Prevailing mindsets limit opportunities to advance change	36%	74
Lack of shared vision of what the change initiative was trying to achieve	31%	64
There is too much resistance to change	29%	61
Poor or inadequate communication	27%	56
Prevailing mindsets about the approaches to teaching and learning that are effective are limited	26%	54
Staff are not capable to execute	25%	53
Political instability	25%	51
Poor understanding of the process of teaching and learning	25%	51
Weak analytic capacity among those making decisions	24%	50
More innovative ideas are necessary	23%	48
Critical stakeholders were excluded from the process	23%	48
Insufficient technical understanding of the problem we are trying to solve	21%	44
Corruption	20%	42
A mindset that impedes change is the acceptance of the status quo as natural as the way things ought to be	20%	42
Staff are not motivated to execute	20%	41
Ineffective negotiation among stakeholders	18%	38
Lack of clarity of what the change initiative was about	18%	38
The representations that parents and teachers have of what good education looks like configures a culture of education that can impede the adoption of new practices	18%	38
Lack of ethics of key players	14%	30
Among various education organizations that should coordinate there are very low levels of trust	13%	28

Table 1. Continued...

The teaching profession is not valued where I work	13%	26
Prevailing mindsets about the roles that young people could and should play in society are limiting	12%	24
There are very low levels of trust in the society	11%	22
I am unable to influence key people	9%	18
Education is a very low priority in the setting where I work	7%	15
In my organization there are very low levels of trust	6%	13
Intolerance and hatred are rising in the context where I work	3%	6
I am afraid	2%	5
People I should influence do not trust me	1%	2

What are the trajectories of their careers?

For some of these leaders, their careers are non-linear. They do not involve joining an organization and advancing through the ranks but rather engaging in a variety of roles, often taking professional detours and alternating between working in the public and private sectors. Two in five of the respondents have made at least one career switch from the public to the private sector or vice versa. For most of the survey respondents (54%), their career's progress from influencing less to influencing more students, however, one third of them report no consistent pattern in their career in this respect, and one in ten indicate that their careers progressed from influencing more to influencing less students.

The essays written by these leaders show how these detours are the result of challenges accessing the leadership roles they seek, or responding to the unpredictability that results from the influence of politics in educational programs and appointments. Often, these changes are the result of the continuous self-assessment these leaders make of their impact as they reflect on the work they do. For example, one of these leaders became an entrepreneur creating innovative programs to support literacy instruction in Mexico when she found it challenging *"to enter the small and closed communities of people working in education... I applied to many job positions without being even called to interviews because I had no friends inside."* Speaking about the upcoming Presidential impeachment in her country, the Director of Curricula for Basic Education in Brazil said it would be unlikely she could complete a full year in that role.

Balancing the unpredictability in the tenure of their roles, particularly for those in high-level positions of decision-making, most of these leaders engage in multiple roles at the same time and speak about the flexibility necessary for them to have impact. This allows them to have a "portfolio" of work and relationships, that provides a buffer to the impact of politics on their careers and to adapt to changes beyond their control. For instance, an education development Foreign Service officer with the United States Agency for International Development explained how resources and goals often shift with changes in presidential administrations. Another education advisor with USAID spoke about the need to be intentional in responding to these changes in context:

"A career in international education development is cobbled together, and not always a straight line. In some cases we need to move opportunistically and based on timing, but being purposeful about our choices, we should ask ourselves key questions along the way."

A constant in the career trajectories of these leaders appears to be the focus on accomplishment and results; it is the achievement of those results that gives these leaders the credibility to access higher positions of influence. They are driven to achieve results in terms of learning opportunities for children, and it is those results that allow them to keep extending the reach of their influence. Often, this focus on results causes these leaders to push boundaries, to challenge existing cultures and to foster innovative and unconventional ways.

"Having zero experience in the public sector, I resorted to my entrepreneurial background and told my team, "We are always in startup mode." While the public sector seems to be the very opposite of a startup environment, I thought that this mindset would help us overcome initial inertia and assume the risks that were necessary to produce change. It would allow us to innovate, experiment and pivot. It would also isolate us from the perilous path of conforming to existing practice because "This is the way it has always been done." It would let us use our power and escape our helplessness, while at the same time having the urgency of every startup: scale or die."

What lessons have they learned?

These leaders are insightful about the challenges they face and use reflections to draw out lessons that can help them enhance their effectiveness. The lessons they offered based on their experience advancing educational opportunity globally can be grouped in ten categories:

1. Lead ethically.
2. Understand the education challenge you are trying to solve.
3. To understand the challenge, understand the people involved. Map key stakeholders.
4. Understanding how to solve an education challenge requires continuous learning.
5. Collaboration is key to learn and to act: There are opportunities in Collective Leadership.
6. Collaboration requires good personal relationships
7. Attend to execution and to the details of getting the work done.
8. Communication is critical to learning and to execution.
9. Balance patience with setbacks and processes, with impatience for results.
10. Do we need to educate for a new kind of education leadership?

Lead ethically.

Leading educational change is not only about getting others to know what to do, but it is also about motivating them to do it. Leaders need to figure out what motivates those they are trying to lead. Ethical frameworks are often core to how people define their identities, and some of the leaders speak of the power of building a narrative of change around clear ethical frameworks.

"I've come to realize that educational leaders must not back away from crafting an institutional narrative that is focused on values. Whether in for-profit or not-for-profit schools, financial and curricular decisions can be framed in terms of sustainable social impact and an ethic of care."

"Leading and coordinating the work of UNESCO in Africa in the area of sector-wide education policy and planning has required me to seek a balance between

investing in supporting the strengthening of capacities in technical planning skills and techniques, with stimulating more profound dialogue at each stage of the policy and planning cycle. Going beyond econometric analytical tools, financial simulation models, logical frameworks, and results matrices, to dialoguing and building consensus around the purpose and potential of education in transforming individuals and societies and creating global citizens that beyond bearing a sense of responsibility, feel gratification in rendering service to others."

Several of the leaders in this book spoke about the need to have clarity about the values and ethics that are the foundation of their own leadership, as a way to get through setbacks and get the courage to lead, as well as a way to convey an authentic sense to others of who they are.

"To be in service to others requires that we find and remain true to our authentic selves. It does not mean that we attempt to like and be liked by everyone; it is about organizing your life and how you are with others—around a core set of principles—that will manifest in your decision-making and actions."

"Be clear about both purpose and values. The work of education is value-laden. It requires personal conviction, determination and clarity of vision. A clearly articulated purpose—that higher call to action that forces us to think and act beyond ourselves for the greater good—is essential."

"The main thing I learned was to remember constantly that the reason we are all in this work is for children. This is why I started working in education, and have dedicated my life to it. Working at a big bureaucratic organization will sometimes make you forget that. There is a lot of red tape around the work we do, and moreover, even my own professional development and type of contract. Centering yourself, taking a deep breath, and remembering the mission behind all this work puts me in the right mindset to approach work."

"The principles that have served me best in the long term are honesty and transparency. Honesty, because personal reputation and work ethic are what keep you employed in this sector. Transparency, because most people in our globalized work environments appreciate someone who works with confidence, and takes responsibility, if things do not go according to the plan.

"We must encourage the younger generation to pursue their dreams to resolve big societal problems. This will come through an emphasis on global education and

creating a sense that they belong in the world as global citizens, and that everything is interconnected."

These leaders see learning and the development of students as a holistic process that involves the development of a range of capacities, cognitive as well as socio-emotional. They see international covenants, such as the Universal Declaration of Human Rights, Education Conventions, or global compacts such as the Sustainable Development Goals as ethical north stars that facilitate collaboration:

"A power of the Sustainable Development Goals is that they provide an overarching commitment that pushes departments and ministries to collaborate with each other, pool statistics efforts, and justify decisions to their constituents. I've seen these Goals and other external forces, such as the Global Partnership for Education, move conversations forward that have been stuck in circles because of people having their hands tied."

Understand the education challenge you are trying to solve.

In order to produce change, these leaders map the systems that undergird the challenges they are trying to solve. This helps them focus on root causes and not on superficial fixes of these problems. An education officer for USAID, for instance, speaking about the challenges of improving literacy instruction, described a system that had to be brought into alignment in order to produce meaningful transformation in opportunities for children to learn to read and write at scale. Similarly, a leader working in a new program of teacher education in Peru mapped how this program fit into a system of various initiatives to improve teaching quality. Seeing this system causes some of these leaders to understand that no single agency has the formal authority to generate change, and brings them to engage in efforts of collective leadership to produce cooperation and alignment among various organizations and sectors:

"Get past the spin, skip the fad, attend to the conditions. There are people who wake up every morning thinking about how best to pitch the next big thing in education. Some continue to pitch and cherry-pick evidence well past an idea's 'sell by' date. Their persistence eventually breaks down donors' defenses but the fact that their innovations never take root or get taken up should make education equity activists cautious. They may have found something that does work for a certain population at

a certain time but my experience has taught me to look at the conditions as much, if not more than, the edupreneur. The organization Bridge Academies, for example, which offers low cost for profit education to poor children in Africa, will never be Escuela Nueva, an organization that for over six decades has offered public schools professional development to change the culture of schools to make them more effective."

To understand the challenge, understand the people involved. Map key stakeholders.

Part of understanding the system is mapping the stakeholder groups which are affected by the system in place, and could potentially be affected by efforts to change it.

"An in-depth understanding of the roles and interests of the different people, organizations, and governments that can effect policy change in a given context proves invaluable in the generation and continued cultivation of consensus surrounding improving education quality."

A number of these leaders speak about accepting and understanding others as a basis of their leadership, and to explore the purposes and needs that motivate them. This does not mean accepting poor performance, or their resistance to change: it means addressing the sources that may undergird such resistance.

"…I have learned that each individual has their strengths and weaknesses. This is true for those whom lead and those who one leads. Along with personalities and personal histories and experiences comes one common link – purpose."

"I have learned that it is extremely important to try and understand the perspectives of the local people with whom you work. Understand their perspectives and goals and you will better understand what they want and how you can work toward mutual benefit… A government official might want to show results toward a policy. A contracting officer needs something "real" to contract. A program officer might need a way to show progress toward strategic results… If you can deliver on these things, give them an answer, find the place where we can satisfy all our binding rules, regulations, and policies, and help them be successful in their jobs, you will be able to create even more space for education to happen."

"Be mindful of others. Just as we plot our own careers and experiences, we must be particularly understanding of the perspectives, interests and motivations of key

actors in the field in which we work. Different individuals at ministries of education, political actors, NGO leaders, scholars, journalists, teachers, and union representatives each play an incredibly important role in their respective education systems, and in the success of any given education program funded by international donors. It is important to remember that they each have a particular job to do, probably care as much as if not more about children learning as you do, though it is not always clear to us what pressures or contexts they face. Being an effective leader in this field means being respectful, creating spaces for "informed dialogue," and creating strong working relationships based on human connections."

Understanding how to solve an education challenge requires continuous learning.

To understand a problem, in particular to understand how to solve it, requires learning. Often this learning requires acting to solve the problem, rather than extensive contemplation or study. Leaders speak about leadership as creating opportunities for others to learn, as well as managing their own learning.

There are limits to the power of mandates, policy directives, regulations and money to induce change. At the end of the day, change in opportunities to learn requires that students and teachers engage in different ways to learn, and those depend on capacity and the motivation to learn.

Many of these leaders have mastered ways to help adults learn, including the capacity for themselves to learn continuously. Some of them have also instituted practices in the organizations they lead so the organizations support collective learning continuously. When done systematically, this is called capacity building and systems strengthening.

"My work with GPE has given me a better appreciation of the scale of the global education challenge and a practical understanding of the centrality of systems strengthening to tackling the challenge."

Effective capacity building requires approaches to adult learning that work. Socratic, participatory methodologies, discovery learning, approaches that honor the knowledge and experience of adults, as well as their interests and learning styles, can be more effective than didactic approaches that assume that learners are blank slates.

"Being a young leader, I had to divorce myself from the old idea of leading people by power and learned a method that is democratic in nature... one thing I have learned is that adults don't like being told what they should do. In the fight for education equity, inevitably we need to get a lot of people on board and we cannot do it alone. We have to convince people to join our movement and believe in our ideas. However, adults are far less likely to put in their 100% into something that was prescribed to them."

Capacity building is especially important in a context in which outsiders advise an education system. An education specialist for UNESCO describes this as working for local ownership:

"...Whole-heartedly commit to local ownership, doing whatever it takes to build the capacity required to produce quality products – and in an inclusive way that involves all stakeholders."

These leaders manage their own learning, through reflection, engaging with mentors, or participating in supportive networks. Most importantly, these leaders see action as an opportunity to learn.

Learning from action and from failure

Many of these leaders share a bias toward action, and comment that it is easier to learn things along the way and make constant and continuous improvements, than to wait until all the conditions are perfect. Several of them comment that as leaders, they are committed to stepping up and taking action given the urgency of the task ahead, and that this involves being comfortable with uncertainty and a capacity to constantly innovate, prototype and improve as the projects and programs go ahead:

"Another lesson has been to err more often on the side of action than on waiting for clarity. While I have had the good fortune to work with amazing, smart and talented people, I have also come to find that it is rarer than I expected that any one of us is the super-knowledgeable, super-experienced person we need for any specific topic. In addition, as was true in my business career, it is rare that the steps in the path to the vision are obvious. Waiting for that level of clarity to materialize (or for someone else to give it to you) in order grab hold and move ahead is not a good use of time. We

all come armed with the abilities to research, to learn, to seek out help from our networks and to think creatively and pragmatically. I have found that it is better to act."

The commitment of these leaders to ambitious goals and to action, as opposed to mere contemplation of the challenges they must address, involves taking the risk to fail. Many of them see these as opportunities for learning. They adopt a growth mindset.

"I am convinced that entrepreneurship is a powerful avenue to advancing educational opportunity. However, it requires the understanding that it is precisely the lack of impact in the early days that enables and unleashes the transformative power of scale. The paradox of pursuing change by producing none has been my greatest lesson in starting educational organizations."

"In the almost ten years since graduating from the Harvard Graduate School of Education, I have learned that resilience is the most important skill needed to endure the challenges affecting long-term change in public education. Setbacks are constant, but keeping a focus on the children, whose education one is working to improve, and on the importance of the mission to build the kind of society one wants to live in and wants to leave for our own children, helps to bounce back ready to take on the next challenge."

Learning from action means being open to changing one's mind and deciding that it may be necessary to course correct.

"A third lesson is recognizing when it is okay to move on from an intervention that may not be working."

A leader from India who thought the priority for the education of low income children in that country should be to teach them the basic literacies, describes how she changed her mind and how this led her to embrace a different line of work:

"My opinion on this matter shifted when I studied International Education and understood the importance of Global Citizenship Education (GCED) and 21st century skills. And now, working on the curriculum for Mission Possible and preparing to educate students, I am a strong proponent of GCED and 21st century skills being integrated into the mainstream."

Learning with others and from others

Learning is central to the education enterprise. This is true not only because education is about ensuring that students learn, but because achieving this requires that those who support the enterprise learn as well. To a great extent, this need for continuous learning of the adults supporting teaching stems from the rapid changes in society and increased and new demands on schools. It is this inherently continuously changing nature of education that explains why some leaders speak about top-down and standardized approaches as inherently limited, and why many see implementation more as the creation of systems of continuous learning and improvement rather than as the execution of predetermined steps.

The founder of an organization to empower parents describes this as follows:

"Success cannot be achieved at scale with standardization or centralization of control. Agile organizations that build decentralized structures will withstand pressures of expansion, changing readily to demands and needs of their stakeholders."

To support their own continuous learning and the learning of their organizations, a number of these leaders participate in communities of practice and other networks from which they receive support and feedback.

"It has been extremely important for Vía Educación to be part of networks and alliances to keep looking at the large scope of things, with organized leadership and consistent support for what is important in both the short and the long run."

"It has been working around the challenges described above and by being part of the highly enriching network formed by the Synergos Institute, that I have become aware that there is a great need for a different kind of leadership in our society."

Many of these leaders speak also about the value of learning from those they seek to serve; this is especially important when their own life experiences are different from the experience of those they work to serve:

"The importance of seeking input from those who are closest to the work. At Room to Read, we have country-based teams that implement and execute our work on the ground with schools and children. Unlike some other organizations, all our country-based staff consists of professionals from that country. The rationale for this is simple: people from that country are the ones who are most familiar with the language, culture and context, and are therefore best positioned to successfully implement the work."

Collaboration is key to learn and to act. There are opportunities in Collective Leadership.

Expanding educational opportunities requires collaboration and a form of leadership that enables and facilitates collaboration across and within institutions.

Children develop holistically, not in the silos government and private organizations have created to organize their work. Too often, development is impeded because these silos work at cross purposes, or do not sufficiently integrate their work. For instance, the education and health communities need to develop more effective ways to integrate their work to support children. Similarly, education institutions need to find ways to more effectively integrate parents in the efforts to support the development of children.

Too often, collaboration is impeded by prejudice and ideology. The view that what one institution does to advance education is the only or the most important way to advance it gets in the way of establishing productive collaborations with others. This prejudice is common between those who work in government and those who work in the private sector. These essays show that the leaders reflected in this book follow careers that often take them to cross sectors, often at the same time, and that the knowledge and experience they gain from doing so only helps them develop a more integrated and comprehensive view of the systems that undergird educational opportunity, or the lack thereof.

Collaboration is also impeded by a lack of trust; these impediments are reinforced by membership in communities of like-minded individuals and by insufficient opportunities to engage with those who think differently. Several of the leaders spoke about the value of building coalitions and of public-private partnerships, as ways to achieve impact of a depth and scale that would otherwise be elusive to their own organizations.

"Leadership is not only individual but is also collective, requiring a shared vision for change and the collective conviction that we can reach it. It also requires being in constant learning mode, and building strategic partnerships. Education is transformational and is key to achieving all the Sustainable Development Goals. We therefore, cannot work in silos but must join forces across sectors (health, labor, energy, environment, justice…) in an integrated manner."

Collaboration requires good personal relationships.

Leadership requires followership, which means it is essentially an interpersonal process, and as such one bound by the norms and expectations that we have for how to treat and be treated by others. A number of the leaders in this book speak about how they take the time to build good will by attending to the needs of and supporting those around them.

"I have certainly learned many lessons doing this work, but my biggest takeaway is that the power of education relies on the human connections that we are able to build across the entire educational system. It does not matter if our goal is to spark deep lasting change within an educational community, or to develop a compelling curriculum that ultimately transforms lives, it is the personal connection that we develop with the educators and students around us that allow us to advance our work."

"Significant relationships underpin all our work, but they aren't easy to build. Educators are used to being right and not being questioned and the value and prestige associated with education is low. People have disliked me for being ruthlessly focused on impact and making their lives difficult; it is the collateral damage of bringing change."

"To mitigate some leadership challenges, I have learned a number of things, particularly about the importance of fostering relationships. For those working in education leadership anywhere in the world, relationships are vital as education is inherently about people."

"People matter. People matter in the most fundamental sense from the authentic engagement of individuals and communities (parents, teachers, heads, community leaders) in the work of reform to the mobilization and empowerment of staff to execute on goals. Recruiting a diverse base of staff and volunteers—people who complement each other in background, perspective, and skill—investing in their development, and ensuring that they have space, agency and voice to innovate and actualize goals is critical."

In addition to personal relationships, cultural and institutional norms can also influence collaboration. The provost of an institute of higher education in Mexico said:

"The most difficult leadership challenges I face are in managing people and creating a space that supports teamwork and collaboration. In a society like Mexico's, where power distance relations prevail, there are a number of obstacles to engendering collaboration."

Attend to execution and to the details of getting the work done.

These leaders focus on results for children and they achieve them by translating ideas about change into implementation strategies that help the various stakeholders involved in making change happen know who needs to do what and when in order to support the change efforts. This requires good management skills and often good project management skills as well.

"Excellent administration and management can greatly advance teaching with efficient organization, supportive mechanisms, and a positive atmosphere. By contrast, unsatisfactory administration hinders teaching and brings up unnecessary tension."

"The devil is in the details – [for example] before you can start to measure skills, it is important to know what they are. While this seems simplistic, taking a step back to define and refine what is being measured will help to prevent confusion and miscommunication amongst stakeholders about what skill is being captured."

"It is important to combine academic preparation, networks, work experience and personal commitment. In the professional area, besides the technical and academic preparation, it is fundamental to understand policies, administrative and financial procedures. Most of the good ideas cannot be implemented without knowing the processes, bureaucracy and financial management."

Communication is critical to learning and to execution.

These leaders understand that leadership is influence, and influence requires communication, which is a two-way street travelled often:

"It is always a challenge to communicate enough and to be sufficiently clear in the message. This is why there must be a robust communication strategy that is revisited often."

Communication can be challenging, whether it involves identifying the interests of others or ensuring that words are used to convey similar meanings; leaders are attentive to how they communicate and with what results.

In describing frustrations with responses to her project evaluation reports from some clients, one of the leaders explained the power of depersonalizing communication with more transparency throughout the evaluation process:

"Little by little I started learning how to adopt techniques that would help me with my reporting to make the partner more accepting and open to what was revealed through the data collection and analysis and make sure nothing is personalized in the process."

Balancing patience with setbacks and processes, with impatience for results.

These leaders are aware of the need to significantly transform educational opportunities for children and youth. They speak about these needs with urgency and often with pain. At the same time, they understand that the scale of the enterprise requires patience with themselves and with others, respect for process, and attending to the development of institutional capacity, so that change can be enduring. These leaders strive to find a balance between these conflicting views.

"…Educational policy results cannot be measured in short periods of time, they are processes and as such, they take time. Actually from the moment they are designed

(thought of, dreamed about) until they reach students, they change many times in many ways."

"I have learned that passion, perseverance, and patience are three key assets needed to effectively deal with challenges that arise. Passion refers to my personal commitment to ensuring a quality education for as many students as possible around the world. This passion is the force that drives my day-to-day work and helps me weather unexpected challenges. My passion for education also fuels my ability to persevere through challenges until I have found solutions that meet the needs of ministries, funders, and most importantly, students and educators. Perseverance is not only the ability to keep working, but the ability to also be creative, innovative, and forward-thinking so that students and teachers receive the best possible outcome from a difficult or challenging situation."

Educating for a new kind of leadership

The leadership that accompanies the kind of work necessary to advance the global education movement as described by some of my former students, one that can foster genuine and sustainable collaboration and partnership, is different from the traditional vision of leadership in a number of ways. Several of the leaders in this book speak of the value of humble and authentic leadership that inspires collaboration with others because of a genuine value on diversity, on bringing people together, and on finding collective vision that inspires collective action:

"It has been working around the challenges described above and by being part of the highly enriching network formed by the Synergos Institute[17], that I have become aware that there is a great need for a different kind of leadership in our society. A leadership based on establishing clear relationships of trust and reciprocity among the various personalities involved in addressing our common educational needs. A leadership that genuinely cares for the points of view, feelings, fears and hopes of those who play a part in the solution of our shared challenges, including their own. A leadership that is patient enough to go slowly but together with the rest towards the ultimate goal, instead of trying to get there first and alone. A leadership that is convinced of the benefits of cross-sector collaboration and facilitates systemic thinking when building the civic capacity of a group or community."

---

[17] Synergos Institute. "Institutional webpage." synergos.org. http://synergos.org/ (accessed July 13, 2017).

"Be open to being influenced; be willing to compromise: a critical aspect of leadership and how I lead is the willingness to step away from even those ideas which 'I know to be true.' It leaves me open to being influenced by the ideas and experiences of others. This, over time, becomes a way of being that makes me willing to hear other perspectives, especially in contexts of historical and cultural experiences, that are different from my own. The lesson for leaders is try not to be so certain that you lose sight of how you might be wrong."

"First, only through humility is it possible to make changes that benefit most children. If in a dialogue one part sees itself as the owner of truth, and will of doing things right, there is no possible middle point. Second, education is the key to changing society. Through education we can give the population the skills needed to make a more generous, less judgmental, and more tolerant society. Third, collaboration leads to longer lasting programs. The public sector has the power to scale programs, but is also tied to regulations that lead to the rotation of personnel and programs. Through partnerships, it is more likely that programs have a longer life; most results in education take several years to happen."

"To lead" requires passion and perseverance, self-confidence, and a collective humility that we can sustain only if we are our authentic selves and if we continue to believe and to dream. Success often comes solely through struggle and sometimes setbacks. Knowing when to stop and when to push through is a developed instinct and not as much a science one can learn. It comes from experience and walking the walk, not just talking the talk. Above all, leadership means having the courage to make decisions, to take action, and to commit to positive change along with others."

Based on the lessons about leadership which these leaders have discussed in their essays, I asked those who responded to the survey to indicate to what extent they agreed with the importance of these elements of effective educational leadership. Their responses are presented in Table 2. Leading ethically, taking the time to understand the challenge, map stakeholders, learn continuously, and create opportunities for others to do the same and communicate effectively are the practices which most of the respondents recognize as effective in leading educational change.

Table 2. To what extent do you agree with the statement that effective education leaders lead in the following manner.

Effective Leaders...	Complet ely agree	Agree to a great extent	Agree to some extent	Disa gree
Lead Ethically	70%	19%	10%	1%
Take the time to understand the education challenge they are trying to solve	82%	10%	8%	0%
Take the time to map key stakeholders and to understand the people involved	72%	21%	6%	1%
Learn continuously	86%	12%	2%	0%
Create opportunities for others to learn continuously	77%	17%	5%	1%
Don't wait for complete knowledge, but act and learn from the results of such action	31%	36%	28%	4%
Exercise Collective Leadership	39%	40%	20%	1%
Have good personal relationships with those they influence	42%	35%	22%	1%
Know how to develop implementation plans	42%	34%	23%	0%
Know how to manage projects	43%	35%	21%	2%
Listen well	78%	18%	4%	0%
Communicate effectively	83%	14%	2%	0%
Are patient with setbacks	37%	35%	24%	3%
Are impatient about results	5%	15%	40%	40%

Survey respondents were also asked to indicate to what extent they agreed with the new form of leadership proposed by one of the respondents in the essays, their responses are presented in Table 3 below.

Table 3. To what extent do you agree with the need for a new form of education leadership?

Completely agree	Agree to a great extent	Agree to some extent	Disagree
A leadership based on establishing clear relationships of trust and reciprocity among the various people involved in addressing our common educational needs.			
56%	34%	9%	0%
A leadership that genuinely cares for the points of view, feelings, fears and hopes of those who play a part in the solution of our shared challenges, including their own.			
60%	29%	10%	1%
A leadership that is patient enough to go slowly but together with the rest towards the ultimate goal instead of trying to get there first and alone.			
43%	35%	16%	6%
A leadership that is convinced of the benefits of cross-sector collaboration and facilitates systemic thinking when building the civic capacity of a group or community			
68%	24%	8%	0%

Changing my mind about how to educate leaders of the global education movement

One of the valuable results of following and listening to our former students is that it can give us some indication of whether the long-term outcomes of our teaching, those we most value, are in line with our expectations. Listening can also teach us how the world our students are trying to influence is changing and therefore how preparation for them to be a force for good in the world must also change. As a result, we can course correct and try to better help our students become contributors to a better world.

This is one reason I communicate with around a hundred former students each year, the other being that I enjoy it. In order to benefit from this feedback, it is helpful to have clear hypotheses about how it is we hope our teaching contributes to the long-term outcomes we value. We can then think of our teaching as an ongoing experiment, where successive iterations benefit from what we are learning.

When my colleagues and I designed the International Education Policy Program in 1998, this design was based on the hypothesis that if we attracted a group of talented students to Harvard each year who had the ambition of significantly advancing social progress around the world as a result of expanding educational opportunities, and provided them a rigorous academic preparation, then we would accelerate progress around the world. We spent some time thinking through the type of competencies that would help these professionals pursue careers in government and in international development institutions, informed by our experience and that of our colleagues working in and for those institutions. Clarity about such competencies then helped us design the overall program and each course, so that they would all collectively build the skill sets we thought would assist our students in gaining essential professional skills.

Other elements of that original hypothesis included attracting a diverse group of candidates to the program, in terms of gender, national origin, religion, race, and professional and personal background. We know there is potential for leadership in all communities and we thought that more diversity among professionals with the ambition and the skills to advance global education would help government agencies and international development agencies better represent and serve the populations they were aiming to serve. We also knew that such diversity would enhance the preparation of our students, helping them benefit from a richer array of viewpoints and experiences, and stimulating their critical and creative capacities in thinking through how to best advance educational opportunity around the world.

Those core elements of our "program theory" are revisited each year when faculty and staff meet to discuss applicants to the program and decide who to admit. These ideas also inform the nature of the course requirements for students, and inform how academic advisors discuss with students their proposed selection of courses.

Other aspects of that initial program hypothesis included creating as many links as possible between the program and the core courses students take, and institutions and professionals involved in the practice of international development education. We host guest speakers from those organizations, arrange internships for students, organize workshops and conferences to bring our students in conversations with leaders of practice, and often invite visiting faculty who are leaders in the practice of international education.

We also invite ownership and leadership of the curriculum by our students. We support them as they create student organizations, which focus on the study of education in particular regions of the world or in key global education topics and issues. Through these initiatives, students organize a range of events and build even more connections with practice, resulting in a rich set of co-curricular activities.

Given the wide range of international projects, centers and activities at Harvard University, students are well supported in co-constructing a curriculum that established connections between their interests and those resources, in addition to those connections they establish with outside organizations. It is, of course, extremely helpful that we can do this work in a University that is committed to the development of global leadership and that has a clear aspiration to be of service to the world. In many ways Harvard embodies the aspirations of the modern university of the enlightenment, which Humboldt crafted for the University of Berlin and which John Adams had hoped for in creating the American Academy of Arts and Sciences: to cultivate the capacity of critical thinking, to advance truth on matters of consequence, and to educate the public on such matters. Harvard is, as are most modern universities and the enterprise of science more generally, a cosmopolitan institution from where we see that in our respective fields of research and teaching, our larger obligation is to humanity and to this planet we share. Because Harvard aspires to educate all of our students as global citizens, a program that deliberately brings students who aspire to advance the global education movement is not an oddity. Appropriately, the theme of the campaign of the Harvard Graduate School of Education is "Learn to Change the World." The students in the International Education Policy Program are right at home at Harvard, not only because as an institution we value and support their professional goals, but because many in this community understand that they are a very valuable resource to help educate their fellow students as global citizens.

An important component of the original program theory was the idea that our graduates would, over time, play an important role in inducting new graduates of the program into the field, and that the community of graduates would serve as a resource for each other, supporting continuous learning and career advancement.

We never set an explicit target of how many graduates of the program it would take to make a significant difference in educational opportunity around the world, although implicitly I thought for a long time that I should do all in my power to reach a thousand graduates. I don't really know where that number came from. Twenty years ago, it seemed like a big enough number. Maybe I figured that an average of five graduates of this program per country in the world would make a difference. Perhaps I based my estimates on the 32 million students my colleagues and I were influencing through our work in Mexico with the World Bank, and thought that a thousand colleagues doing the work that I was doing could influence the educational opportunities of one billion students in the world. Whatever the basis of the calculation, the number of 1,000 remained a north star for me for a very long time. Since there were only twenty-one students in the first class of graduates of the program, a group of pioneers who decided to follow the curriculum we had designed and be part of an unofficial program before applicants to the school could apply formally to the course, a thousand seemed to be an ambitious goal.

After our most recent graduation in May of 2017, 902 global education leaders had graduated from this program, plus the original 21. This means we will reach a thousand graduates in May of 2018, when the 79 students who will enroll this fall, graduate, twenty years after I joined the Harvard faculty. I suppose this is one motivation for me to take stock of what these graduates are doing and to reflect on the goals I had set out to achieve twenty years ago.

I have learned much from my students and from my graduates, including lessons about how it is that we make a difference in education. I am now more persuaded of the power of doing this "one student at a time," but I have changed my views on some aspects of the original hypothesis that served as the foundation of this program.

One of the ways in which I have changed my mind is in thinking more broadly about the competencies that matter to lead the global education movement. In part this shift follows the development of my own research interests in the areas of citizenship education, global citizenship education, and 21st century education. Those have helped me understand that cognitive skills are only part of the mix, and that a balanced education should include also the opportunities to develop self-knowledge and the skills to relate to and collaborate with others. I think an ethical compass is also critical to carry people through work and life, and universities should take responsibility to help students develop ethically. As a result of this evolution in my thinking about what competencies matter, some years ago I invited my faculty colleagues who teach students in the program to a conversation about what those competencies should be, and we drafted a document which we have since shared with every incoming cohort of students in the program, asking them to hold us accountable to helping them develop those skills. That framework is presented in Table 4.

Table 4. Framework of Core Competencies guiding the International Education Policy Ed. M. Program at the Harvard Graduate School of Education

Professional Ethics
- o Commitment to supporting the education of the most disadvantaged students
- o Drive for results and effective use of resources
- o Accountability
- o Proactive acquisition of responsibility
- o Professional integrity and trustworthiness

Professionalism
- o Entrepreneurial mindset / Growth mindset
- o Ability to receive formative feedback and draw out implications for professional improvement
- o Inter-cultural competency
- o Ability to cope with pressure and setbacks
- o Capacity to adapt to and respond to change
- o Capacity to learn independently and desire to continuously learn

Technical Skills
- Ability to frame an educational challenge into a tractable problem through policy and program interventions
- Ability to draw on empirical research and documented good practices to inform the identification of possible levers to address an education challenge
- Ability to conceptually define causal pathways, and to evaluate empirical research in terms of its adequacy to support causal inference
- Knowledge of contemporary key challenges to educational opportunity in the developing world
- Understanding of how different disciplinary perspectives inform understanding of education institutions as they influence learning and its social consequences for students, as well as the relationship of education institutions to larger social institutions

Table 4. Framework of Core Competencies guiding the International Education Policy Ed. M. Program at the Harvard Graduate School of Education

and the process of development. For instance, basic familiarity with concepts used in economic analysis of education such as:

- o Supply and demand as they relate to education
- o Teacher labor markets
- o Incentives
- o Production function approaches to study educational effectiveness
- o Human capital theory

Similarly, familiarity with basic concepts used in sociological, anthropological, psychological and historical analysis of education, and appreciation for how these various perspectives are complementary.

- Understanding of alternative perspectives of development and of the role of education institutions
- Knowledge of how various governmental and civil society organizations at the subnational, national and supra-national levels influence education policy and programs that affect educational opportunity at scale
- Comparative knowledge of global education policies, systems and educational innovations, and frameworks to learn from comparative perspective and to transfer ideas about good practice across contexts
- Understanding of program and policy evaluation, and of how to collect and analyze data to assess program impact
- Capacity to think logically about education challenges, to think about cause and effect and to develop interventions that can plausibly address the causes of the challenges and achieve their intended results and scale

Table 4. Framework of Core Competencies guiding the International Education Policy Ed. M. Program at the Harvard Graduate School of Education

Leadership and Management

- Communication / Leadership
    o Writing in different genres, including writing op-eds or using social media
    o Using various media to communicate, including video and social media
    o Public speaking and presentation skills
- Negotiation skills
- Ability to collaborate in groups and lead groups towards successful achievement of a goal
- Ability to map relevant stakeholders to an education issue/policy, and to build coalitions and plan a strategy for policy advocacy or to support policy change.
- Understanding of project management
- Ability to listen to different perspectives and to make decisions that advance the productivity of the group
- Ability to achieve results in inclusive ways in diverse groups
- Social pro-activity, or capacity to relate to others in constructive ways towards the achievement of shared goals
- Ability to influence and persuade others in a professional setting

---

Underlying these competencies are a set of values about what kind of world we hope our graduates will help build. Over time we have become more intentional in engaging them in reflection about those values. Covenants such as the Universal Declaration of Human Rights and the UN Sustainable Development Goals have immense potential to inspire such reflection. I greet each incoming class of students into the International Education Policy Program by providing them a postcard with the Sustainable Development Goals, and explaining why they matter. I know helping them think with moral clarity about the important consequences of doing the work they want to do, will carry them far and help them navigate the many ethical dilemmas which fill rich professional practices.

I also know the use of a language that permeates many institutions in the international development community will help them "see" the coalitions that need to be built, and perhaps help them lead them. In a seminal book, ethicist Sissela Bok once argued that the most challenging problems in the world could only be solved through collaboration among people from many diverse origins, which required a set of common values.[18] I agree with her views, and think that compacts such as the Universal Declaration of Human Rights or the UN Sustainable Development Goals are very good approximations at those frameworks of common values. Higher education institutions should use them to guide their efforts to educate global citizens.

When we designed the program, the original set of competencies we had intended to cultivate were primarily academic competencies intended to help students gain technical skills that would help them conduct policy analysis. Over time, I came to understand that we could not take the inter-personal and intra-personal skills that allow a person to put technical skills to good use for granted and that we should help students develop them. This is why we created a student advisory board to the program which is asked to work with all members of the cohort each year, planning activities that will enhance the curriculum, and it is the reason we encourage each student to take up leadership roles in creating activities that foster conversations and collaboration with fellow students and with leaders of practice in our field. We hope that sharing leadership for the program with our students in this way provides the opportunity for collaboration and for proactively taking responsibility to improve one of the communities of which students are a part.

I also gradually expanded my view of our focus on preparing policy analysts to preparing leaders of policy reform. Leadership requires more than good analytic skills, although those are essential. In a number of the courses students take, there are opportunities for them to develop skills to design programmatic solutions and interventions to education challenges, going beyond the analysis of the challenges themselves. In

---

[18] Bok, Sissela. 1995. *Common Values*. Columbia, Mo.: University of Missouri Press.

my work in higher education over the years, at Harvard, in collaborations with other universities, and in my service as a member of the Massachusetts Board of Higher Education, I have observed that there is too much of a contemplative bias in the curriculum of higher education institutions, more emphasis on understanding problems than in learning to solve them. There is, of course, no direct path from understanding why a problem exists, to having the capacity to solve it. The following example will illustrate the distinction between understanding and designing solutions to problems.

I used to teach a course on education, poverty, and inequality. The course provided students an opportunity to discuss theoretical and empirical work examining how schools that serve the children of the poor help them get out of poverty. Much of the scholarship examined the multiple avenues through which growing up in poverty constrains the opportunities of the children of the poor to develop skills that will help them break the cycle of poverty, including the fact that too often they attend schools of very low quality.[19] I was, and remain, deeply interested in understanding these issues and the students found the course valuable and interesting. But a number of them remarked, in the course evaluations they wrote at the end of each semester, that they found some of the issues we examined in class overwhelming. It is easy to become overwhelmed as we spend time thinking about the many ways in which poverty influences the lives of children. Personally, the course had the effect of getting me down a little. I would finish this class with a nagging sense that the barriers to overcome in order to provide effective, high quality, education to all children were too many. A serendipitous event caused me to try a rather different way to engage my students with these issues.

I had been working with a group of colleagues from different professional schools at Harvard launching a program to attract to the university people who had retired from a primary career and wanted to spend a year at Harvard figuring out how they could make a significant impact in addressing some social challenges. As part of the curriculum

---

[19] Reimers, F. Educating the children of the poor: A paradoxical global movement. In Tierney, W. (Ed). *Rethinking Education and Poverty*. Johns Hopkins University Press. 2015.

for this group, I engaged a group of graduate students in preparing short case studies of individuals who had made a significant difference in the field of education to be used in a three day Think Tank on education I was planning for this group of Harvard Advanced Leadership Fellows. This work, and the conversations with my colleagues on the board of the Harvard Advanced Leadership Initiative, opened my eyes to the field of social entrepreneurship and social innovation.

I decided then to tweak my course on education, poverty, and inequality, including in it some of the case studies of innovators who had made a difference creating educational opportunities for the children of the poor. I observed that, in that section of the course, the students became animated and hopeful, rather than overwhelmed, about the possibility of addressing some of what had previously seemed to be intractable challenges of education and poverty. I too found myself more hopeful, happier, with the discussions of those cases. So I decided to retire my course on education, poverty, and inequality, and replace it with a course on educational innovation and social entrepreneurship. The course has evolved over the years, but it is essentially a course designed to teach students to create innovations in order to advance educational opportunity, rather than teach them to understand the scholarship of what factors constrain the learning opportunities of the children of the poor.

I have learned much about human centered design, and design thinking in the process of teaching this course on educational innovation, and now integrate some of those insights into other work I do with students in the International Education Policy Program. For example, during orientation, as I welcome the incoming class of students into the program, I teach a short session on design thinking as I engage them in solving an education challenge they think is pressing. Last year, I worked with a group of students in my education policy class, designing a K-12 curriculum aligned with the Sustainable Development Goals[20] which we published as a book. I find that engaging students in solving real problems, as part of their professional education, is an effective way to help them develop some of the essential skills to lead: creativity, the

---

[20] Reimers, F. et al. 2017. *Empowering Students in Sixty Lessons.* Create Space.

capacity to innovate, problem solving, human centered design, and collaboration. Engaging with opportunities to solve real problems helps students develop agency and self-efficacy, which are necessary to lead. Doing this kind of collaborative problem solving in a program that is intentionally culturally diverse also helps students develop valuable inter-cultural competencies.

My thinking about what we are preparing our students for has evolved also from thinking we were preparing them to pursue careers in government and in international development institutions, to understanding that there are many more avenues from which students can advance educational opportunity.

I now understand the task of advancing the global education movement less as the sole responsibility of governments and development institutions, and more as the result of an ecosystem which includes civil society organizations, the private sector, and various levels of government, local, state, national, and supra-national. I have also in part changed my views about the process of educational change because the development of communications technology, and the ubiquity of capital and knowledge, enable relatively small groups of individuals to undertake projects of ambitions previously available only to very large-scale organizations. With the recognition of a pluralist ecosystem as the locus of educational advancement, I have become more interested in the idea of collective impact, the impact that results from being able to connect the dots across organizations and sectors.

Over the last two decades, I have also become more aware of the fluidity and unpredictability of affairs, both local and global. Learning to deal with this fluidity and ambiguity is critical in a field which prepares students to lead institutions that are about the future. Given our growing uncertainty about the future, it becomes essential to prepare those who are to lead education so they can learn continuously, be comfortable with such ambiguity, be flexible, be innovative and creative, understand complex systems, and act in ways that have systemic impact. It is clear that our graduates will have to continue to learn and re-learn all their professional lives, which means we should equip them with a foundation that helps them manage and direct their own learning.

This awareness has made me become more interested in how to support the lifelong education of our graduates, rather than focus only on their initial education, even at the graduate level. It is not that I think undergraduate or graduate studies are unimportant, it is just that we need mechanisms that are equally effective in supporting professionals as they continuously develop skills to do their work. University instruction is heavily biased towards serving people in early stages of their lives and of their careers, and does not give the same importance to lifelong learning. Some professional schools have understood that we need to rebalance this emphasis, and have created good programs of executive education, but for the most part those do not receive the same priority in higher education. As a result of spending considerable time working in this area, I now know that we could have much greater impact advancing the global education movement if we developed educational opportunities to sustain the existing communities of leaders who do this work. Some years ago, in partnership with UNICEF, I developed a multi-month program of leadership development for senior education officers in the organization. Most of this program took place online, with a short stint when about 100 participants each year converged in Harvard for a week during the three years we ran this program. The program was designed to support the development of many of the competencies discussed in this book as necessary to lead global education. The feedback from the participants and from UNICEF was very positive, and the program was renewed for three years, until about half of the education staff of the organization had participated in it.

I developed another project along similar lines collaborating with a public university in Brazil, the Universidad Federal de Juiz de Fora in Minas Gerais, designing a two-year master's program in education leadership for educational administrators in various municipalities and states in that country. Participants signed up for the program not as individuals, but as teams, that included a mix of people at various organizational levels: school principals, supervisors, and secretaries of education. Most of the instruction took place online, with brief stints in person when all participants converged in the University. I insisted that this program involve several departments of the university, as well as partnerships with non-governmental organizations involved in school improvement efforts. The results were very positive. Some of the districts where large numbers of people participated achieved remarkable gains in student learning outcomes in subsequent years.

It should not be surprising that if we provide rich opportunities for people to improve their skills in close partnership between their job contexts and universities, they should become more effective. What is still not widely accepted in higher education is the idea that this is work that universities should do. I believe it is for all professional fields, because a profession depends on the use of expert knowledge and, along with Max Weber, I believe universities play a central role in the advancement of expert knowledge. But to do this well, universities must guard against the risks of excessive isolation from the fields of practice they are trying to influence, they must learn from the field, and from those who lead practice in the field. This is the reason universities create professional schools; it is the reason the Harvard Business School and the Harvard Graduate School of Education were created, along with other professional schools. To stay relevant to the field, we need robust and pervasive ways of communicating with the professions that shape the field. We need to not only advance knowledge through research, but also to engage in translational research that helps practitioners access this knowledge in ways that are relevant. The traditional emphasis on professionals at early stages of their careers in graduate schools of education is limiting in this respect, because it fills our classrooms with people who are candidates to enter the field, rather than practitioners or leaders in the field. Executive education can change this balance for the better, and online instruction can help us reach professionals where they are. I have taught online at the Harvard Extension School for about a decade the same courses I teach at the Harvard Graduate School of Education, and this allows me the opportunity to reach education leaders who are already in positions where they have significant influence over large numbers of students, as opposed to students who aspire to be in those positions in the future.

More fundamentally, I think the sisterhood between the projects of democracy, public education, and higher education can only survive the current attacks of the populist movement that glorifies ignorance and attacks on "elites," if we build relationships of mutuality between these institutions. Universities could do substantially more than they do to improve public education, and they should make this task part of their core mission, as much as they should embrace the mission of strengthening democracy, when it is threatened. To do this well will require designing new avenues to pursue the enduring mission of the University, including giving much greater attention to educating the larger public and supporting the lifelong learning of education professionals.

There was one additional element of our original hypothesis that seems so flawed, twenty years later. It was the idea that the job would be done when 1,000 students had graduated from the program. It is certainly the case, as Margaret Mead once stated, that a small group of people can change the world, and the graduates of this program have done their share to improve it. For this I am deeply grateful. The trust of each one of the graduates of the International Education Policy Program has been an undeserved privilege.

But it is a big world and the fragility of the global education movement, and of the liberal values that inspired it, suggests we need to think in much bigger numbers. We must increase the capacity to prepare leaders of this cosmopolitan global movement exponentially, not incrementally. I trust that some among the graduates of this program will be discerning how best to do this. Maybe I will get to play a part in this reinvention of the extraordinary movement that began seven decades ago, when humanity decided that we had to educate all so we could have peace in the world.

As I look forward with confidence and excitement to that road ahead, the road I have been lucky to travel humbles me. It has been a long way from those afternoons of typing lessons in high school, and from the long bus rides that led me away from home and towards higher education. I have been fortunate to travel that road in the company of my students, now colleagues and partners, in a shared quest to educate all children and create a more peaceful world. As we have traveled together, my students have taught me, one student at a time, that education is, in fact, the most remarkable human invention to improve the world.

Fernando M. Reimers is the Ford Foundation Professor of the Practice of International Education and Director of the Global Education Innovation Initiative and of the International Education Policy Master's Program at Harvard University.

Professor Reimers is an expert in the field of Global Education. His research and teaching focus on understanding how to educate children and youth so they can thrive in the 21ˢᵗ century. He studies how education policy and leadership foster educational innovation and quality improvement. As part of the work of the Global Education Innovation Initiative he leads, he and his colleagues conducted a comparative study of the goals of education as reflected in the curriculum in Chile, China, India, Mexico, Singapore and the United States, published as *Teaching and Learning for the 21ˢᵗ Century* by Harvard Education Press, a book which has also been published in Chinese, Portuguese and Spanish. A forthcoming book, also to be published by Harvard Education Press, studies programs around the world which support teachers in developing the professional competencies to teach holistically for the 21ˢᵗ Century.

Two recent books present innovative global citizenship curricula. *Empowering Global Citizens* a complete K-12 curriculum of global citizenship education, examines why global citizenship education, aligned with helping students advance human rights and contribute to the achievement of the Sustainable Development Goals is an imperative of our times. *Empowering Students to Improve the World in Sixty Lessons. Version 1.0*, presents a strategic framework and protocols to help teachers and school leaders develop strategies and curriculum for global citizenship education. Two recently edited books compile the results of informed dialogues, designed to foster collective impact in the areas of teacher education in Massachusetts (*Fifteen Letters on Education in Singapore*) and in the area of Scaling 21ˢᵗ century education programs (*Empowering All Students at Scale*).

He recently chaired a Global Alliance which produced a framework for collective impact in strengthening teacher preparation and support (*Connecting the Dots to build the future teaching and learning*). This report has been translated and published in Arabic, Portuguese and Spanish and used to steer national dialogues on how to create conditions to strengthen the teaching profession and improve the relevance of instruction.

Professor Reimers has worked to advance the contributions of colleges and universities to develop leadership that advances cosmopolitanism, democracy and economic and social innovation. He has led the development of several innovative programs at Harvard University, including the master's degree program in International Education Policy and various executive education programs, including a program to support education leaders working for UNICEF and a collaboration with the Universidad de Juiz de For a in Minas Gerais, Brazil, to develop a master's degree program in education leadership. He is a founding co-chair of the Advanced Leadership Initiative, a program which brings to the university outstanding individuals who have retired from a primary career and who are interested in devoting themselves to addressing significant social challenges. As chair of the Strategic Planning Committee of the Massachusetts Board of Higher Education he works with all public institutions of higher education in the State developing institutional strategies to enhance the relevance of their programs. He has advised a range of institutions of higher education on strategies to advance the global awareness of undergraduates and serves on the board of Laspau, a Harvard affiliated organization whose mission is to strengthen institutions of higher education in Latin America.

He has advanced the development of programs to provide students and recent college graduates opportunities to engage in service and to develop civic, global and leadership competencies through his service on the boards of numerous education organizations and foundations including Teach for All, World Teach, the Global Scholars Program at Bloomberg Philanthropies, Envoys, and the scholars advisory council of Facing History and Ourselves. He is a commissioner in the US Commission on UNESCO. In 2017 he received the Global Citizen Award from the Committee on Teaching about the United Nations for his work advancing global citizenship education. In 2015 he was appointed the C.J. Koh Visiting Professor of Education at the National Institute of Education in Singapore in recognition of his work in global education. He received an honorary doctorate from Emerson College for his work advancing human rights education..

SCHOOLS

Back to Preschool

By Kevin Kalra

Goals and Work

My journey in international education started in the oil industry. As a geographer, I designed maps of new drilling sites and later applied geospatial technology to track the impact of my company's social investments in global education. During this process, I discovered that my company struggled to find effective partners to deliver relevant education. And despite good intentions, my colleagues found it challenging to work with international education systems plagued by teacher absenteeism, low standards, and corruption. I was motivated to pursue graduate studies to explore education in-depth and to understand how the business community could play a meaningful role in addressing the learning crisis as well as make the best use of its investments.

In 2013, I graduated from the Harvard Graduate School of Education and was invited to serve as Lead Consultant for *The Smartest Investment: A Framework for Business Engagement in Global Education*, a joint initiative between the UN Global Compact, UNICEF, UNESCO, and the Office of the UN Special Envoy for Global Education. The document was the UN's first guide for business investment in education as part of former UN Secretary General Ban Ki-moon's *Global Education First Initiative* to overcome the global learning crisis. The report offered a three-part process to help the business community engage responsibly in global education and led to an increased interest by the global business community to engage in education in a coordinated way. As the former Secretary General described, "...corporate philanthropy is critical, but we need more companies to think about how their business policies and practices can impact education priorities."[21]

---

[21] Ki-moon, Ban. "Remarks to Global Business Coalition for Education Breakfast." Global Business Coalition for Education Annual Breakfast, 27 September 2012, NYC, NY. Keynote Address.

My assignment also led to an opportunity with the Global Business Coalition for Education (GBC-Education) in New York City, a US-based nonprofit that "brings the business community together to accelerate progress in delivering quality education for all of the world's children and youth." At GBC-Education, we mobilized the business community to collaborate on an international scale targeting the education of underserved children and youth. Over my two years, I actively interacted with CEOs of global corporations and their philanthropic leadership to create awareness of the learning crisis and channel funds for education. GBC-Education was instrumental in advocating for the creation of the *Education Cannot Wait* fund, which is raising nearly $100 million in support of education during crises around the world. Most recently, GBC-Education helped champion education as a priority investment by G20 countries.

Soon, I realized that many challenges in education should be addressed in the earliest years. It also makes financial sense because for every $1 invested in early education, society benefits by nearly $8.[22] Many mentors in the business world were encouraging me to return to the private sector. Through GBC-Education, I also learned that education—particularly in my own home country of the United States—was a local issue and that "Act Local - Think Global" is a critical mantra in international development work. To create sustainable impact, education leaders need to start working in their own backyards. So, I returned to work at a preschool in my own hometown of Houston, Texas.

I intend to create a global network of preschools that cultivate a global outlook and build a strong academic and socio-emotional foundation at an early age. Although K - 12 schools worldwide have access to public funds, early childhood education has been left to parents to fund on their own. Also, there is a growing 'childcare crisis' worldwide and not enough organizations to meet the growing demand for quality preschool.

---

[22] Executive Office of the President of the United States. (2015). *The Economics of Early Childhood Investments*. Washington, DC.

In 2015, I joined Montessori Children's School Inc. in Houston, Texas, USA, which has been in the early education industry for over 20 years. This Montessori school emphasizes developing a global outlook in the early years and helping children tap into their unlimited potential. My family, who shares my vision and ownership of the school, provides the support and flexibility to pursue my goals. The school permits me to incubate new early education ideas that could be scalable as the company grows globally, from teaching computational thinking to launching parent-infant classes. Also, as a lead member of our local Chamber of Commerce Education Committee, I have a platform to raise awareness of early education and its impact on the business community, employees and local families.

Impact

Since 2016, through my work in early education and with my students and their parents, I have been able to share my message and develop influence with over 1,000 children. My goal is to reach over 5,000,000 young children in a decade. Actually, one of my teacher mentees, whom I hired, was so motivated by our model that she decided to move to India where she intends to start her own Montessori preschool. I hope to use this school platform to accelerate investment in early education educators and entrepreneurs who can address the need for quality early education in a meaningful way. Although the childcare crisis is global, the solution lies in the work of local entrepreneurs, where these challenges can be profitable and socially impactful.

Challenges

The demand for early education, although well recognized, is not particularly valued by the investment community. Generally the focus is on secondary and higher education, when it is too late to intervene. Our greatest challenge is creating awareness of the important contribution of early educators as well as early education entrepreneurs. We need to develop specific social and financial indicators to measure the impact of early education business success and its impact on society. Unfortunately, a strong government emphasis on regulations by state agencies without any financial assistance to implement them further impedes developing quality early education centers.

The fragmented ownership of early education centers does not allow for coordinated implementation of new ideas and technology that could improve operational efficiencies and communication. Improved research, investment and grants would allow centers (and their owners) to implement and learn new technology, which could eventually make early education less labor-intensive and more affordable.

Quality early education teacher training is also limited and fragmented. There is an urgent need for a public sector initiative to improve the quality of early education training. Society cannot afford to leave our children unprepared for kindergarten and beyond without affecting our position in the global market.

Early childhood education also needs an active collaborative effort between the health and education communities. My experience working with young parents revealed that they lack good information to make informed decisions about early childhood development and early education for their children. Parents need to be provided with more resources after a child's birth until they have an opportunity to enter an early education center.

Despite these challenges, there are several opportunities for leaders to transform the sector and innovate new solutions. We need leaders willing to take financial risks and realize the business and social value of the sector.

Lessons Learned

Through this journey, I learned that leadership in international education relies on a strong team. Leaders in education must learn how to work with diverse people and assemble world-class teams.

I also learned that leadership in education requires good skills in advocacy and an interdisciplinary mindset. Whether one is working at the local or global levels, education initiatives are often in competition with initiatives in the health, nutrition, gender, and environmental sectors. Good education leaders speak up and make pragmatic arguments, framing the case to invest in education from multiple international development perspectives. Education leaders need to make a compelling case that investments in education (especially early education) are just as critical as other development sectors.

Education leaders also need to take smart risks. Good leaders listen to their colleagues and take calculated risks for greater rewards. In the education sector, we often over-analyze data and uncertainty, which slows progress and limits the risks we do take.

Lastly, leadership in international education cannot rest on its laurels. As UN Special Envoy for Education Gordon Brown often says, "Education is the civil rights struggle of our generation," and this requires that we, as global education leaders, celebrate our collective victories but continue fighting for children's rights.[23] Whether we work in the for-profit, nonprofit or government sectors, we are all ignited by a passionate desire to help every child reach their full potential.

Our fight has only just begun.

Bio

Kevin Kalra graduated from the International Education Policy program at the Harvard Graduate School of Education in 2013. He serves as Director of Innovation and Global Strategy at Montessori Children's School Inc. Kevin is founder of the Global Teaching Network, an NGO focused on education for all, and leads the World Economic Forum Houston Hub. In 2004, Houston Mayor Bill White declared March 30 as Kevin Kalra Day for his work in sustainability.

---

[23] Batha, Emma. "Education is civil rights issue of our age: U.N. envoy Gordon Brown." *Reuters* 16 Sept. 2016. *Business Insider.* Web. 19 July 2017.

At My Core, I am a Teacher.

By Maya Thiagarajan

Goals and Work

While I have, over the years, branched out and done a number of other things as well – I've written a book, I've trained other teachers, I'm now consulting for schools – I ultimately define myself and my impact on the world through my work in the classroom.

For the last seventeen years, beginning with Teach For America and continuing on to the United World College of South East Asia in Singapore, I've been teaching high school students. At this point, I have taught nearly two thousand students around the world.

A Calling: Lessons Learned in Teaching and Leadership

On some days, I wonder why I became a teacher in the first place.

There is no money. Papers keep coming in, and the marking never ends. *Where's your thesis? Work on your transitions. Why are there still comma splices in your writing?* At three o'clock, I'm utterly and totally exhausted.

What is it about this profession that keeps me coming back to the classroom year after year?

When I first started teaching, I taught because I wanted to create a more just and equitable world. Over the years, I have taught because I loved literature, poetry, and language, and I wanted to share my passion for words with others. I believe that through literature and language, students can think deeply about the human condition and grapple with issues related to social justice and identity. Through deep and rich discussions of literature, students can seek truth, beauty, and goodness.

Most recently, however, I have realized that I teach because of the kids. One of the biggest lessons that I have learned about effective teaching is that you *have* to teach because you care about kids. The kids have to matter more than the texts, more than any outside goals or ideologies, more than just about anything.

Ultimately, teaching is about forging a strong relationship with kids, meeting them where they are in the learning process, and then, to borrow Kahlil Gibran's words, "leading them to the thresholds of their own minds."[24]

Teaching is a uniquely human profession, and to be a good teacher, most of all, you have to be a living, breathing, honest human, with passion and feeling and energy and idealism. You have to share your experiences and questions, your ideas, and even your failings. You have to be compassionate and kind. You have to be real.

And this, perhaps, is what I love most about teaching: the relationship between teacher and student. And I am extraordinarily fortunate. Over the course of my career, I have taught some amazing kids.

Kids who get totally engrossed in the heat and energy of a good classroom discussion. Kids who stand up and share a poem with their peers, despite the knocking knees and trembling hands. Kids who listen quietly and kids who challenge everyone.

So why do I teach now? I think it is because of the kids I love.

Perhaps one lesson that I have learned along the way – from all the work I do, but particularly from my work in the classroom – is that, at the heart of leadership is empathy. When we forge strong relationships with people, it becomes very easy to lead – and it does not matter whether we are talking about kids or adults. Leadership happens most naturally and powerfully when there is respect, trust, and caring.

---

[24] Gibran, Kahlil. *The prophet*. London: Heinemann, 1966. Print. Chapter "On Teaching."

The Central Challenge and the Central Goal: Re-Thinking What Teachers Do

Over the course of my teaching career, I have realized that teaching is perhaps one of the most complex professions in the world. As educators, we need, not only a strong and sophisticated knowledge of the content and skills that we teach, but also an expertise in terms of how we teach, and how we build and nurture our relationships with students. We make a million decisions each day, and each decision has the power to impact our students in significant ways. Teaching is, in fact, a highly complex craft and a vocation that demands hard work, adaptability, compassion, intellect, leadership, and skill.

Yet, I often find that, not only the outside world, but teachers themselves often fail to recognize the tremendous complexity of the teaching profession. **One of my primary goals is to transform the way teachers see themselves.** Over the last five years, I have conducted numerous workshops for teachers both in Singapore and India, and in the next academic year, I will consult full-time with schools in India to train hundreds of teachers.

While my training and coaching sessions focus on a wide range of topics (how to create reading cultures in the classroom, how to facilitate critical thinking and conceptual learning, and how to empower students to take initiative and design their own projects), the single most important goal I have when I work with teachers is to convince them of the tremendous importance and urgency of our jobs. I want my fellow educators to recognize that we have the power and responsibility to shape and transform young lives, and the work we do is extraordinarily complex and intellectually demanding.

Teachers make a huge difference in students' lives – our impact can and should be transformative. And I think that once teachers understand and internalize the importance and urgency of the profession, they will become great teachers of their own accord.

IMPACT: The Classroom and Beyond

In addition to teaching and teacher-training, I have also written a book about parenting and education.

Beyond The Tiger Mom: East-West Parenting for the Global Age is a book that reflects upon various approaches to parenting and education in both the East and West. For my book, I interviewed a wide range of parents and educators in Singapore (of Chinese, Malay, and Indian backgrounds) to give them a voice and reflect upon their stories. The thesis of my book is that both East and West have tremendous strengths when it comes to education and parenting; therefore, parents and educators on either side of the world can, and should, learn from each other.

Given my own global experiences–I have lived and taught in India, the US, and Singapore–I am well aware of the wide range of approaches to education and child-rearing, and I am fascinated by the idea of blending the best of all approaches to raise and educate well-adjusted children. Through interviewing other parents and educators, writing about education, and speaking at events and conferences, I have moved beyond my own classroom to share my insights and thoughts with a wide range of people. Over the last fifteen years, I estimate that I have impacted over 2000 students directly as a teacher, over 400 teachers through my teacher training workshops (and indirectly, their students), and over 3000 parents through my book and parent workshops. One could view the numbers as small – a drop in an ocean, perhaps – but for me, every individual interaction with a student has meaning. Every child counts.

Teachers need to feel empowered in many ways. We need to see ourselves as significant agents of change, as role models, as intellectuals, and as community leaders. When we begin to see ourselves in these ways, we not only inspire our students but we also feel energized and excited about our work, our purpose, and our own ability to add value to the world.

Bio

Maya Thiagarajan is an education consultant based out of India. She trains teachers and helps schools design curriculum. Prior to this, she taught high school English in the US and Singapore, and she also wrote a book titled "Beyond The Tiger Mom: East-West Parenting for the Global Age." She graduated from the International Education Policy Program at the Harvard Graduate School of Education in 2001.

Leading Change by Becoming a Teacher

By Mingyan "Ophelia" Ma

Goals and Work

I am a teacher.

It took me a while to own up to this identity. When I first returned to China after graduating from the Harvard Graduate School of Education (HGSE), I was often asked this question: "Isn't it a waste that you went to Harvard just to become a teacher?"

Truth be told, I did not go to Harvard to become a teacher. I wanted to be a researcher—to study policy papers, analyze data and provide the Chinese government with suggestions to improve its education system. I wanted to have impact on a large scale. What HGSE taught me was that even though I could talk convincingly about education reform, my knowledge is purely conceptual, and I had very little idea what good education actually looks like. Moreover, my hope for impact was more about seeking personal accomplishment than about impacting students' learning. I needed to be grounded, which I realized would come from teaching on the frontline, from being in the classroom.

Now, three years out of HGSE, I work for Beijing No.4 High School International Campus (IC). My title is Director of Curriculum Development, but more importantly, I am a teacher. A few weeks into teaching full time, I discovered something: the word "student" is no longer a faceless concept I encountered in my policy papers, but represents lively individuals each with their own back stories, laughter and sorrows, struggles and triumphs. I started imagining how Sophie or Sam might respond to the activities. I became more in tune with emotional signals from Daniel or Diana, even when they have nothing to do with what I am teaching that day. I began investing in the dreams and aspirations of Tom and Tracy. When I put on my teacher hat, the world from a student's perspective unfolded in front of me, but residing in it, I somehow maintain the knowledge and maturity of an adult. I see what each student wants and needs. It is strange and wonderful.

This discovery affected how I viewed my other responsibilities. When I think about curriculum development I ask myself, "What experiences do our students want that will also cultivate them into life-long learners and global citizens?" The IC is a western-facing program within a Chinese public school and even though our students are extremely academically qualified, we have found that they struggle to fully participate in the intellectual community when they get to university. I designed a reading seminar program to address this challenge. My teachers and I knew that students were interested in discussing values, ethics, and salient global issues, and reading textual materials is thus a perfect springboard for engaging in such conversations. Now, each reading seminar class centers around a driving question — How do immigrants make sense of their identity? What is a hero? What does it take to change the world? What does society tell us about happiness and how might it mislead us? At the end of each semester, students carry out personal projects to showcase their understanding of these questions. They publish magazines, make movies, organize campaigns, and design board games. Over 300 students have been through this program and we witnessed them start to share their opinions more comfortably, cite textual evidence to support their ideas, respectfully disagree, grow in their knowledge of the world in a personally relevant way and perhaps most importantly, curiously want to explore more.

I also piloted a 5-week independent studies program that we are calling iProject. We wanted to give students the opportunity to take seriously their quest to discover an interest that they hold deeply over a long period of time. It was a joy to see the energy outburst from some of our less engaged students – some designed and painted graffiti, some took on a healthy lifestyle challenge, others choreographed and shot music videos to their favorite songs. One student said that iProject helped him figure out what he is passionate about, and he started seeing his academic obligations in a different light: "I finally understood how my classes are relevant." Another student learned to embrace failure: "It's the tears, the breakdowns, and hardships that drive us forward." All of them grew in confidence, courage, and creativity. Also, through appreciating the talents of their peers, a new sense of community emerged.

Impact

The programs I designed and implemented impacted about 300 students last year, and will hopefully impact 1500 students in the next 10 years. I have also spoken at conferences and online seminars to share ideas with other teachers, and an estimate of 1200 students were indirectly impacted through the roughly 300 teachers who attended these sessions. Through translating and promoting Professor Fernando Reimers' books on global education and citizenship, I hope to impact even more teachers.

Challenges

In a government school with 110 years of history and a national reputation, change comes slowly. Prestige can become an obstacle in advancing educational opportunities; people take so much pride in how things are done that it is difficult to think differently. I wrestled with the mission-centered philosophy that HGSE taught me, and accepted that the missions-aligned reason might not be the most compelling to my stakeholders. For example, when I pitched for my school leadership to join Global Online Academy, I highlighted the importance of networking with prestigious prep schools and mentioned only in passing the benefits of innovative blended and online education. I learned to insist on my objectives (which always intend to serve students) without explicitly arguing it, knowing that sometimes the conversation about mission has to wait until people see the positive student results.

If I can be resigned to "right choices for the wrong reason," how do I reconcile myself to the wrong choices? Leading ethically is the biggest challenge, as well as the first priority. We are faced with tough decisions every day. Should we allow a student to transfer in exchange for not reporting a disciplinary probation on her university application? Should we admit a student unprepared for our program because his family can bring resources to the school? How many resources should we devote to psychological counseling and other support programs? The ostensible mission statement does not always align with values reflected in the decisions we make, and that can be a difficult critique to voice.

Lessons Learned

I have come to embrace my identity as a teacher. In fact, I believe that if educational leaders forget that we are teachers first, we will surely let the students down. Jack Ma said that one of the core values of Alibaba is "costumers first, employees second, shareholders third," and this simple statement helps people stay grounded. Education, like business, is a complex process with many stakeholders involved. Perhaps educators also need to remember "students first, teachers second, other interests third." Whether we are administrators, researchers, policy makers, or entrepreneurs, we must always analyze, imagine and deliberate how our decision-making affects each individual student. As we balance competing priorities and maneuver treacherous political water, we must always remember the students. Ultimately, change at any scale happens one student at a time, and that is how the value of our work should be judged.

At age 26, I am trying to lead change from within the classroom. The rest of my career could have many possible trajectories. Perhaps one day I will find myself in policy-making or advising, or starting my own company or school. One thing I do know: I will always keep the personal experience of every learner at heart. I will always remember, first and foremost, that I am a teacher.

Bio

Mingyan "Ophelia" Ma graduated from the Harvard Graduate School of Education with an M.Ed. in International Education Policy in 2014. Born and raised in Shanghai, she has lived in the United States as well as Israel, and has worked for schools, policy research organizations, and non-profits. Her passion is to develop global citizens through teaching, curriculum design, and cross-sectoral innovation. She currently works at Beijing No. 4 High School International Campus as the Director of Curriculum Development. Ophelia also holds a B.A. in Asian Studies from Pomona College.

Leading From My Roots: Creating Safe Spaces for Students in Palestinian Classrooms

By Haneen Sakakini

Like many who go into the field of education, it was a teacher, who made an impact on my life, and which sparked my initial interest in the field.

This teacher showed me firsthand the lasting imprint an educator can have when the time is taken to not only teach but also to listen and understand a student and his/her background, ultimately using the information learned to create an inclusive and safe learning space.

Goals and Work

Upon graduating with a degree in elementary education and a minor in special education, I decided to move from the US to Palestine, the birthplace of my parents, and the country that defines a huge part of my identity.

I began my career in education as an elementary school English teacher and a summer camp director for a school in Ramallah, Palestine, during which I had a unique opportunity to see firsthand the impact education can have on an individual, a community, and a nation.

I worked with adults and children impacted by the ongoing occupation of Palestinian land. This 60+ year-old conflict continues to leave its mark on the Palestinian people, affecting every aspect of life from freedom of movement to access to quality education.

It has also led Palestinians to value the education they receive, because despite the destruction that comes with living in a conflict-ridden country, the knowledge gained from an education is seen as one's sole possession that can never be stolen.

As a Palestinian American who has spent a lot of time in Palestine, I believed I had a clear understanding of the history of Palestine, its people, the culture, and the impacts this conflict continues to have on the people. However, it was not until I experienced the day-to-day life of my students, that I realized there was more to consider than I had anticipated.

I began to comprehend the immense influence my role as a teacher could have, not only on my students, but also on the situation as a whole, as the role of a teacher has the potential to influence the trajectory of our world today.

This is why, I believe it is essential for all international teachers to make an effort to have a comprehensive understanding of the location he/she will be teaching in, its history, culture, and its people prior to starting the role and developing lessons.

Work and Challenges

From my first day in the classroom, I had the autonomy to customize the content I taught to fit the needs of my three classes annually; it was up to me to ensure the content was culturally relevant for my 75 students each year.

I had the freedom to define the learning objectives and curriculum for the English Enrichment Summer camp I directed as well, which included over 100 students and eight international staff annually. I handpicked the content to fit a theme selected for each session and collaborated with teachers to ensure their lessons would resonate with the students in Palestine.

This autonomy brought with it a significant level of responsibility and expectation. This pressure was amplified by being the "new girl" from America who thought differently and used new pedagogical methods. Other teachers and parents in Ramallah were not accustomed to such techniques and I was met with skepticism.

With this skepticism came a great deal of questions and pushback from parents. Although I was fortunate enough to have the support of the school administration, the parents ultimately held a large amount of influential power within the school.

I knew I was pushing the boundaries and even had family members tell me to not be so different and try to keep a low profile, but I was convinced I was giving my students an opportunity to learn content in ways that would relate to them and spark their interest.

At the end of the day, I wanted to find ways for the content I was teaching to make a lasting impression with my students, just as my teachers had done for me years ago.

I regularly had my students navigate lessons, as opposed to me putting my lessons on autopilot, and I welcomed off topic discussions around current events. I truly believe that the lessons that veer off course due to a student's sparked interest end up being the lessons that have a lasting impact.

Where I faced a hurdle however, was navigating through responses to questions referring to Palestine's current political situation. I was unsure how to respond without adding my own bias, nor did I know what the "norm" was for teachers to respond to political questions.

Towards the end of my second year of teaching, the situation in Palestine had escalated, and the situation took a turn for the worse. Israeli soldiers had entered central Ramallah multiple times, many young Palestinians were shot and killed, and Gaza was being bombed daily. The tension of the situation was palpable and brought out anger, fear, and confusion in my students, emotions that I had not known my students possessed until then.

Being their teacher, I saw it as my role to help resolve these emotions; however, I was unsure how to handle this new territory within my classroom. When I spoke with our school counselor, I was recommended not to draw additional attention, unless it was noticeably disrupting my lesson. If it did reach that state, I was told to send individual students to see the counselor for a one-on-one.

Interestingly, it was not only the counselor who advised me to not focus on the issue, but in addition many of my Palestinian colleagues, advised me to continue with my normal lessons. According to their reasoning, in Palestine escalations and de-escalations of the conflict were seen as a "normal" and anfrequent recurrence for the students.

At first, I took their advice, however, as the situation heightened a young boy in his mid-teens, who was a friend to many of my students, was shot and killed. In the aftermath, I quickly shifted gears and did what I thought was best for my students. This caused some heads to turn; however, ultimately it proved to be the best choice for my students and the school.

Impact

The morning we learned about the shooting, I noticed my students' emotions running high during first period, and despite what the school advised, I took it as an opportunity to discuss the situation openly with my students. I had students move their desks into a circle, and told them this was going to be a safe space where they can talk about how they feel and ask any questions.

It was not long before my students began to raise their hands one by one, and as each student shared their emotions with the class, I was shocked to learn of the magnitude in which this ongoing conflict has affected them. The fact that the impact this conflict was having on students had not been discussed for such for a long time was even more troubling.

As our class ended, I learned from the students that discussions around the day-to-day violence in Palestine rarely occur in a formal educational setting, nor did they happen regularly between families, and the students thanked me for giving them an opportunity to express themselves.

For me this was a huge shock as I expected the current conflict in Palestine and its impact to be a hot topic of discussion, since I noticed the trauma this conflict was having on my students trickle into the classroom. As a result, I decided to speak to our school counselor and administration to find ways to help spread awareness of the importance of our students' mental well-being and the importance of teaching them about peaceful resistance.

Directly after speaking with the school counselor and administration and receiving their support, I began to plan a unit around peaceful resistance throughout history. During this unit, we focused on leaders such as Martin Luther King, Nelson Mandela and Malala, and their non-violent resilience. This unit resonated with my fellow colleagues leading them to begin to incorporate similar lessons into their curriculum.

Embedded into the unit was a weekly open forum for students to draw parallels between the lessons within our unit and the situation in Palestine.

These discussions started as round table discussions around feelings, personal stories, and the situation, however, they quickly morphed into planning sessions used by students to bring to life what they learned in their own community.

These planning sessions fed into the summer camp I directed, which most of my students participated in, ultimately resulting in; a student-run clothing and toy drive for children in Gaza and a field trip to visit a local memorial created to commemorate the lives that had been lost since the start of the war on Gaza that summer.

It was amazing to witness firsthand how creating a safe space for students to share their feelings morphed into such an impactful unit.

Lessons Learned

I have frequently been told that with each challenge comes a lesson learned, and for my time in Palestine, the list of lessons learned is endless.

Being a global educator whose reach has the ability to directly impact thousands of students is not easy. It is a role that pushes you out of your comfort zone and tests your mental strength, patience, and perseverance.

For me, being an international teacher, who impacted over 1,000 students while I was in Palestine, forced me to contextualize how I taught subjects to the situation. It also showed me that adapting standardized models to new situations is not easy for a global educator, even if one is familiar with the culture. This is not due to a lack of skills but due to the variety of unexpected contexts encountered and the lack of practice we give trainee teachers in the application of such techniques.

It was due to these lessons that I decided to return for my masters and dedicate it to international education policy. It is also why I returned to the Middle East post-graduation, in hopes of making a lasting impact on the wider education sector: by raising awareness of the importance of creating safe spaces in every classroom, where students feel their voices are being heard, and know that the content they are learning is relevant to their lives.

Bio

Haneen Sakakini is currently a Dubai based consultant for EY, where she continues to thrive to make a lasting impact on the education sector in the Middle East. In her role, Haneen advises governments and the private sector on the importance of contextualizing contemporary education methods to local situations. Haneen received her BA in Elementary Education with a minor in Special Education from the University of Maryland in 2012 and in 2015 graduated from the International Education Policy Program at the Harvard Graduate School of Education.

Bringing Excellent Education to Underserved Children in India

By Suman Barua

Goals and Work

I moved back to India after graduating from the Harvard Graduate School of Education (HGSE) and joined a non-profit called Reality Gives, as the Director of Education to follow my dream of bringing excellent quality education to underserved communities in India. I lead a team of 45 people, including teachers and senior managers, through three programs with an annual budget of 250,000 US dollars. We serve children, teenagers, and adults in the urban slum regions of Mumbai and Delhi. I set the vision, goals, and quality for all the programs, as well as build capacity in teachers and managers to meet the gap between excellence and reality.

Our School Program is for children ages three to ten and runs pre-school to Grade 4, with 30 teachers and a school leader. Our classrooms are child-centric, inclusive and have an experiential pedagogy. I work with the teachers by conducting intense week-long training three times a year, where we build technical skills and discuss larger education issues in the world. We engage in debates, sharing circles, meditate, and talk about our lives. Then we do weekly observations and feedback sessions and they follow a growth plan to become better teachers and leaders. With the school principal, I work on overall management structures and systems that make the daily operations smoother. Deciding targets, assessments, and collaboration forms a huge part of this.

We have an extracurricular program for ages nine to sixteen and offer football, cricket, and dance classes. This program's aim is to give opportunity to beneficiaries to explore their passions through professionally conducted activities, which are hard to get access to in their schools in the under-resourced areas. Our big success is the football for girls that serves as a great empowerment tool for the girls, who often find themselves lacking the chance to explore activities outside their homes. We hire experienced coaches who are monitored by our managers, and often engage with other local clubs for healthy competition. Some of our dance students have been selected by an institute for dance scholarships to become professional dancers.

The Youth Empowerment program, our flagship, gives an opportunity for youth from the slums from age 16 to 35 to learn computer, life skills, and English, therefore meeting the skills gap for employment. We have developed the curriculum for all three in partnership with experts from the UK and local community champions through a cyclical process of identifying needs and international standards and then making a bridge. Our lessons are rooted in the daily context of our beneficiaries but based on benchmarks. For example, our English course is divided into four levels and based on the European language framework (CEFR). The initial teacher training is conducted by an TESOL expert from the UK and ongoing development is taken care of by me, which involves weekly English and exposure sessions, observations, and monthly meetings. The idea is to ensure that our teachers grow faster than the students and therefore are always more comfortable teaching.

We do monthly meetings with the managers of all the programs where we reflect, share best practices, and discuss challenges. My job is also to identify skills the managers need to strengthen and support them in doing so.

We believe that community capacity building is the only sustainable way to bring communities out of poverty, and therefore hire all our teachers and junior staff throughout the three programs (about 40), from the community we work in. Often we recruit people who have been our students, and we also see them grow into managerial positions. The challenge that comes with this model is the lack of these teachers' exposure to excellent quality education, and that is where my role comes in. My job is to create training and support systems for all our staff that builds excellence in them and therefore our beneficiaries get the best. It is a long-term approach and the results are very obvious at the beginning, but the idea is to make the staff so capable that no matter where they go, the benefits keep coming back to the community.

Impact

In the last year, my work impacted more than 1,100 people directly including 30 teachers, 400 children, and 700 youth through the programs. We are slowly expanding our programs and adding more cities; in another 10 years we will impact over 20,000 lives directly, and 100,000 indirectly, considering their families who will be influenced by the benefits.

Challenges

I have faced two major challenges in my role; the first is to get people onboard with what I believe to be "excellent education" and the second is to lead people of mixed age and skills. Because of the community-inclusion model in our organization, most staff come with nearly no exposure to good quality education, whereas I have seen the opposite extreme while working at Teach for India and then studying at Harvard. My idea of excellent education has been informed by all of that, and my job is to bring it to our classrooms. My challenge is, how do I simplify and contextualise quality education, convince the staff that it is a good idea, and then bring up their capacities to plan and deliver such high-quality work? The second challenge I face is leading a group of teachers and managers who are not only very different than me, but also are far more experienced in life. Being a young leader, I had to divorce myself from the old idea of leading people by power and learned a method that is democratic in nature.

Lessons Learned

While addressing the above challenges, one thing I have learned is that adults do not like being told what they should do. In the fight for education equity, inevitably we need to get a lot of people on board and we cannot do it alone. We have to convince people to join our movement and believe in our ideas. However, adults are far less likely to put 100% into something that was prescribed to them. People need to believe that it is their idea and that they are completely invested in it. So my first task whenever I want do something, is to convince the people I lead by showing them what the benefits are and pitching it is as "one of the ideas" and not the one and only. After that, I encourage all of us to come up with more ideas and think about implementation methods, using their experiences and ideals. Finally, we decide on a version of the original idea that everyone is passionately driven towards. I have seen this work with most adults I have encountered in all spheres of my life.

Also along similar lines, advancing educational opportunities is a really tricky job. Often investing in people in the field can be rendered wasteful if they leave the organization or the mission. Therefore, it is vital that leaders invest a significant portion of their time in building a strong values-driven culture of collaboration, love, and excellence. Positivity is what they should start and end their days with and that is what should be the anchor of every conversation. The benefits of education are only visible long-term and you want to ensure that your people stick around to see that.

The third and most important is that we need to train and build capacity in others, imagining that they will not work for us soon after. Being a leader in education organizations we face two options, either teach others what is required for the job or teach what is required to advance education for everyone. I would always pick the latter and put in more time and energy because it is the right investment in the future. The battle of education equity is so long and hard that we have to ensure that we are building skills that are sustainable and usable no matter where they go.

Working in the field to bring great quality education to everyone is what we are taught to do in grad school, but honestly the nuts and bolts of it gets clearer the moment you do your first leadership project in the real world. It is important that we do not give up our dreams and succumb to the realities and work out a balance between ideal and practical, philosophy and delivery, theory and practice.

Bio

Suman Barua graduated from the International Education Policy Program at the Harvard Graduate School of Education in 2016. He has previously taught for two years in a low-income school in Mumbai, as a Teach for India Fellow, and also worked as a Software Engineer in a technology firm, before realizing his passion for education. He hopes to do whatever he can to achieve education equity for all children.

Navigating a Place in Global Education

By Austin Volz

"In China, friends don't say 'thank you,'" EnHui Shen told me after our first few months of friendship in Beijing. Through my years living in Greece, Germany, China—even at times visiting my small hometown in Colorado—nuggets like this have consistently undermined my assumptions about the world. And so I have spent the better part of the past decade outside the United States, learning to navigate new cultural territories, reconstruct my worldview, and help students do the same.

In 2013, I graduated from the Harvard Graduate School of Education and moved to China for the third time. As the recipient of a Harvard-China Scholarship, I joined Fudan University's Higher Education Institute to research models of liberal arts education emerging in China's universities, and I deeply embedded myself at Fudan. I met with deans, sat in on curricular meetings and residential life meetings, attended the Teaching Assistant trainings, interviewed numerous students, and befriended the Communist Youth League Deputy Secretary, who was responsible for coordinating the campus's social clubs.

I began to understand the successes and challenges of Fudan's liberal arts program, and I wanted to transform my insights into practice and finish my year with more than a publication. But yet, my role was clear. While I was able to deeply become a part of Fudan, I had no place working to change how things were done. I was meant to be an observer from the US.

The realization that publishing offered limited fulfillment, and that my American identity could shape my role apart from any skills or knowledge, led me to my current role at Avenues: The World School. As a Senior Learner Experience Designer in the Research and Development Department, my core responsibilities have three parts. First, I develop education plans and manage policy research to expand Avenues' international network of campuses. Second, I design new learning models ranging from new programs to entirely new kinds of schools. Third, I conduct research on the best ways to facilitate children's learning.

Over the past year, I have worked on drafting a set of global graduation learning outcomes to unite and guide teaching and learning at Avenues's current and future campuses. On the research side, I ran a study on teaching pinyin (a Romanized alphabet for Chinese) in first grade that will help us determine the best way to teach Chinese to all our Chinese track first-graders.

In January 2017, I went with an Avenues team to Uganda to pilot a program that would expand education to those currently without access to quality learning. We partnered with Project Hello World, an organization that builds internet kiosks with communities, so I could do two pilots of a curricular unit where students built their own instruments for measuring the weather and then made a weather report of the past 7 days. I also conducted open-ended family interviews to better understand how families think about education's value. The results were highly encouraging, both in terms of student learning and reception, from the community.

Leadership Challenges

Spending my career abroad has taught me what it means to lead in a globalized context. There are decisions that I have no place making because I am not from the country. In some cases, like Chinese government relations, this is because of skill limitations: not fully understanding how the system works or having the relationships in place. In other cases, though, I may have the ability to make the decision, but I do not have the right since I am not from the country. For instance, with Project Hello World in Uganda, we do not decide what internet content was accessible on the kiosk. That is always the communities' decision. Drawing the line between these is immensely complex. It is further complicated by issues of privilege and rising nationalism.

A similar challenge comes up in my work on education plans for campuses around the world. It is an unfortunate effect of language that local can be perceived as the opposite of global. As a World School, existing government policies are frequently restrictive, whether it be which nationalities of students are allowed to study together, or a required national curriculum, or in some cases, even the use of the word "world" is not allowed in the school name or course titles. Some national governments can perceive global education as a threat, or as more appropriate to higher education than primary or secondary education.

To address this challenge, I have found it necessary to be very clear about how global goals match with national goals and also to better articulate global education. I believe that for something to be truly global, it must also be local. "Global" does not mean "somewhere else," but it means that it affects here, and there, and everywhere. Legitimate, complicated questions exist around how to make sure students have roots and a strong foundation, but global education is not necessarily opposed to these things. Instead, the aim is to foster students' curiosity about the world and help them develop a concern for addressing some of the world's most pressing issues, not just those that affect themselves.

Lessons Learned

Relationships motivate.

It is easy to simplify people's motivations and think that they act for material gain or prestige. While these are definitely factors, in working across a variety of value systems and cultures, I have found that community and camaraderie can be equally motivating. Others want to work with you if they feel you are genuinely interested. And, vice versa, despite other motivations they may be disinclined to work with you if they feel like there is actually an ulterior motive.

It is a common saying that people do not quit jobs, they quit their managers. In order to understand the education environment of cities around the world, I have relied heavily on interns I have hired who have a deep knowledge of the country. Because the stipend they receive is modest, I focus on developing a relationship with them. I ask if they are getting what they want out of the experience and work with them to make sure that they understand how decisions are made and what the big picture is. My expectations are high, and the work they produce has generally been exceptional.

Welcome discussion.

Leadership requires making controversial decisions. Developing new programs can create tension within the organization because these programs depart from the standard way of doing things. Similarly, running pilots for new programs that students can opt into can introduce ambiguity that not all parents are comfortable with. In most cases, I have found it possible to explain how the decision was made, acknowledging that there are pros and cons, and listening to any frustrations or uncertainty. Intelligent people can disagree. Welcoming discussion invites others to disagree while creating a space where we can understand the differences in one another's reasoning.

Be very, very clear on the goals.

Without a clear goal, I have found it nearly impossible to make decisions, reach consensus or lead effectively. When proposing a new program, one of the first steps is painstakingly wordsmithing and iterating on what the goals are. Before we go into any details of how we will go about the program, we spend a significant amount of time making sure that we have the goals right. Developing a new program means venturing into uncharted territory with numerous options for how things might be done. By being clear that the goal of a program is to pilot a new curricular model and develop relationships in a given city, as opposed to create a sustainable financial model or generate revenue, I am able to make decisions around how to allocate resources. I am also able to assess what was successful and adjust the strategy accordingly.

Bio

Austin X. Volz graduated from the International Education Policy Program at the Harvard Graduate School of Education in 2013. He is an educator and researcher with an international background in higher education, education research, and program design. As a Senior Learner Experience Designer in the Research and Development Department of Avenues: The World School, he is responsible for global campus development, new education models and empirical research.

Promoting Teachers' Professional Development

By Ming Jin

Goals and Work

As Associate Director for the Teaching Affairs Office at an international senior high school in Beijing, I worked to improve teaching quality and management at the school level. The senior high school has more than 1,000 students, and it is part of a K-12 school group with 2,400 students. The school has gone through 20 years of development, with China's fast economic growth and Chinese parents' increasing demand for quality education. I believe a superb teaching force is the key to quality education and I have made every effort to promote teachers' professional development at the school. In my work, I see the need for teaching and administration to develop hand in hand, the importance of being both goal-oriented and detail-oriented, and the benefit of continuously applying research skills that I built up at the Harvard Graduate School of Education.

The Importance of good administration for good Teaching

Excellent administration and management can greatly advance teaching with efficient organization, supportive mechanisms and a positive atmosphere. By contrast, unsatisfactory administration hinders teaching and brings up unnecessary tension. I think it is important to empower teachers and provide them with sustainable professional development opportunities. Next, I discuss a few programs I have led to advance teachers' professional development.

In our school, we encourage teachers to observe each other's classes, exchange feedback, and learn from each other. It is designed to raise openness and continuous learning opportunities about teaching practice. I focus on teaching objectives, teaching content, teaching design, pedagogy, teaching aids, teaching art, teaching effectiveness, etc., and worked out a class observation form with indicators and questions to reflect on. Nonetheless, there is no single standard to determine a good class. Class observation is also a good way for school administrators to know about the teachers and their teaching practice. From my standpoint, I always appreciate the teachers' hard work and give recognitions along with constructive suggestions. I also listen to the teachers, putting pieces of information together and seeking to align administration with teaching.

In particular, new teachers may need practice and guidance to overcome their initial frustrations. The context in our schools is also special, as most of the students are English as Second Language learners and have limited English proficiency. I also work on a mentoring program for new faculty. The program assigns experienced teachers as mentors to new teachers so they can provide support. The new teachers will observe their mentor's classes, while the mentors work with their mentees on teaching planning and design, observe their classes, and give feedback and suggestions. For this semester, I just checked the progress and observed each mentee's class for a mid-term summary. Some teachers are working closely with their mentors and teaching very well, some are teaching OK but did not form a close mentorship with their mentors, and a few teachers are having problems with their teaching. I met with each group, summing up and discussing the next steps.

There is one foreign teacher who I heard was not very cooperative and by way of example, was not checking his emails. Nevertheless, he always replies to my emails within seconds. His teaching is fine, and his students like him as suggested by the student evaluations, which I am also responsible for. I could see he was making efforts and was even a little stressed and nervous. After our conversation, he felt much better and said things would have been much better if he could have this kind of individual meeting with me right at the beginning. He suggested that every new teacher talk with me first, and said very politely that I might be too busy for that. Actually, I did have an orientation for the mentor program, but he missed it due to some physical condition. We must be aware of the importance of having empathy for students and boosting their self-confidence, along with the danger of labelling them with any negative words. Likewise, teachers need to feel understood, encouraged, supported, and respected, while seeing a higher standard to strive for. Many teachers see the need for ongoing professional learning opportunities, and I also actively work with other institutions and organizations abroad to extend resources available for our teachers. For example, I led a team of 11 school leaders to attend the Think Tank on Global Education at the Harvard Graduate School of Education in 2016. We all felt very much inspired. One of the participants was an 11th grade leader who started a grade-wide initiative after he came back to school. The students posted Sustainable Development Goals (SDG) in front of the classrooms, designed SDG passports and fun games, and conducted research on each goal. After a series of events, the students presented their findings with pictures, diagrams, and texts, sharing their thoughts about how to make a difference. I felt so touched by their sincerity and creativity. I could see them growing into global citizens and global leaders.

Big Goals and Small Details

After graduating from Harvard, I started my career in education with several goals. However, I found myself busy responding to urgent requests and obsessed with all the details of making things go smoothly. We may not be in a position to make decisions in our work at first, but clear goals and conscious planning, like lighthouses, will lead us to go further and deeper. As my leadership in the school increases, I find it useful to turn to log frames, SWOT analysis and other tools that I learned at the Harvard Graduate School of Education. What's more important, clearly defined goals and plans are essential for conformed and effective collaborations.

In the meantime, the work cannot be done just through clear goals or good plans. All those details make the quality of one's work and count to make changes happen.

Research and Practice

Being an education practitioner, I work on the frontline of education and may find limited time to keep up with the research in the field. However, it is truly of benefit to read books and journals, work out a research-based proposal, and collect and analyze data. For example, I conducted research on teacher evaluation, and saw that recent research favors a formative evaluation with the goal to promote teachers' professional development. A summative high-stake teacher evaluation may lead to many negative consequences. We need to be careful and draw lessons from previous research.

Impact

The teachers I have worked with show positive working morale, reflected on their teaching with enthusiasm, aspired to progress professionally, and actively participated in the school life. This in turn impacted their classes and their students. What is worth mentioning is that a new faculty member in the mentor program this semester competed for the position of Social Science Department Head and was successfully elected. I feel so happy to see that he adapted to the school so quickly and embraced new challenges.

Challenges

Teachers may already have demanding teaching tasks. The challenge is how to make administration most effective and friendly. School leaders need to devote time to understand and accommodate different situations in time. We need to listen and at the same time give helpful suggestions and even modify school policies or programs when necessary.

Lessons learned

Promoting teachers' professional development and promoting teaching as a profession are essential for education. To build a teacher-friendly ecosystem, we need to give attention to administration alongside teaching and define our goals, while at the same time looking into details and leveraging academic research to advance our practice.

Bio

Ming Jin was Associate Director for the Teaching Affairs Office at the Beijing Royal School (10-12th grades). She has just been appointed as Vice Principal at the Beijing Royal Middle School (6-9th grades). She has previously interned with UNESCO-IBE in Geneva, and worked at Lingnan University in Hong Kong and Ewha Womans University in Korea. She had her B.A. in English at Peking University before doing her master's degree in International Education Policy at the Harvard Graduate School of Education.

Building Institutions that Elicit Greatness

By Ethan Van Drunen

Goals and Work

The international school sector is one of Asia's most remarkable growth stories. The International School Consultancy Group reports that Asian international school enrollment has grown by over 55 percent in the last five years. They estimate that by 2026 there will be 16,000 international English-medium schools worldwide teaching 8.75 million students and charging $89 billion dollars in annual school fees.

Once the exclusive domain of children of missionaries, diplomats, and multinational business executives, international and English-medium schools in Asia have now become the preferred education option for upper middle class and upper class families. Parents know that this investment will likely be well worth the cost. These international schools provide their children with the knowledge, skills, competencies and English language abilities required for success in today's global economy.

International schools are at the leading edge of Asia's rapid urbanization and industrialization—but how many of these new learning communities are driven by a deep sense of institutional purpose? How many of these schools' leadership teams are empowered to make decisions that are based upon values and social impact rather than merely upon examination results or the financial bottom line?

Since graduating from Harvard's International Education Policy Ed. M. program in 2010, I have worked for education charities, for-profit proprietary schools and not-for-profit schools in the United States, Myanmar, and India. The socio-economic and cultural gap between the international schools and the monastic schools in which I have worked could not be greater, but regardless of the type of institution or the socio-economic status of the staff and clientele, I have been struck by

127

the power and importance of developing an institutional culture that is based upon social impact, human commonality, and service to others.

Impact

While in Myanmar from 2011 to 2016, I worked to establish a teachers' training institute for a group of 85 monastic schools located in underserved communities across the country. The Studer Trust began as a charity focused on building schools in remote communities. Their motto, "Respect the Spirit of Helping," reflects the altruistic values of the teachers and monks who run these schools. Myanmar's monastic school teachers have a deep sense of religious duty to teach the students well, but the resources and skills to do so are sorely lacking. Textbooks are antiquated, and rote learning is the predominant pedagogy.

After building over 60 schools, the Studer Trust pivoted from expanding access to improving the quality and relevance of the taught curriculum in 2012. We established a Teachers Training Centre in the central city of Mandalay that since 2014 annually educates four cohorts of 27 teachers in a residential ten-week immersive certificate in teaching. We also offer week-long trainings for school principals and Buddhist monks on topics ranging from school finance to curriculum development and instruction techniques. This Teachers Training Centre annually trains 130 educators and directly impacts 6,500 students per year.

The work with Studer Trust was only my night job in Myanmar. My day job was to serve as the director of a proprietary British curriculum school in Myanmar's commercial capital of Yangon. There, my ownership board consisted of local businesspersons and former military leaders who were members of both the military government and of the opposition party of Aung San Suu Kyi. Informed by Buddhist values and a sense that Myanmar needed a school that could cater to all students including those on the Autism spectrum, the school leadership team was able to build a genuine narrative of how our school was fitting into Myanmar's broader social change. Teachers, parents, and students would regularly use their weekends to offer English classes and professional development for monastic school teachers. We were also able to advise the government on new legislation pertaining to inclusive education policies and practices. Our work with the government had an indirect impact of increased access to quality learning resources for just over 15,000 children with disabilities attending non formal primary education (NFPE) and monastic schools. These activities helped develop a sense of identity in our young and rapidly growing school community. The emphasis on community service was an effective tool for recruiting and retaining quality staff. Despite the challenges of low salaries by international standards and the sometimes-challenging quality of life in Yangon, we were able to move into a new campus and grow our school from 320 students to 660 students from 27 countries.

In 2016, my wife and I decided to move our family back to a boarding school in the Indian Himalayas where we had met as young teachers 12 years earlier. As Woodstock School's Vice Principal and Deputy Head, I oversee the academic and enrichment program of the oldest international residential school in Asia. Woodstock is a place with a profound sense of purpose. In response to the refugee crisis and travel bans initiated in 2017 by the United States, Woodstock School recently designated USD 1 million per year for a "Scholarships for Peace" initiative that targets students facing displacement, insecurity and a loss of educational opportunity. By prioritizing funds for this purpose, we have been able to attract worthy students on full scholarship from Syria, Somaliland, Yemen, Gaza, Afghanistan and refugee communities in Lebanon. Woodstock has three outward-facing service-oriented centers on campus: the Hanifl Center provides outdoor education training for local government officers and mountain guides and an annual celebration of mountain arts and culture; the Center for Imagination invites resident scholars onto campus to look at a social problem or a research question alongside students, with a mind to foster in students a sense of vocation and agency for social entrepreneurialism; and the Community Engagement Program trains hundreds of local teachers and principals each year, connecting students with local development projects that operate on a long-term partnership basis. While Woodstock consists of only 510 students, the annual direct impact of the school's intensive partnerships extends to 850 teachers and government officials and over 10,000 students within the Tehri Garhwal District of Uttarakhand.

Challenges

Like many international schools, Woodstock students come from around the world; however, this diversity of geography and religious background can bely a social homogeneity of global elites and western youth culture—a consumer mindset that is antithetical to Woodstock's core values. The school's curricular focus on community engagement and a strong scholarship program only goes part way towards ensuring that students are comfortable with diversity and ambiguity—understanding that other people, with their differences, can also be right.

In Myanmar, the retention of monastic teachers was a main concern. Teachers typically work for less than USD 80 per month, and classroom temperatures regularly reach 35-40 degrees Celsius. The Studer Trust's social networking, salary scheme and Teachers Training Center went some way to address these concerns, but with the private sector opening up it was clear that many of the best teachers would soon be drawn out of the profession.

Lessons Learned

My experience of school leadership in Myanmar and India has shaped my belief that regardless of their economic stratus or religious and secular affiliations, schools must draw upon the wellspring of service leadership. International schools can become distracted by an emphasis on the luxury of the learning environment, their deeper purpose in this world hidden beneath a focus on university placements and IGCSE, A-Level, Advanced Placement, or International Baccalaureate external examination results. This focus can distract international schools from the opportunity to facilitate the values of international mindedness and global citizenship. Parents, teachers, and leaders are motivated by values more than finances. The result of this is a learning community that is both dynamic and compassionate.

I have come to realize that educational leaders must not back away from crafting an institutional narrative that is focused on values. Whether in for-profit or not-for-profit schools, financial and curricular decisions can be framed in terms of sustainable social impact and an ethic of care.

130

I feel that international schools worldwide should place an increased emphasis on their social responsibility as elite educational institutions. Imagine the impact in 2026 if there were 16,000 international schools with sustainable local development at the core of their strategy and mission, all committed to graduating students who care and are equipped with an ethic of global citizenship for the good of our planet.

Bio

Ethan Van Drunen is the Vice Principal and Deputy Head of Woodstock School in India. Since graduating with an Ed.M. in International Education Policy (IEP) from Harvard in 2010, he has worked in international school leadership and for charitable trusts in the USA, Myanmar, and India. Ethan is married to Jamie Vinson, who is also an IEP alum.

DEVELOPING PROGRAMS AND PRODUCTS

Empowering Youth to Drive Social Change

By Joel Adriance

Goals and Work

After graduating from Harvard in 2010, I was hired to work at the International Youth Foundation on a program called YouthActionNet. YouthActionNet equips the world's greatest asset—young people—to solve the world's greatest challenges. We do this by supporting youth as advocates and drivers of community development, growing the social impact of youth-led organizations and building a supportive ecosystem that allows youth leadership to flourish. Our work includes a global network of 23 national and regional institutes supporting young social entrepreneurs and their ventures; activities that engage young people to think entrepreneurially and contribute to social change; and activities that engage adult practitioners to better understand the unique needs of young people and effectively support their growth.

I never imagined when I was hired that seven years later I would still be at the same organization and working on the same program. One of my key realizations in this time has been that professional growth doesn't necessarily require shifting positions or employers. Much more important, in my case, has been connecting with a mission that continues to inspire me, working with a high-performing team, taking on new responsibilities that allow learning over time, having the conditions to do creative, impactful work, and being given the opportunity to be entrepreneurial within an established organization.

I am currently the Director of Training & Learning for YouthActionNet. In this role, I provide leadership on how to best support the learning, growth, and development of our program participants. This includes work on training design and delivery, online learning, the development of curricula and lesson plans, and the design and management of non-formal learning programs that use approaches like mentoring or coaching. I also oversee the work of twelve of our national and regional institutes in Latin America and Spain, coordinating with local counterparts and partner organizations to grow the impact of their work in support of youth-led social innovation.

Impact

Each year through YouthActionNet we support the growth and development of more than 1,500 young social entrepreneurs in 90 countries who have participated in our fellowship programs to date and form part of our network. Our fellows and alumni, through their social ventures working in areas like health, education, and the environment, together impact the lives of more than 1.7 million individuals each year. We have worked with an additional 6,000 young people, many of whom are university students in the developing world, to acquire change-making skills and reflect on their roles as citizens and leaders. Finally, we work with hundreds of adult practitioners each year to help them understand social innovation, design youth-centered programs, and better support youth voices. I hope that my work will continue to impact tens of thousands of lives in the years to come.

While my focus may be somewhat different than International Education colleagues who work mainly within school systems or explicitly on education policy, I do think of my work as impacting educational opportunity for youth and adolescents. Specifically, I am working to support young people as they develop the skills and capacities that enable them to become active citizens and problem-solvers who can drive social change. I am convinced that the inherent enthusiasm and energy of young people, combined with on-the-ground understanding of the challenges faced by their communities, uniquely position youth to generate solutions to social problems. At the same time, young people face a series of obstacles that often prevent them from fully employing this potential. School systems that are disconnected from real-world contexts; community institutions that treat youth as either problems to be solved or as token participants; as well as a general lack of access to the funding, visibility, and support systems that are necessary to grow and sustain youth-led social initiatives.

I think that the answers to these problems must involve formal educational systems but cannot be limited to those systems. We need curricula that adequately develop civic skills and help young people reflect on how their interests can intersect with real world problems, educators that understand how to effectively engage their students in participatory learning and support leadership growth, and spaces in the community where youth can roll up their sleeves and learn by doing. We also need to work at a systems level with a wide range of private, public, and civic institutions to make it easier for young people with promising ideas to receive support and be effectively engaged in social processes.

Challenges

I think that one of the biggest leadership challenges that we face in this space is changing mindsets—among both youth and adults—about the roles that young people can, and should, play in society. In working with adult practitioners—teachers, counselors, youth workers, program administrators—across multiple regions of the world, I have seen again and again that many of those who work closest with young people can still harbor unconscious negative bias about who young people are and what they are capable of. Young people themselves often need a boost of confidence to realize the significance of their work and how far they can go if they apply themselves. They need to connect with like-minded peers, develop positive relationships with adults, and have the chance to take on increasing levels of responsibility that allow them to grow over time.

Another leadership challenge is helping educators—who were themselves educated in traditional academic systems that emphasized rote learning—to understand and effectively employ the active, participatory and peer-to-peer learning approaches that seem to work the best in developing civic skills amongst young people. While there are no easy answers here, I have seen the most success in situations where we first allow educators to live these methodologies as participants, then open space for critical reflection on the "how" and "why" of the teaching approaches used, and finally put in practice new techniques with the close support and guidance of more experienced mentors.

Lessons Learned

In both cases, it is important to recognize the adaptive rather than technical nature of these challenges. Educators, practitioners, and young people themselves need more than just new information to change mindsets or deep-seated ways of doing their work. They need support and structure to think critically about who they are, how they view the world, and how they can change elements of their environment.

One of the critical ingredients in a successful adaptive learning process is the quality of the relationships that support the learner and help them to process situations that may pull into question elements of their own identity and beliefs—as often occurs in situations of personal growth. In this sense, I am convinced that the most powerful learning experiences occur in environments where we feel deeply connected to other human beings—whether they are peers, mentors, educators, or others. We need educational systems, as well as training and non-formal learning opportunities, with more heart, more humanity, and more authenticity. I think this is a critical ingredient in creating a world where young people are truly empowered to solve our greatest social challenges.

Bio

Joel Adriance is the Director of Training and Learning at YouthActionNet, a program of the International Youth Foundation. He graduated from the International Education Policy program at the Harvard Graduate School of Education in 2010, where he was a Reynolds Fellows in Social Entrepreneurship. As a trainer, Joel specializes in non-formal and participatory learning processes that support personal transformation, leadership growth, and skills development. As a manager, he has worked in over 15 countries overseeing programs focused on education, civic participation, social innovation, and youth development. Joel is currently based in Ecuador and works across Latin America.

Improving Children's Reading Skills and Habits in Marginalized Areas of Mexico

By Maria Elena Ortega-Hesles

Goals and Work

I grew up in a country full of contrasts and disparities. My parents always told me that education was a treasure, something no one could take away from you. Nowadays, I wake up in the mornings thinking of how to share the treasure of a good education with more people.

While studying to earn a BA in Economics I found out I had a deep interest in education policy, so I decided to pursue graduate studies in this area. In graduate school, I learned a lot from professors and classmates. That experience prepared me to go back into the field to plant a seed for the advancement of educational opportunity. Daily experience on the ground also turned into a great teacher. In this search for how to share education, I have tried multiple things; some of them have worked whereas some others failed, but they have all taught me something, especially to "dream and try."

Three years ago, another researcher and I saw an international call for proposals. Even though everyone told us it was a waste of time we decided to try and sent our idea. We received the grant and designed a program called "Mundo de Libros"[25] which aims to improve the reading skills and habits of students enrolled in Grades 1 to 3 in Spanish-speaking countries. This free program seeks to foster parents' engagement in their child's reading and complements it with a web-based platform (www.mundodelibros.mx) and access to interesting, level-appropriate children's books at a community library. After only a year, we have started seeing changes in the reading habits and abilities of many of these kids, who are now enjoying reading and some of their parents (and grandparents) who are devoting time to take their children to the library and reading to or with them. Giving children in

---

[25] This is Spanish for World of Books.

marginalized areas access to books has been a way to expand their educational opportunities outside the school setting.

In another area, after graduate school, I started connecting with people working to advance educational opportunity in Mexico. I found out there are many organizations trying interesting approaches, but many lack the technical capacity to design and evaluate their programs. Recognizing that need, I have worked with three different organizations to help them design, monitor, and evaluate programs ranging from teaching basic skills to mentoring. Through them, I hope to positively influence many children, young people, and parents. Continuing with this task, another Harvard Graduate School of Education (HGSE) alumni and I are starting an education "think-and-do tank" to connect organizations, create synergies, build capacity, and produce ideas that can transform into practice.

Impact

As a researcher in the last year, I created 10 libraries in marginalized areas of the State of Mexico. About 850 early grade readers and their families benefit directly from the *Mundo de Libros* program, with over 11,000 book loans and about the same number of books read on-site. Among active users we have seen an improvement of reading skills and a change in their reading habits; now reading is part of their daily activities. Since libraries are not restricted to those in the program, every day we see children from other ages (and even adults) enjoying the books. I hope the program continues growing to reach more families.

As a consultant, it is difficult to estimate the indirect impact of my work because I have provided technical assistance to organizations with 200 students and to local governments with thousands of schools. What I can say is that, in the last six years, I have worked on the design and/or evaluation of three programs from non-profit organizations, four programs from ministries of education, and three programs from international development banks. Through them, I hope I am changing the educational opportunities of many.

Challenges and Lessons Learned

In my short experience, I have faced some challenges, but I feel I am continuously learning from them.

- *Building a career.* One of my most difficult challenges has been going back to my country and building a career almost from scratch. When I left, I was an economist working at the Central Bank in areas not related to education. At my return, I attempted to enter the small and closed communities of people working in education. Having a degree from Harvard sometimes helped but other times it was perceived as a threat. I applied to many job positions without being even called to interviews. I finally took the learning of one of the projects I had evaluated: "if you cannot enter the system, be an entrepreneur." I am very happy on that path, building a career at my own pace and now being sought after by people who did not want to speak to me before.

- *Going against the current.* I found out that dealing with bureaucracy and changing the status quo is always difficult, especially if you are alone. It has been challenging to show people that what gives you votes and money is not always what is needed by the society. That is why you can find schools with a classroom full of computers, but no electricity. Going against the current is difficult, but it is worth trying. The first step is to start talking and explaining the reality that they ignore. In such a task, find a mentor to ask for advice and allies who share your goals and give you energy to continue.

- *Preparing for the unexpected.* Things never happen 100% as planned. When designing and implementing programs, no matter how many details you plan on paper, you do not realize how many details you have not considered until you go into the field. For instance, you can assume that kids would like to go to the library during the summer vacations, but then realize that rain can stop them from going. The best contingency plan is to be flexible and prepared for adjustments.

- *Raising your voice while keeping the balance.* Being a woman in a patriarchal society imposes a challenge in many dimensions. At the beginning, it is difficult to be heard and you must work harder to gain trust and respect and make your ideas count. For example, in a meeting with stakeholders, they would assume that the male researcher was the one leading the entire project and I was there just to take notes. Then, once you get heard, you need to search for family-work balance. This is the time to remember that you must learn to share responsibilities and build networks of trust. As someone once told me, "to keep balance while riding a bike, you have to keep moving."

Bio

Maria Elena Ortega-Hesles graduated from the International Education Policy Program at the Harvard Graduate School of Education in 2007. After that, she obtained a EdD from the same institution. She has worked as a consultant for non-profit organizations, governments, and international organizations. She is co-founder and Director at PraxEd, a research organization dedicated to improving education in Latin America.

Supporting the Development of Skills for the 21st Century

By Gilda Colin

Goals and Work

The 21st century sets new demands and expectations on our children and young adults. First, young people should be adequately prepared to participate in the global economy. Second, youth should also be prepared to act as responsible global citizens who can work to improve their communities. This means that in order to succeed in the real world, today's learners should be equipped with both the technical skills they need to participate in a rapidly changing economic environment, as well as with a set of interpersonal and intrapersonal skills that will empower them to connect with a diverse, complex, and changing world.

Over the course of the past few years, I have worked on two different projects: the McKinsey Social Initiative (MSI) and ConnectEd. Each project is focused on developing one of the skillsets I have just described, serving different populations and aiming for different objectives. However, I consider that the two projects share a similar element: they are both focused on improving the relevance of what is being taught in the school setting and beyond.

Through the first project, MSI, I have engaged in the re-definition of the type of technical and behavioral skills, as well as mindsets, that young adults truly need to succeed at a personal and professional level. The second project, ConnectEd, has allowed me to re-think the skills, mindsets, and character traits that young people require to actively participate in their communities and make a difference.

As a part of the MSI's Global Curriculum Team, I have worked on the design of a youth employment program called Generation. The program is aimed at closing the skills gap in 5 countries – Mexico, India, Spain, Kenya, and the United States. By delivering high quality learning experiences that provide young adults around the world with the opportunity of finding a job and participating in the global economy, we support our students in achieving personal and professional success, fundamentally changing their life outcomes.

As part of this organization, I have worked on the design of youth employment programs in different industries, including technology, retail/sales, and skilled trades, among others. I have also participated in the development of teacher training experiences and resources that ensure that our instructors are adequately equipped to deliver the Generation curriculum globally.

The second project I have worked on is ConnectEd, a global citizenship program that I have developed and tested with different groups of high school students in Mexico. The program allows students to acquire an understanding of global and local issues, develop empathy and responsibility for these challenges, and take action in their communities to build a more just and sustainable world. Throughout the course, students work on projects using technology and digital media to understand, inspire and change their communities. They develop the skills, mindsets and character traits to become active global citizens.

Although I am a strong supporter of hands-on, experiential education, I started teaching this course when I was still based in the United States. Therefore, the course relies heavily on a diverse array of technological resources to connect with students on a weekly basis and create an engaging learning experience for them. Working on this project has been a fulfilling adventure, for it has allowed me to create technology-based learning experiences that help develop caring, kind and empathetic human beings.

Impact

Over the course of the last year, my work at MSI has directly and indirectly impacted more than 9,300 learners around the world. However, we are the fastest growing youth employment organization in the world and our vision is to support 1 million young adults in finding career-launching jobs in the coming years.

At this point, the ConnectEd project is still running as a pilot and over the course of the last year it has reached over 60 learners directly and indirectly. However, I trust that when the project is properly launched and implemented in more schools, it will have the potential of reaching hundreds or even thousands of learners per year.

Challenges

The work that I have undertaken in these past years has been very fulfilling; however, there have also been many challenges along the way. Although there are widespread ideas about the need to innovate within education, the first challenge I have faced is a hidden resistance to change amongst many of the actors involved in education. The clearest example of this is realizing how much teachers can struggle to adopt new teaching methodologies that differ from the ways they have taught in the past.

A second challenge I have faced has to do with truly understanding the end-user's needs for each learning experience. Given that I have worked with youth ranging from ages 14 to 29 in five different countries, I have found that understanding the learners' developmental stages and cultural contexts is crucial to designing and delivering high quality learning experiences for different groups.

Finally, a third challenge that I have encountered is being able to create learning experiences that truly connect with the whole person. Education is much more than just teaching and learning a set of technical skills. The most transformative learning experiences often happen when we as educators also consider the socioemotional state of our learners, and work to support their own personal growth and development, beyond the technical curriculum.

Lessons Learned

I have certainly learned many lessons doing this work, but my biggest takeaway is that the power of education relies on the human connections that we are able to build across the entire educational system. It does not matter if our goal is to spark deep lasting change within an educational community, or to develop a compelling curriculum that ultimately transforms lives, it is the personal connection that we develop with the educators and students around us that allow us to advance our work.

After working with different stakeholders in education, including students, teachers, and school leaders, I have come to realize that often people are willing to learn and improve, but what they really need is to connect with one another and feel appreciated for who they are—before any real learning takes place. Keeping in mind that an educational process becomes more powerful when we develop human relationships with others has made a big difference in my work, like one of my students once told me: "Education empowers us when we are able to connect with others, learn from their perspectives, and together create something that is greater than ourselves."

Bio

Gilda Colin graduated from the International Education Policy program at the Harvard Graduate School of Education in 2015. She is a Global Curriculum Designer at McKinsey Social Initiative and leader of ConnectEd. Her work is focused on the design and implementation of 21st century education programs that help students succeed in a globalized world.

Preparing Egyptian Students for Higher Education and Promoting Learner-Centered Teaching in Egypt

By Nelly ElZayat

Goals and Work

During my class on Social Entrepreneurship in Education at the Harvard Graduate School of Education, I heard the term "serial entrepreneur" many times. It seemed that most of those entrepreneurs we met and/or learned about could not help themselves from embarking on yet another educational adventure. Little did I know back then that I would become a serial entrepreneur myself.

I started off by co-founding a start-up with two of my classmates. We tried to build a social platform that would offer online tutorials to teach youth in the Middle East North Africa (MENA) region 21st century skills; we called it T21. Our goal was to bridge that ghastly gap between the skills employers are looking for and the skills that public universities in the Middle East equip their students with. For many reasons, and after several difficult lessons, this start-up fell apart. Before it did, I had partnered with my husband on another educational start-up whose goal was to prepare Egyptian students for studying abroad. Having been international students ourselves, we thought we owed it to our people to expand their access to better higher education opportunities.

Newton Education Services, the company I created with my husband, began by offering test preparation courses to students who needed to take the SAT. For quality assurance, we partnered with an organization in the US who had designed an SAT curriculum suitable for students from the Middle East. For the first time in Egypt, students were using mnemonics and other learning strategies to build vocabulary and cognition. Soon, we began offering advising. We would help students research the right universities for them, guided them in narrowing their choices down, reviewed their personal statements and put together winning application files. Two years down the line, we submitted our first proposal to manage a prestigious scholarship offered by the Sawiris Foundation for Social Development, a pioneering Egyptian NGO. We

147

won the proposal, and are now in our third round of managing the scholarship that funds two Egyptian students every year to pursue a Masters in Development Practice at the University of Minnesota. Around the same time, we added our fourth service of offering recruitment services to universities abroad. We organize high school and university visits for universities who are interested in recruiting Egyptian students.

While Newton was growing, I was approached by a then five-year-old start-up, Tatweer. Like T21, Tatweer, offered youth e-learning solutions to address the gap between what public universities offered, and what the labor market was seeking. I worked on changing the general perception about e-learning in Egypt. It was a great experience partnering with Misr ElKheir, one of the largest NGOs in Egypt, to offer youth a scholarship to learn those sought-after skills via e-learning. We also offered our services to private sector and government organizations by producing tailored e-learning content for their respective constituents. Those included the Commercial International Bank (CIB), which is the second most profitable bank in Egypt. It was a testament to the quality of our work that a bank like CIB trusted us to train their staff.

Today, I continue to work on Newton, and I have pursued a few other projects. The first is advocating learner-centered teaching at the Executive Education program at the School of Business at the American University in Cairo. My role is to evaluate instructors on their capacity to incorporate learner-centered teaching, and to orient them on the pros of this approach, and the rationale behind using it. As of now, I have conducted evaluations for 26 instructors, and I have taken part in orientation sessions for around 45 instructors. This particular endeavor has a direct impact on the whole teaching process, and is disrupting the ingrained teacher-centric culture.

The other avenues I am working on involve revolutionizing K-12 education in Egypt. The Nile Egyptian Schools are one arm of education reform in Egypt. The schools offer fully bi-lingual curricula designed by Cambridge University in the UK but for the Egyptian context, giving the middle class access to improved education options. I reviewed the curriculum framework, teaching guides, and testing specifications of the Entrepreneurship and Innovation curriculum. Currently, there are five Nile Schools across Egypt; there will be three more this September, and 25 more over the next few years. I am now also part of a new team of consultants working with the Egyptian Ministry of Education to forward educational reform across public schools.

Impact

During my two years with Tatweer, we served around 2,200 users between recent graduates and junior employees. Newton has served over 230 students since its inception in 2013. Our goal is to have served over 2,000 students in the coming ten years. I am also hopeful that the consulting team I am part of with the Ministry of Education will impact the lives of thousands of Egyptian students and families positively.

Challenges

The challenges have been many, and I expect them to only metamorphose, not disappear. With T21, there was the challenge of focusing on the learnings, after the failure of the start-up. At Newton, the challenge continues to be how do we go to scale without jeopardizing the quality of the service we offer? Guiding instructors on learner-centered teaching has been a balancing act between introducing a foreign concept to experienced teachers, without undermining their expertise. The biggest challenge, however, has been to contribute to education reform in Egypt, without being disheartened by the size of this daunting task.

Lessons Learned

My biggest takeaway from these challenges has been to make sure I focus on the bright spots and to build on them. That is not to say I would ignore the instructor who resists adopting learner-centered teaching; I would still seek other ways to help him or her see the value in this teaching method. But I would also celebrate those who embrace it. I would not dismiss the numerous obstacles to education reform in Egypt, but would revel in little pockets of hope like the Nile Schools. I could, and I sometimes do, lose sleep over our not-so-large numbers at

Newton, but I also read heartfelt emails from students who laud their experiences at the great schools they ended up at because of what we do. This gives me the stamina to help many more.

Bio

Nelly ElZayat graduated from the International Education Policy Program at the Harvard Graduate School of Education in 2012. For the past 18 years, Nelly has been working in international education, specifically in student advising, scholarship management, admissions, curriculum design, learner-centered teaching and on bridging the gap between education and the job market. She is the co-founder of Newton Education Services and is a consultant with the Egyptian Ministry of Education.

Improving Access to Quality Education Through Technology

By Pam Vachatimanont

Goals and Work

I did not expect to fall in love with education. But while taking time post-university to consider a career in academia, I found myself in a second grade classroom and loving it. The opportunity let loose a deep passion for supporting others to learn, to grow, to be, and to live. As much as possible, I have tried to dedicate my energy to supporting more vulnerable populations, and working on improving social justice and equity in education. My reflections here are personal, and an amalgamation of the opportunities I have had in global education over the past eight years.

Currently, I have been working at Enuma, Inc., an ed-tech start-up for the past year. Our company works to develop quality learning tools (applications for smartphones, tablets, smart watches, etc.) to better support young children's learning needs, including in literacy and numeracy. In creating these tools, we specialize in improving accessibility and universality by creating tools that can appeal to all children, regardless of their ability, needs, or learning context. We hope that in leveraging ongoing advances in technology, we can continue creating new possibilities in access to learning and improved education quality across the globe.

Impact

Technology as a system provides incredible opportunity for scale. Millions of children can be immediately and positively, influenced by the release of a quality app onto smartphones and tablet devices. We are working with partner organizations to bring access to those that are disadvantaged by the digital divide (which is difficult, given the multi-variable web of challenges many struggling communities face in accessing quality technology). As part of my work involves implementing field tests of our tools, 500 or more children have been directly involved in my work in the past year. Within the next year, I expect those numbers to more than triple, though the likelihood of my getting to meet each child will increasingly dwindle. Within a decade, through the scalability of technology, those numbers could reach the multi-millions, which is very exciting.

Prior to my current role, I worked at Sesame Workshop's Office in China; more than hundreds of thousands of young children engaged with our T.V., print and digital products. Prior to that, I was with UNICEF China, and given the demographic weight of the extremely populous country, the scale of our work was with hundreds of thousands of children, and indirectly with millions of children as we supported the government in regional and national education policies. Right after HGSE, I started out my career with UNESCO's headquarters, and I worked on global education policy, trying to influence the billions of learners across the globe indirectly through our advocacy work with governments; given the scale and the policy nature, it was difficult to measure the direct impact of my role there. My career journey has increasingly reduced my involvement with education systems in some ways, but has deepened my involvement with learners directly.

Challenges

Managing politics

In one of my roles, I was tasked with leading partners, including governments, to execute donor-funded programs. The politics involved in such a multi-party initiative were many, and oftentimes, priorities were not aligned. There were differences in what groups would benefit, in how and when activities could be implemented, and with who we could work to design and implement activities. While most parties had the best intentions for learners, they had different visions for what "best" meant, and how to get there. Most parties also had additional needs and interests to take care of such as fulfilling Public Relations needs and responsibility to investors; choosing communities where they felt success could be more guaranteed (and therefore resources more wisely used); and working with experts they felt they could trust, though technically may not have been the best fit for such a project. The most difficult task is not necessarily finding the solution, but in its execution in a particular reality.

Managing risk

Across all my roles, I have also struggled with the issue of risk: how much risk am I or the organization willing to take in trying to advance education opportunity? Sometimes we are aligned and sometimes we are not. Sometimes I am more risk-averse, sometimes the organization is more risk-averse. I have been blessed with the opportunity to work in a variety of organizations: more traditional as well as more dynamic ones, huge entities and small, budding entities. Often, it is more difficult for the larger, more established and traditional organizations to take on risk. And this usually makes the work move more slowly and less creatively. I would get frustrated by the lack of innovation, and the unwillingness to push the boundaries in order to effectively reach those in need. But then, in more dynamic organizations, their willingness to take on risk was often greater than my comfort level. Those innovative projects could have an immense impact on learners, but without a proven track record, there is a higher risk of failure. And in the realm of educational opportunity, not executing with an appropriate degree of risk (either too much or too little) could mean lost learning opportunities for children. The balance of risk is often a fragile one, and I think especially so in the realm of education, given the expected outcomes, and the funding nature of many projects often grant for work targeting vulnerable groups.

Lessons Learned

While working with a group of interns, I recall sharing how one of the most challenging aspects of working in education for development was how much gray there was. Decisions were rarely black or white, or a clear right or wrong. Work was clouded with risk and with politics, and all that gray could be extremely unsettling when children's education was at stake.

But precisely because children's education was at stake, there was a bottom line to which we could hold ourselves-to do what was best for children. The shape of the project or product might be slightly or wildly different from what I had initially planned for, but as long as we kept measuring ourselves against what was best for children, we could wade through the gray more easily and justly.

Bio

Pam Vachatimanont graduated from the International Education Policy Program at the Harvard Graduate School of Education in 2009. She received a B.A in Art History and Asian Studies from Williams College in 2007. Originally from Bangkok, Thailand, she's had opportunities in the classroom and worked for UNESCO, UNICEF, and Sesame Workshop in cities across the globe. She currently resides in San Francisco, where she works for Enuma, Inc., an ed-tech start-up, and is on the board of the Jump! Foundation.

Developing Innovative Products to Expand Educational Opportunity

By Ana Gabriela Pessoa

Goals and Work

I am currently the VP of Product and Innovation for Emerging Markets at Pearson Education. The way I see my work advancing educational opportunity is through working across 6 geographical regions (Hispanoamerica, Brazil, Hong Kong – China, the Middle East, India and South Africa) offering the best products and services for K12 education, English learning, and Higher Education. I work very closely with students and teachers in these locations to understand the necessities around curriculum needs, as well as new subject matters, and the most effective ways of teaching and learning across different cultures. We apply a design-centered approach to product development where we listen and create products together with those who will use it, be it teachers, students, parents, or school owners. I believe the work we do addresses three aspects: expanding access to education, improving the quality of education, and improving the relevance of what is taught. Today we are reaching students across the world who would otherwise not have the opportunity to be exposed to a curriculum that is curated by experts globally. We are also providing digital assets that when distributed across a large network of schools become accessible financially. We work both in the private sector as well as with public schools, and the vision is that we are able to provide measurable results on the progression of learning through an efficacy framework that we apply locally as an evaluation system to our products.

Previous to Pearson I was an education entrepreneur, having founded in 2008 one of the first personalized learning platforms in Brazil, focused on teaching English online. The purpose of Ezlearn was largely around providing access to content in a structured way that would help professionals acquire simple English knowledge focused on the work environment. We offered courses online and through mobile devices at a fraction of the cost of a traditional face-to-face school.

Impact

Over the last year, I believe we have reached close to 10 million students. Over the course of a decade, I believe we have reached over 50 million students. However, my hope is to reach one billion learners!

Challenges

There are two types of leadership challenges I have faced over the last 10 years, since I graduated from the International Education Policy (IEP) program in 2007.

On one hand, there are managerial leadership challenges. When I first started my company Ezlearn in 2008, I faced all of the challenges of a brand new startup, in Brazil, where at that time the culture of startups and access to venture capital was incipient. I had to find the right investors, fundraise, build a team, build a product, find a distribution channel, and break-even as fast as possible, so the company could survive. These are many challenges bundled together and I had to learn to be laser focused on where to spend my time and energy. For me the most important thing was to attract the right investors and the right team to build a solid product. However, we were doing something very innovative for the time in Brazil, and finding the right people to join this dream took a bit of time. Since our business model was also quite new at the time, figuring out where to find our customers and how to sell to them (this was around the time the Lean Startup movement was starting http://theleanstartup.com/) took many trial and error efforts. I needed to keep my team happy and motivated, but also focused on making money to pay their salaries at the end of the month.

In a large organization, such as a multinational, the fear of not having enough money at the end of the month is practically non-existent. However, the managerial challenges are similar in many ways. For me it was always about building the best team and bringing together the best people I could. The biggest difference in this case was that at Ezlearn we were 23 people, while my team at Pearson, running product development in Brazil, has 300. So it was a huge step for me in people management and really trying to understand how to be more efficient with our delivery of products to the market. I learned about creating new processes with a cost-savings mentality.

There is also another big leadership challenge, and this one is around the purpose of the work. I have worked in education my entire professional life because I believe in the purpose of the work I do. I believe access to high quality education is the only way people grow, the only way a country develops. So it's the most important job in the world! The leadership challenge I face is the pace at which change happens, globally. Quite frankly I think we as a society are moving too slowly. The world has drastically changed and will continue to do so with the fast advancements of technology, artificial intelligence, and greater competition for jobs. This means we must take time to think about what kind of education system we need for these future jobs, and what types of values we need the younger generation to be exposed to in order to build a better, more sustainable world.

Lessons Learned

I believe we need more design and more play. Many of the products (the way content is delivered) available today are not the best design-oriented to address the real needs of students and teachers. Through technology we are able to personalize learning and show learner progression in a very detailed way. However, most schools still do not have access to this technology. The world has changed, the work environment will be quite different with a larger freelance population and students that grew up in a world with games, mobile devices and a shared economy. If learning is not fun and engaging, students and teachers are disinterested. The jobs of the future will require much more critical thinking, creativity and curiosity, and less repetitive skills that can be substituted by a machine.

We must encourage the younger generation to pursue their dreams to resolve big societal problems. This will come through an emphasis on global education and creating a sense that they belong in the world as global citizens and that everything is interconnected. Socio-emotional learning must be incorporated within the school environments.

Access to capital is readily available; there are many private investors, venture capital funds and non-profit organizations looking for good opportunities and entrepreneurs. If there are more education entrepreneurs spending time in schools with teachers, students, and parents and having a design-centered approach to solving their real problems, we will have even better solutions. It takes people working together, but also realizing that we need to move fast.

Bio

Ana Gabriela Pessoa is the VP of Product and Innovation for Emerging Markets at Pearson. Ana graduated from the International Education Policy program at the Harvard Graduate School of Education in 2006. Shortly after, Ana founded Ezlearn, one of the first edtech startups in Brazil, which was acquired in 2013. She is a graduate of the University of Pennsylvania, and selected as a Young Global Leader by the World Economic Forum.

Leading Educational Innovation in the Arab World

By Shatha AlHashmi

Goals and Work

I work for the Mohammed Bin Rashid Center for Government Innovation (MBRCGI) where I have led a team in the development, design, and launch of Massive Open Online Courses (MOOCs) on Innovation in Government in 2016. This year we are developing a second MOOC on how to conduct an innovation lab and how to use innovative methods and tools to inspire innovative ideas and find solutions to the challenges that face government entities. The MOOCs are intended to build on the United Arab Emirates' (UAE) expertise and leadership in the arena of innovative government and governance. The online courses will serve both to create a freely accessible Arabic resource to help spur innovation in governments across the region, and also as a component of government innovation training programs for UAE government employees and all Arab speaking employees around the world. We sought to build a solid pedagogical foundation throughout the courses that ensures the MBRCGI's learning objectives are met. These MOOCs include videos, interviews, case studies, reading material, animation, slides, discussion forums, infographics, and assessment, all developed according to global standards. The MOOC was developed in collaboration with Edraak, a current educational platform that has a significant number of learners (approximately 1.2 million). Edraak is a massive open online course (MOOC) platform that is an initiative of the Queen Rania Foundation (QRF). The Edraak platform has significant traction and brand recognition regionally and globally, as it is developed according to global technological standards. We at MBRCGI also aim to develop our own education platform that can support a minimum of 100,000 registered learners and support a minimum of 10,000 concurrent users at any point. We also plan for it to provide detailed demographic data on learners registered in the MOOC, as well as provide assessment and grading to the learners. Also, we aim to embed discussion forums where learners can interact with instructors and with their peers.

Impact

The MBRCGI provided the first world class MOOC on government innovation in Arabic. Through the MOOC, the MBRCGI intends to reach Arabic speaking learners across the world and play an integral part in advancing innovation in governments across the region and the world. The MOOC was developed in a fully digital and interactive format that has attracted more than 75,000 people from all over the world (12,000 people from the UAE) and we aim to reach 150,000 people after launching the second MOOC in September of 2017. The geographic distribution of the learners shows that the learners are from all seven continents, which suggests that it has attracted learners globally and not only from the Arab region. The MBRCGI has a significant social media presence to ensure that it reaches a larger number of learners.

Challenges

The MBRCGI was established to become a center that encourages innovation in government work. Through the Center, the UAE seeks to develop a comprehensive system of modern tools to help government entities innovate in areas such as policies and strategies, organizational structures, operations, procedures, and services provided to the public. Through these tools, the Center aims to transform government innovation into an organized institutional work system that serves as a key pillar of the UAE Government strategy.

The MBRCGI is the practical implementation of His Highness Sheikh Mohammed Bin Rashid Al Maktoum's vision to develop government work internally and improve the competitive level of the UAE internationally. His Highness also sought to move from individual innovation initiatives to a comprehensive institutional innovation framework through the Center's adoption of modern innovation theories that reinforce the UAE's standing as one of the best governments in the world.

To achieve our vision and spread our message, the MBRCGI provides world-class spaces for innovators to test ideas and empower individuals through the establishment of a connected community of innovators.

This in turn helps enrich the culture of innovation in the UAE. The Centre's business model includes three main pillars: innovative ideas, innovative capabilities, and innovative culture.

One of our challenges is linking the main objectives of our Centre to the development of the different MOOCs that could help in achieving the objectives of our business model and enable capabilities and experimentation with ideas, since the MBRCGI aims at providing training and preparing government employees through a comprehensive system of innovation tools, scientific materials and the best innovative practices. This enables employees to use relevant knowledge and skills to innovate in the area of government services. We also aim to test innovative ideas by providing world-class spaces for innovators to develop, test, and spread ideas locally, regionally and worldwide.

We face many other challenges such as:

a. **Developing an effective innovation framework** and how to inspire and motivate others to ensure they are engaging with the trainings provided, and encourage them to interact with the instructor.

b. **Driving change** in the culture is also a challenge when it comes to innovation and how to include e-learning as one the main components of the educational and/or training system.

c. **Guiding change** is the challenge of managing, mobilizing, understanding and leading change. This includes knowing how to mitigate consequences, overcome resistance to change, and deal with employees' reactions to change.

d. **Mentoring and coaching the employees** (other elements of enabling capabilities and developing government employees).

e. **Managing internal stakeholders and politics** is the challenge of managing relationships, politics, and image. This challenge includes gaining managerial support, managing up, and getting buy-in from other government departments, groups or individuals.

Lessons learned

a. Within the next decade, extremely powerful information technologies will become ubiquitous in educational settings and will create fundamental changes in learning environments at all levels.
b. The eLearning concept and the range of computational devices and their applications are expanding at a geometric rate, fundamentally changing how people think about communication, connectivity, and the role of technology in society.
c. Educational innovations are developed in a way that requires a continuous infusion of outside resources to keep them going (greater accessibility, educational effectiveness, scalability of the new systems, incorporation of the stakeholders' views and comments).
d. Leveraging content that is mobile-empowered for MOOCs.
e. Creating an educational ecosystem that is sustainable and scalable.
f. Building personal learner efficacy and capacity for self-directed learning.

Bio

Shatha Alhashmi is a public sector innovation specialist. Over the course of her career, she has held several positions in the Federal and local government of the United Arab Emirates. Shatha is also interested in social entrepreneurship and is passionate about youth development. She graduated from the International Education Policy Program in 2014.

CREATING
ORGANIZATIONS

A decade after HGSE: Building organizations to empower children and youth

By Luis E Garcia de Brigard

I graduated from the Harvard Graduate School of Education (HGSE) 10 years ago in June 2007. I have always felt that my experience at Harvard was analogous to the gravity assist maneuvers often used in space travel; it influenced my path much in the way gravitational fields alter the speed and direction of a space craft. My time at HGSE changed the direction of my career and accelerated the pace of my personal and professional life. Harvard was, to me, an incredibly powerful force that propelled me into professional ventures and experiences that have been challenging, gratifying and unexpected.

I applied to HGSE a few years after going through a career change; I had decided to abandon my job as a corporate lawyer to become a school teacher and was convinced that my time at Harvard would allow me to return to teaching and climb the ranks of school leadership. Instead, I embarked into a somewhat chaotic career characterized by a series of overlapping and non-linear educational pursuits. During the past ten years, I have been involved in entrepreneurial endeavors in both for- and non-profits, have served in the public sector and engaged in philanthropic initiatives. During that period, I founded or co-founded companies and organizations that have collectively impacted more than 100,000 students, employed more than 5,000 teachers, and operated in more than 15 countries. I also had the opportunity to serve as Deputy Minister of Education of Colombia, where I was responsible for the schooling of more than 8 million students. During the same time, I have had the privilege to sit on numerous boards of educational organizations.

This range of experiences, from seeding a tiny educational startup, to being responsible for the operation of an entire nation's schooling system has been an enormous privilege and an opportunity to learn about the challenges in advancing educational opportunity. The following reflections illustrate some of the lessons learned from ten years of **starting** organizations, pursuing **change**, and **bridging** across sectors in my ever-evolving quest to make a difference through education.

START: Entrepreneurship and the challenges of resilience and scale.

While completing my master's program at HGSE I learned about the work of WorldTeach, a Harvard-affiliated organization with over two decades of history recruiting and placing volunteer native English speakers as teachers in underprivileged communities across the globe. I decided to contact them with a proposal to start a chapter in Colombia. I was promptly rejected; Colombia's reputation made international organizations reluctant to operate in the country. Furthermore, WorldTeach made it clear that it preferred to launch their programs through partnerships with ministries of education. I persisted. After months of conversations, they agreed to launch a pilot program with four volunteers in partnership with Volunteers Colombia (VC), an organization that I co-founded to provide WorldTeach with some degree of institutional support and an assurance about our commitment to bear the costs of the program. The reality was that our resources were minimal; seed funding to finance the cost of placing the teachers came from a small loan from my parents and all the work necessary to run the organization came from unpaid volunteers. I did, however, have a goal in mind: this pilot had to grow into the largest educational volunteering program in the country and we would convince the central and regional governments to fund an ambitious expansion of the initiative. Today, VC is indeed the largest international volunteering program in Colombia; it employs over 120 staff and works with different government agencies to place over 800 volunteers per year in public schools around the country. VC was also the pathway for me and a group of colleagues to launch Teach for Colombia, the 19th country to join the Teach for All network.

I spent almost half of the decade that has elapsed since graduating from HGSE launching companies and organizations. In each case, the story was much like that of VC, an early idea that was always met by obstacles of funding, credibility, experience, or market. In each case, the initial impact was negligible: four volunteers, one client, one school, one employee. Modest figures that contrasted with my dreams of system-wide impact, scale, innovation, and genuine transformation. In looking back, I can see that the survival and success of those endeavors was always associated with resiliency and a mindset that steady progress, rather than initial perfection, was the only possible avenue for growth and impact.

I am convinced that entrepreneurship is a powerful avenue to advancing educational opportunity. However, it requires the understanding that it is precisely the lack of impact in the early days that enables and unleashes the transformative power of scale. The paradox of pursuing change by producing none has been my greatest lesson in starting educational organizations.

CHANGE: public sector and the paradox of power and helplessness

I was sworn in as Deputy Minister of Education in September 2014. I suddenly controlled the largest budget in the nation (surpassing that of defense for the first time in history) and was responsible for the operation of tens of thousands of schools that served millions of students and hundreds of thousands of teachers. I was quickly overwhelmed by the paradoxical feeling of having the tools and formal authority to implement real change, while at the same time being paralyzed by a feeling of helplessness resulting from the sheer magnitude of the school system, depth of bureaucracy, and consequence of the stakes. There was an irony in knowing that every decision I made would greatly affect the futures of many children and being petrified about making those very decisions at the same time. I immediately understood the reason why the prevalent view of the public sector is one of inefficiency, paralysis, and impossibility. It is humans, after all, who run the public sector—humans who are prone to fear, who are risk averse, and who have a survival instinct. Humans that are only so strong and that are suddenly tasked with altering the course of a gigantic organization.

Having zero experience in the public sector, I resorted to my entrepreneurial background and told my team, "We are always in startup mode." While the public sector seems to be the very opposite of a startup environment, I thought that this mindset would help us overcome initial inertia and assume the risks that were necessary to produce change. It would allow us to innovate, experiment and pivot. It would also isolate us from the perilous path of conforming to existing practice because "This is the way it has always been done." It would let us use our power and escape our helplessness, while at the same time having the urgency of every startup: scale or die.

Living up to this mindset was not easy. I constantly succumbed to a "cruise control" mindset because of pressure, inexperience, or sheer exhaustion. And every time it happened, the impact —or lack thereof— in the lives of children became obvious. It is easy to be in the public sector and conform to practices, standards, and mindsets that have caused the educational systems of countries like mine to perpetuate inequities for decades rather than correct them. It is easy to stay the course, and yet remain busy. I had frenetic days when I achieved nothing; I called those the "bureaucrat" days. I had equally intense days when I knew a difference had been made; I called those my "startup" days.

I believe advancing educational opportunity requires us to constantly battle the idea that we should stay the course. Even incremental changes require tremendous agency. The public sector is a testament to how little one can achieve while endowed with vast resources. It is also an example of how much can be transformed by managing small but thinking big.

BRIDGE: the (false) dichotomy of social and financial returns

I started my career as a corporate lawyer, working with clients to structure mergers and acquisitions. This experience gave me an insight into the world of business and the potential for value creation of corporate structures. I also grew up in a family of educators that were skeptical about for-profit educational companies and believed that education should be left to governments or non-profits. It is probably because of this tension, that I have spent all my career with one foot in each world. I have started for- and non-profits, served on paid and unpaid boards, invested in educational companies, and contributed to educational causes.

This duality has allowed me to see the best and the worst of both worlds. I have witnessed the ruthless pursuit of profit and the unnecessary tradeoff between financial returns and educational quality. I have been disappointed by the inefficiency, conformity and self-righteousness that can permeate the non-profit world. I have been inspired by the genuine altruism of organizations committed to delivering services, advocating for change and advancing knowledge in places where no government or corporation would ever go. I have seen the unmatched ability of private equity structures to deploy financial resources and create the incentives to attract talent and unleash human potential and innovation. But what has surprised me most has been the lack of conversation between these two worlds. Mutual suspicion, skepticism, and contempt has created and amplified a useless schism that has held back the advancement of educational opportunity around the world.

I have fought all my career against the binary logic behind the false dichotomy between social and financial returns. I have witnessed the benefits of laying bridges, instead of walls, between these distinct yet compatible approaches to impact education. In doing so, I have seen one particularly powerful effect— the unrestricted flow of human talent. Over the past decade, I have had the privilege of working with extremely talented individuals who have been attracted by the versatile nature of a group of organizations that allow them to pursue their professional, personal, and financial goals through an open flow of career opportunities in diverse sectors. They have fulfilled their commitment to education by traversing around government, non-profits, investment funds, and educational companies, while remaining true to the purpose of advancing educational opportunity. Compartmentalizing and isolating denies the sector from synergies, restricts the flow of human talent and ultimately detracts from our collective ability to transform education for future generations.

Become a gravitational slingshot.

I had the enormous privilege to spend a year at HGSE and experience my personal gravity assist, one that enabled me to continue traveling through life with renewed speed and energy. The last decade has been professionally challenging and personally fulfilling and for that I am grateful. As I look into the next decade of my life, I cannot help but think that the upcoming challenge is no less than to *become* a gravitational slingshot for others: to facilitate path-changing experiences through entrepreneurship, public service, philanthropy, and a continued exploration of avenues to educate all children.

Bio

Luis E. Garcia de Brigard graduated from the International Education Policy program at the Harvard Graduate School of Education in 2007. He is an educational entrepreneur who has founded multiple organizations including Enseña por Colombia, Volunteers Colombia, Appian Education Ventures and Envoys. He served as Deputy Minister of Education of Colombia and has been a member of numerous boards of educational organizations in Colombia and the United States.

Advancing Educational Opportunities for Disadvantaged Children and Youth in Mexico

By Mariali Cárdenas Casanueva

Goals and Work

Mexico is one of the most unequal countries in the world[26] which affects the distribution of educational opportunities.[27] The complexity of our socio-economic conditions has widened the gap between those who have access to quality education and those who do not, mainly because they are living in underprivileged conditions.

When I started my career as a field researcher in education projects, I saw how children belonging to remote indigenous communities or those living in rural communities in the mountains, as well as those children who grew up in marginal-urban communities with high rates of violence, had less opportunities to learn than those with less socio-economic constraints. However, I always questioned, in my mind, the validity of the premise that limited resources or the place where one is born determines the possibility of obtaining an education that can generate life opportunities. I wanted to challenge this premise, especially after also having had the opportunity to see very closely the talent and the ability to learn that many children have, even in such unfavorable conditions.

Since then, I have worked to create educational alternatives that can expand opportunities for children to become who they are meant to be,

---

[26] CEPAL and OCDE in PNUD-OEA (2009) La Democracia de ciudadanía: una agenda para la construcción de ciudadanía en América Latina, Washington.
https://www.oas.org/dsp/documentos/publicaciones/la_democracia _de_ciudadania.pdf

[27] Reimers, F. (2001) *Unequal Schools, Unequal Chances: The Challenges to Equal Opportunity in the Americas*, David Rockefeller Center Series on Latin American Studies, Cambridge, MA.

regardless of a lack of resources, their background, or their socio-economic conditions.

I work to advance educational equity, which requires bringing the best to those who need it the most and designing innovative educational models that are implemented in underprivileged public schools. These models incorporate three elements: a) confidence in human capacities despite limited socio-economic conditions, b) a deep understanding of reality, and c) renowned educational theories and frameworks, which when combined are capable of transforming pedagogical practices and school culture in order to expand learning opportunities.

Through the design of pedagogical models, I have worked directly in improving the quality of pedagogical practices, designing methodologies that derive from theory, and making them accessible and relevant to teachers and facilitators to improve learning opportunities for children. I have also worked to reformulate the relevance of citizenship competencies beyond the acquisition of factual knowledge to the possibility of developing skills, attitudes, and values while transforming reality. The designed models consider that students should learn to face obstacles and generate opportunities, think critically, to use their creative potential, to analyze and act collaboratively with others, and to develop a sense of agency to improve their own conditions and those of their communities in search of a common good.

My work is done within Vía Educación[28] where we design models and test them through formative and summative evaluation[29] for further dissemination. These are five examples of the kind of work I do:

---

[28] Via Education is a non-profit organization based in Mexico which I co-founded with two other Harvard Education graduates, Armando Estrada and Emanuel Garza. www.viaeducation.org

[29] Reimers, F., Ortega, ME., Cárdenas, M., Estrada, A., Garza, E.(2014) Empowering Teaching for Participatory Citizenship: Evaluating the Impact of Alternative Civic Education Pedagogies on Civic Attitudes, Knowledge and Skills of Eight-grade Students in Mexico, *Journal of Social Science Education*, Volume 13, Number 4,

- Designing a Curriculum for Democratic Citizen Education: The pedagogy used involves the development of projects where the student exercises citizenship skills while improving his or her community.
- Leading a Professional Teacher Development Program: Pedagogical skills for the teaching of democratic citizenship implemented at a nationwide level with teachers in service and in formation.
- Expanding Social Participation for Parents: Development of leadership capacities for the organization of parents' participation in the educational community.
- Formulating Afterschool Project for the Development of Democratic Citizenship Capacities among disadvantaged youth.
- Collaboration in the design of the National Curriculum of Civics and Ethics and Socio-emotional development.

Impact

The implementation of the models I helped design have directly reached around 300 teachers this past year and indirectly reached about 10,000 students and parents. This is not considering all the learners from Mexico's Elementary Public Schools (nearly 20 million students), who are going to use the National Curriculum in Civics and Ethics and Socio-Emotional Development designed for them beginning in autumn 2017.

Over the past decade my work has directly reached almost 800 teachers and facilitators and more than 24,000 students. My work has indirectly impacted 80,000 members of school communities.

Challenges

The main leadership challenges I have faced are related to managing resistance to change, identifying variables that can be modified in the system and that really strengthen it, and empowering the main actors of that system to discover ways in which they can expand the impact of their work by their own means and in collaboration with others.

At the beginning of my career I realized that people who work to educate the poor balance two issues, the motivation that comes with the satisfaction of seeing the development of human potential, even with the contextual limitations, and the burden involved in facing daily difficulties. Many of these educators try to advance educational goals with very limited resources, which is valuable work. Nevertheless, sometimes their motivation may decrease when, despite their efforts, they are not reaching such goals that could actually generate more and better educational opportunities.

In this way, a system is maintained that is working less effectively, but for longer than it should and it creates a frame of mind where high achievement results are no longer expected and where the experience of struggle and failure has taught people that that is all they can achieve. This makes it very difficult for them to see the potential of change, or they see it as a great effort to do things in a different way. This results in a resistance to change, that is understandable, because what has so far been achieved might be lost.

Lessons learned

I have seen in my work that this resistance to change sometimes represents the commitment of people to educational development. That is, they value the work they are doing and the potential impact it represents, so the resistance is based on a desire to do things well. In this case, my work has been to help them think about how their own efforts can have different results through carrying out different actions, and I have learned that this process requires dialogue and reflection as well as a true sense of empathy and a horizontal relationship of learning in order to create alternatives together. In this way, the resulting alternatives will represent the needs of the community and in this way the community will be more engaged in implementing and sustaining them.

To meet these challenges, it has been useful for me to follow this process:[30]

Paradigm shift
1. Resistance to change
    a. Value the work that is done
    b. Recognize the difficulties involved in achieving the objectives
2. Understand the reality:
    a. Identify the main obstacles to overcome
    b. Identify which of these obstacles can be overcome by the own actors as leaders of this process along with the accompaniment of the facilitator
    c. Find opportunities for change in the system through analysis and dialogue
3. Work together to define the desired change: establish common goals and involve the rest of the community.
4. Act: develop social capital, establish a plan of action with specific goals, leadership development, and deadlines, and carry out the plan.
5. Reflect on the learnings and the results obtained in order to make adjustments, then celebrate successes and begin again.

Bio

Mariali Cardenas is from Mexico, graduated from the Teaching and Learning Program at the Harvard Graduate School of Education in 2000. Her focus of study is the design, implementation and evaluation of innovative education strategies that can expand teaching and learning opportunities. Ms. Cardenas' current work is related to the understanding of how students can develop citizenship and democratic capabilities while working together on initiatives to improve their communities and contribute to a common good.
Note: While Mariali did not graduate from the IEP Program, as the program did not formally exist while she was a student at HGSE. I was her academic advisor and she took courses that were part of the 'pilot' of the IEP we ran that year. She encouraged her fiancée and his best friend to apply to the program, and returned to HGSE as they all worked in developing Via Educacion. Fernando Reimers.

---

[30] Developed with insights from Prof. Marshall Ganz's <u>Organizing notes, Mapping the social world</u>, 2000, Harvard KSG, Cambridge, MA.

Empowering Parents of First Generation Learners in India

By Ghazal S. Gulati

Goals and Work

I am a child of migrants. More than 25 years ago, my parents moved to Delhi from violence-hit Kashmir. They moved to a new city with a young child, armed with little else other than professional degrees. Twenty years later, I received an acceptance letter from the Harvard Graduate School of Education (HGSE), which gave me an opportunity to receive high quality training in the field of education. It was the perseverance and dedication of my parents that paved my path to Appian Way.

After a vibrant and enlightening year at HGSE, I moved back to India to work on a research project with J-PAL (Poverty Action Lab). I traversed thousands of kilometers across one of the largest states in India, collecting data from government schools. Hoping to understand their perspective on the education system, I sought out parents in every district I visited. I met parents who had high hopes and aspirations and parents who were willing to make hard choices and tough sacrifices in the hope for a better life for their children. Every interaction continued to remind me of my own parents. A deep chasm separated this set of parents from my own – education.

In the effort to provide education for all, an increasing number of children are going to school today. Children are going further in school than their own parents. Struggles of parents of first-generation learners are insufficiently studied. In my experience, all parents, regardless of socio-economic status, understand the value of education. However, what happens when they have never been to school themselves? Are they able to hold the schools accountable? Can they assess the quality of education their children are receiving? Is the system able to provide support to these parents? An interview in Delhi exemplified the plight of parents of first-generation learners. Geeta Kumari never completed school herself. She regrets not having completed school every time she's needed assistance in reading even simple messages on her phone. Her dream for her daughter, Jayashree, was simple. She wanted her daughter to be independent and knew it could only be achieved if Jayashree was educated. She ruefully accepted that her lack of education was a barrier to her daughter's future. She is continuously seeking avenues to acquire skills that will enable her to support her daughter effectively.

Months of primary and secondary research made the dearth of support for parents apparent. In the bid to achieve quality education for all, the stakeholder that spent the most time with the children was being ignored. This prompted me to co-found Meraki – an organization that helps parents support their children. Meraki, a Greek term, loosely translates into leaving a part of your soul in everything you do. The word is symbolic of parenting itself. For the last six months, we have worked with 200 families in and around Delhi. Our vision is to ensure quality education for children by equipping, enabling, and empowering parents.

Impact

As a teacher, researcher and now social entrepreneur, I have had the opportunity to influence at least 20,000 children. The last five years in the education sector have been frustrating yet fulfilling. The fact that I am playing a part, however small, in aiding access to quality education fuels my work every day. Apart from gaining high quality functional skills at HGSE, I learned to define and reflect on my leadership style. I understood the importance of context. I now know that it is the time spent understanding the eco-system, its players, and their motivations that builds strong programs and leaders. At Meraki, we spent more than a year interviewing and shadowing parents from different socio-economic statuses, teachers, and school administrators. It is this continuous primary research that guides product development at Meraki.

Challenges

With a background in quantitative methods, implementing data-driven product development and decision-making came naturally to me. What I struggle with every day is how to create a product, guided by context and data, that does not crumble at scale. With Meraki, my aim is to create a sustainable organization that delivers value to its customers at scale. Parents are struggling universally but their struggles are not uniform. The value for Meraki lies in creating a personalized support for parents. The satisfaction and joy of supporting parents with their exact needs is unparalleled. The daily struggle, knowing that personalization may not be sustainable at scale, is also real. We continue to look for ways to achieve the tricky balance between quality (read personalized support) and scale. As we expand, the statement 'quality at scale' almost seems like an oxymoron. My work in India has exposed me to plenty of meaningful, well thought-out education programs that crashed and burned on expansion. The programs could not handle contextual differences across regions and the differentiated needs and preferences across stakeholders. I have seen well thought-out, piloted programs backed by research reduced to mere box-ticking exercises when they finally reached a large number of customers.

Lessons Learned

The search for answers is ongoing but here is what I know. Success cannot be achieved at scale with standardization or centralization of control. Agile organizations that build decentralized structures will withstand pressures of expansion, changing readily to demands and needs of their stakeholders. To translate that for Meraki, we have decided to rely relentlessly on the support of parents to help each other. Meraki will train them on how to look for answers but also take ownership of their problems. Meraki cannot solve all their problems but we can teach them how to seek the support in their ecosystem. This support would grow and become multifaceted as parents organize themselves into collectives, collectives which will be focused on quality education and healthy child development. This movement of empowered parent collectives would draw on the strengths of all its stakeholders. Parents will be able to draw personalized support, leveraging on the collective skills of the community. While the fight to provide quality education to all is ongoing, the small victories Meraki's parents make every day are a step in the right direction.

Bio

Ghazal S. Gulati graduated from the International Education Policy Program at the Harvard Graduate School of Education in 2015. She is founder and COO, of Meraki, a non-profit company in India. Meraki's vision is to improve student learning through increased parent engagement by building knowledge, skills and mindsets of parents of first generation learners.

Creating an Organization to Increase the Relevance of what is taught in Mexican Schools

By Armando Estrada-Zubía

I am the executive director and co-founder of Vía Educación, a Mexico-based nonprofit organization that seeks to unleash the potential of society to transform itself through education. Vía Educación increases the opportunities of students, schools, and communities to engage in the kind of education that helps them understand the world around them, and develops their skills to proactively change it for the better.

Vía Educación began when I was a student at HGSE in 2004 (yes, we were in Cambridge when the Red Sox reversed the curse and won the world baseball championship after 86 years!) along with Mariali Cárdenas, Emanuel Garza and a vibrant group of students from different Latin American countries including Rafael Gomes and Valeria Rocha from Brazil, Ximena Miranda from Costa Rica, Fernando Díaz from Colombia, Cristóbal García (MIT) and Josefina Errazuriz from Chile, Juan de Dios Simón from Guatemala, Elena Simpser from Mexico, and Andrea Schildknecht from El Salvador, all of whom are part of Vía Educación's international coalition.

Goals and Work

We were interested in looking at the role of education in developing citizenship competencies in a time where there was considerable international focus on the subject. Current international challenges make us realize these competencies are now even more important.

The group initially sought to understand the conditions of schools and teachers, and to look at the ways we could interact with the ministries of education. We soon realized that research was the way to start, so the emerging organization conducted a research project in Mexico to identify the pedagogical skills required to teach education for democratic citizenship. Different approaches were tested and one of them achieved significant improvements for both the teachers and the students. The model focused on helping participants learn and practice

181

citizenship competencies by participating collectively in advancing the practical solution of an issue that they themselves had identified as a problem or a challenge within their own context.

The methodology behind the program was developed building on different concepts related to democracy, including Robert Putnam's social capital, Amartya Sen's theories of freedom and opportunities, Marshall Ganz's concepts on community organizing and leadership, Paulo Freire's notion of conscientization, Albert Bandura's theories of self-efficacy, Roger Hart's concepts on children's participation, Peter Senge's contributions on systems change, and Judith Torney Purta's frameworks on education for democratic citizenship, among others.

Vía Educación converted this blend of concepts into a practical, experiential curriculum by using project- and service-based learning pedagogies. The result was a sequence of steps for problem solving and organizing while acquiring a set of skills, attitudes and knowledge for democratic citizenship.

This methodology is relevant because now, more than ever, we can see the importance of the distribution of power and its influences: the power exerted by elected State representatives, government officials, business' agendas, citizens' voices, media content and coverage, technology and interconnectedness, etc. Now we can see that evolved democracies need evolved citizens.

We must have better citizens, individuals, and collectives capable of understanding and transforming the social systems in which they live; prepared to advocate for and challenge the status of things, with a deep sense of responsibility and solidarity; and equipped with an adequate and effective set of skills to be agents of change. The methodology's theory of change addresses this urgent need because it implements an experiential curriculum and pedagogical path to help participants engage in transforming the self-identified challenges of their own environment, while learning and practicing citizenship competencies such as self-efficacy, organizing, leadership and collective action, all in a democratic way.

Vía Educación's methodology is also relevant for improving the way societies rely on the power of education. The role of schools in building new societies is fundamental. However, the real effects of a quality education will not come from the work of schools alone, but from the collection of efforts produced by the broad array of individuals and institutions that make a school culture possible. Teachers play an essential role, but without the power of families, the media, businesses, neighbors around the school, etc., the task will always be incomplete. Vía Educación has experience working on long term initiatives for the *Renewal of the School Culture* using systemic approaches, building the sense of collectiveness, co-responsibility, and shared vision among the different actors involved in education in a particular region. This is why Vía Educación works not just with the school, but the entire community, with youth, corporations, libraries, school administrators, the government, and with students themselves.

Impact

Last year, our 86 colleagues served 25,033 beneficiaries, including teachers trained with our methodologies, students participating in our youth programs, and school administrators who attended our workshops, as well as neighbors and community members who organized participative projects. Operating in five different states across Mexico, our beneficiaries also helped us to indirectly reach 61,048 people. In 2017 the organization started an initiative to expand its impact to three other states in the country as well as the United States and Colombia.

An additional aspect of our impact is our participation as board members or advisors in several networks and alliances such as the Strategic Planning Council of Nuevo León (a first of its kind public-private council for long term strategic planning where we helped established our State's education goals and strategies for the next 30 years); the Consejo Cívico (a citizens' council for the strengthening of civil society organizations where we helped build a strategy to assess municipal and state governments); the Academy for Systems Change, an international network of individuals and organizations focused on advancing the field of awareness-based systemic change in order to accelerate ecological, social, and economic well-being; Red SumaRSE (a network of 25 corporations who, working with USAID, share a 5-year corporate social responsibility project in underserved communities where we serve as the operating partner). We were also part of the team who designed the Mexican national curriculum on education for democratic citizenship and the cross-cutting content in socioemotional learning. Over the last 10 years we have directly trained 66,395 people in our methodologies, who reach more than 189,000 people every year.

Challenges

There have been challenges and uncertainties along the way during these first 12 years. One of the most important I see has to do with building awareness that working in partnerships and alliances for long term impact takes time and consistent commitment. Almost everybody agrees education is one fundamental solution for social change, but only a few are willing to keep working to achieve long term impact. Most funders and institutions in our country who invest in education projects expect to see impact right away which is hard when the system requires major cultural renovations. This is also an issue with government institutions and ministries of education where, in general, there is short attention for initiatives related to education innovation and its impact in the long run. Administrations only last a few years, which barely provides the time to get to understand the system and perhaps attempt a few quick fixes. In other cases, such short-lived administrations lead others to attempt a complete redesign of the entire system through an education reform. Reforms that might look great conceptually, but for obvious reasons will take years to implement, mean that other administrations – most of the time disconnected from the previous one – will have to execute them, or discard them in favor of yet another reform.

Lessons Learned

There are some lessons we have learned to face these challenges. The first has to do with partners and commitment. It has been extremely important for Vía Educación to be part of networks and alliances to keep looking at the large scope of things, with organized leadership and consistent support for what is important in both the short and the long run. Sometimes we started the effort and sometimes it was initiated by others, but the degree of commitment has to be the same if the purpose is worthy. A second lesson has been to work with those who want to work and not to spend much time trying to convince those who are not willing or who are not committed to a shared vision. To focus as much as the organization can, on nurturing and challenging and being ready to be challenged by, the partners (both individuals and institutions) who are doing good work for the right cause, because one committed victory will bring the next one. The good partnerships endure and will always make organizations stronger.

The last lesson has to do with communication and its importance for the strength of the internal team. It is always a challenge to communicate enough and to be sufficiently clear in the message. This is why there must be a robust communication strategy that is revisited often. Every aspect of the organization can be communicated, especially internally in the first place, because it is the team, and nothing but the team who will make possible the changes we all want to see in education and in the world. The values we want to see in the world should be the values we all care about and promote internally. Inconsistency and incongruence are very expensive tickets to failure. In the end, it is the team that enables us all to enjoy the privilege of learning to change the world.

Bio

Armando Estrada-Zubía is the co-founder and executive director of Vía Educación. Prior to Vía Educación, he worked at CEMEX to design the company's process assessment system to measure sustainability at its worldwide operations. He is fellow of Ashoka and the Academy for Systems Change where he also serves as board member. Armando graduated from the International Education Policy program at the Harvard Graduate School of Education in 2005.

Creating Organizations to Foster Educational Opportunity in Mexico

By Emanuel Garza Fishburn

Work and Goals

I am amazingly privileged to be part of many educational endeavors that have one core purpose in common: to profoundly contribute to the empowerment of the children, youth, and adults of my country in order for them to become the architects of their own lives and to become highly-committed citizens engaged in the improvement of their own communities and of society as a whole. I am glad to share with our dear readers a brief description of these efforts.

Universidad Carolina

Launched in August 2014, Universidad Carolina[31] is a social enterprise fostering meaningful educational opportunities for a large sector of Mexico's underserved youth. Based in Saltillo, Mexico, *Universidad Carolina* currently serves more than 1150 students, primarily coming from highly underprivileged contexts, who are in the process of obtaining technical high school or bachelor degrees with strong foundations in citizenship and global education, human development, and the responsible pursuit of freedom. Universidad Carolina is also becoming an increasingly relevant platform for social transformation in our region. Many of our students, faculty, and staff have been providing their leadership in collaborations focused on tackling many of the pressing social challenges we face, ranging from school violence[32] and

---

[31] Universidad Carolina. "Institutional webpage." ucarolina.mx. http://ucarolina.mx/portal/ (accessed July 13, 2017).

[32] Capital Coahuila. "Becan a jovenes en EU por Proyecto contra el bullying." capitalcoahuila.com.mx. http://www.capitalcoahuila.com.mx/sociedad/becan-a-jovenes-en-eu-por-proyecto-contra-el-bullying (accessed July 13, 2017).

anti-corruption efforts to participatory economic-development initiatives in rural communities,[33] among many others.

In addition to the educational programs focused on providing opportunity to our youth, Universidad Carolina has recently partnered with local business organizations[34] to launch Universidad del Trabajador, a platform designed to open access to workers of the rapidly-growing industrial sector of our region. Many had to interrupt their studies earlier in life and are now ready and eager to continue with their educational advancement. This platform is particularly significant because it has become a space for collaboration between businesses committed to strengthening their corporate citizenship and our university that has the honor to serve this purpose.

Via Educación

With my dear friends and colleagues, Mariali Cárdenas and Armando Estrada, I also serve as Co-Founder and member of the board of Directors of *Via Educacion*,[35] a Mexican nonprofit focused on fostering educational transformations, primarily in the field of civic education. In a country where only one out of three citizens engage in actions to

---

[33] Vanguardia. "Dragones al Rescate." vanguardia.com.mx. http://www.vanguardia.com.mx/articulo/dragones-al-rescate-el-valor-de-apoyar-nuestros-vecinos (accessed July 13, 2017).
[34] Our initial local partners for the launch of *Universidad del Trabajador* are ARHCOS (*Asociación de Administradores de Recursos Humanos Coahuila Sureste*) and AIERA (*Asociación de Empresarios e Industriales de Ramos Arizpe*), both organizations providing substantial leadership to the effort. In addition, we had the privilege of initiating the operations of this platform, largely because of the interest and commitment of GST Autoleather, a global business that opened access to this opportunity for the members of its workforce.
[35] Via educación. "Institutional webpage." viaeducacion.org. http://viaeducacion.org/ (accessed July 13, 2017).

benefit their community,[36] it became very clear to us that we shared an urgent need to address the issue of education for democratic citizenship (EDC) in Mexico.

Starting in 2005, *Via* Educación has since launched various initiatives that have been focused on providing opportunities for members of our population to develop the attitudes, knowledge, and skills needed to ignite and sustain civic capacity in their communities, generating lasting impacts in thousands of our fellow citizens.[37] These transformations have been a direct result of the close collaborations that we enjoy with local and international organizations such as Ashoka, Outreach International, Universidad de los Andes, Academy for Systems Change, Fomento Moral y Educativo, Fundación Frisa, Fundación Comunidar, Sumarse, Cemex, Natura and many others that have provided substantial inspiration, resources, and talent to our efforts.

Harmony School

Most recently, I have also joined forces with colleagues in the educational field to launch Harmony School,[38] a learning community that started operations in August 2016, where I currently have the honor of serving as Chairman of the Board. Harmony School has the clear calling to educate global citizens by fostering significant learning experiences for our students. Based on an educational model primarily focused on student-centered learning, we currently serve more than 350 families in the Greater Saltillo area, a community that had been mostly

---

[36] Secretaria de Gobernacion, "Resultados de la Quinta Encuesta Nacional sobre Cultura Política y Prácticas Ciudadanas ENCUP 2012" encup.gob.mx.
http://www.encup.gob.mx/work/models/Encup/Resource/69/1/images/
Resultados-Quinta-ENCUP-2012.pdf, p.32 (accessed July 13, 2017).
[37] Via Educacion. "Informe Anual 2016." viaeducacion.org.
http://viaeducacion.org/downloads/informe_anual_2016.pdf
(accessed July 13, 2017).
[38] Harmony School. "Institutional webpage." harmonyschool.mx.
http://www.harmonyschool.mx/ (accessed July 13, 2017).

limited to a traditional approach to education. With this effort, we hope to greatly expand the quality of the education available for the children of our community, as they prepare to engage as active citizens of the world.

SumaRSE Business Networks

I have also devoted much of my energy to setting up and launching the SumaRSE[39] business networks, both in the states of Nuevo Leon and Coahuila, Mexico, as an effort to foster a culture of corporate citizenship in these states and to integrate large businesses and corporate foundations in joint social investment initiatives. In both states, our social investment initiatives have mobilized resources from more than 60 large and mid-size companies, governmental agencies, and local foundations towards various educational and civic-engagement efforts. In the case of the SumaRSE Network for Coahuila,[40] we have currently partnered with *Profauna Mexico* to provide an environmental-education experience in a nearby natural conservation area to 4800 children from under-privileged schools of our community.

Impact

Through the various collaborations that have provided the foundations and development of the educational organizations described previously, our work directly impacted 26,100 learners, and indirectly impacted 62,900 in the last year. Over the last decade, our work has impacted 67,500 students directly, and 191,300 students indirectly.

---

[39] http://www.sumarse.org.mx/ http://www.sumarse.org.mx/ Red SumaRSE Nuevo Leon. "Institutional webpage." sumarse.org.mx. http://www.sumarse.org.mx/ (accessed July 13, 2017).
[40] Vanguardia. "Se integran 15 nuevos organismos a la Red Sumarse Coahuila." vanguardia.com.mx.
http://www.vanguardia.com.mx/articulo/se-integran-15-nuevos-organismos-red-sumarse-de-coahuila (accessed July 13, 2017).

Challenges

I would like to focus on the following three challenges that we have faced in fostering educational opportunity:

- *The establishment*: Deeply-rooted practices and paradigms enable the reinforcement of the prevailing culture that adversely constrains the possibilities for positive change in the educational field. These elements, and in many times the closely guarded agendas of powerful interest groups, significantly shape the way that bureaucracies and leadership act and react towards the evident needs for change in our education and social systems.

- *The barriers for collaboration*: Lack of trust in and between institutions is a common trait found in Mexico. Self-interest has so many times been placed over the common good that it is uncommon to see leaders reaching across the table to work together towards collective goals. Another element of cultural inertia that affects the possibilities for collaboration lies in the vertical, mostly un-democratic way in which decision-making has traditionally worked in our society.

- *The culture of silence:* For millions of my fellow Mexicans, the poverty and inequality they have experienced in their lives seems to be such a fixed element of their reality and of many generations that came before them, that it is hard for many of them to imagine breaking out of this cycle of poverty. This on-going and seemingly ever-lasting condition of their lives, which is also reinforced by the social and political system in which we live, has contributed to sustain the belief in many of them that the effort necessary to produce change is beyond reach. In other words, that it may be easier and safer to continue going with the flow of things and thus never achieve their dreams for freedom and a better life in the face of such a harsh reality.

Lessons Learned

It has been working around the challenges described above and by being part of the highly enriching network formed by the Synergos Institute,[41]

---

[41] Synergos Institute. "Institutional webpage." synergos.org. http://synergos.org/ (accessed July 13, 2017).

that I have become aware that there is a great need for a different kind of leadership in our society. A leadership based on establishing clear relationships of trust and reciprocity among the various personalities involved in addressing our common educational needs. A leadership that genuinely cares for the points of view, feelings, fears, and hopes of those who play a part in the solution of our shared challenges, including their own. A leadership that is patient enough to go slowly but together with the rest towards the ultimate goal, instead of trying to get there first and alone. A leadership that is convinced of the benefits of cross-sector collaboration and facilitates systemic thinking when building the civic capacity of a group or community. These are some of the fundamental shifts that I have been applying to my own role in the efforts that I am so excitingly involved in and have found to be of lasting impact in the depth and scope of my work.

Bio

Emanuel Garza Fishburn, President of Universidad Carolina, is an educator with special interest in the field of education for global citizenship and in participatory approaches to poverty reduction and community development. Emanuel is happily married to Ana Celia Aguirre and is the proud father of Emma, Angela, Emanuel and Ana Maria. He graduated from the International Education Policy Program at the Harvard Graduate School of Education in 2005.

Education Reform and Youth Development in Jordan and the Middle East

By Nour Abu Ragheb

Goals and Work

I am the Co-Founder and Partner of Edvise ME, a three-year old consulting firm that gives advisory services to organizations working in the education and youth sectors. Our main focus is to develop and strengthen key functions at the organizations we work with to assist them in being more effective and efficient in their education reform and youth development efforts. We are the alternative to hiring specialized teams for higher level functions at the organizations we work with where we plug into the existing structure, work closely with the client, build its employees' capacity and improve its procedures and processes. By making our partners more strategic, competitive, and able to plan and implement their respective initiatives, we are helping children and youth have better access to higher quality education and learning experiences that would make them more skilled and competitive but also better local and global citizens.

Our clients vary from donor and international organizations, local non-profits, non-government organizations, and private sector service providers. The main services we provide for our clients are in the areas of strategic planning, monitoring and evaluation, and business development, all towards assisting the clients in advancing educational opportunity to children and youth. My assignments have varied to include foci on both improved quality of as well as access to educational experiences to children and youth in formal education settings and informal, with Jordanian and with refugee populations, in urban and rural areas.

In addition to my firm-related work, I have recently been appointed by a royal decree on the Board of Trustees of the Crown Prince Foundation in Jordan that focuses on youth empowerment and development and preparing Jordan's future social, political, and economic leaders. This will be primarily through large scale programs that provide youth with access to superior quality technical education, leadership training and citizenship building opportunities, as well as creating and enabling ecosystems for innovation and entrepreneurship. I have played a key role in developing the Foundation's strategy and now, as a member of the Board, overseeing the Foundation's implementation of the strategy through its initiatives, advising on higher level policy issues, and ensuring efficient and effective governance and operation.

Impact

Throughout my professional life and across the jobs and responsibilities I have assumed until today, I have not had direct influence on "learners" per se. I work at the policy and strategy level in support of the partners who implement on the ground and have direct communication and reach with the beneficiaries. Therefore, my reach and influence are estimated based on the number of beneficiaries I know my clients are working with and supporting.

I have worked in the past year with three organizations on projects that would ultimately have an influence on a total of about 45,000 beneficiaries- assuming the partners have implemented the strategies I assisted them to develop and executed the alterations I recommended at the institutional or implementation levels. The assignments, over the past year, included conducting evaluations of two development projects working with children and youth across Jordan, in addition to conducting an assessment on drop-out and disability and developing a strategy in that regard for an education authority of 171 schools that serves refugee populations.

I am constantly looking for higher impact and wider reach projects to work on, through which I can continue to help serve the underserved and underprivileged in Jordan, the Middle East, and beyond. I do plan on working closely with at least three or four organizations on an annual basis that focus on tackling key development and education challenges in our part of the world, and have influence on more than a million young citizens with more hope towards the future, deeper personal purpose, and strength and capacity to make a difference towards a more tolerant and prosperous world.

Challenges

Throughout my professional journey, I have faced multiple challenges that I had to grapple with and find a resolution to, some through internal reflection and untangling, others through trials, errors, and lessons learned. The two that have had the most significant impact on my approach are the following.

The first is, again, the fact that I do not have direct influence on beneficiaries or control over the implementation of the projects I get involved in. My work is a few steps away from the beneficiaries, and execution of strategy depends on the technical and financial capacity as well as the commitment of the partners I work with. This is particularly difficult with assignments that require direct interaction with the beneficiaries, through for example, interviews or focus group sessions, and being bombarded with cases that leave a deep emotional impact on you coupled with your inability to directly help: a teenager who has attempted suicide for fear of consequences to breaking certain social rules, a 5th grade student who is suffering from serious verbal and physical abuse at home, or a 10th grader who has been pulled out of school, despite her passion for learning, to soon get married. I have to continuously remind myself to maintain professionalism, avoid personal involvement, and focus on my role to achieve systems change and policy reform to help such cases.

The second is trying to build a culture of learning amongst the partners I work with. I have found that my honesty in identifying the issues and discussing the needed changes is not always accepted; I have been in situations where I am confronted with defensiveness or complete denial, other times where clients have attempted to discredit the process or underestimate my qualifications and experience to justify their rejection of the findings. These experiences made me realize how delicately those difficult evaluation assignments need to be handled.

Lessons Learned

In spite of these challenges, I keep reminding myself of the gap I am filling that exists in the market and across organizations in Jordan and generally the developing world and the biggest value I can add within the education community. In order to ensure my work is as relevant, practical, and implementable as possible, I am always dedicated to put in the needed time, effort, energy, and genuine interest in learning about our partners, their needs and challenges and engineering solutions for them that would have the most effective and cost-efficient impact on their beneficiaries.

This self-reflection I found positive in many ways especially in ensuring I always carefully assess my choices in terms of assignments to take on and partners to work with: I have to believe in the purpose and mission and also the principles and intentions of the partners. Although business and revenue generation is important for our firm's continuity and growth, my mission and passion will not be compromised. I also find strength in the stories I meet and get exposed to that I cannot individually resolve, a drive to making my work and deliverables at the best standard possible.

The other lesson I learned is how essential it is to adopt additional steps and considerations with clients that may have difficulty learning and changing as a result. Little by little I started learning how to adopt techniques that would help me with my reporting to make the partner more accepting and open to what was revealed through the data collection and analysis and make sure nothing is personalized in the process. I now start by establishing mutual understanding of the purpose of the task and buy-in on the methodology and approach. I also realized it is important to provide recommendations that are easy and practical to adopt so that the organization does not feel overwhelmed or crippled. All this requires more time and thoughtfulness; however, it is worthwhile if it means better impact for the organization and its work.

In my conclusion, I would like to highlight the importance of maintaining very strong knowledge and connection with the beneficiaries, even if your work does not explicitly require that. For every assignment I have taken, I insisted on the need to allocate some level of effort to spend on the ground, with the beneficiaries and other stakeholders – this is what makes the product relevant and meaningful.

We can have the greatest minds with the best educational and professional backgrounds strategizing, but without listening to and consulting with the people who will be most affected by the intervention, or tailoring the solutions to their reality and what they need, the product will not be as impactful or sustainable. Most often, the beneficiaries are the best positioned to clearly identify the needs and also offer the solution, so it is important to put in the time and effort to have their voices heard.

Bio

Nour Abu Ragheb graduated from the International Education Policy Program at the Harvard Graduate School of Education in 2005. Nour started her career at the Ministry of Education in Jordan, moved on to managing multi-million dollar education and youth projects at USAID/ Jordan. Nour now is the Co-Founder and Partner at Edvise ME- a leading consulting firm focused on education reform and youth development.

197

The Importance of Collaboration to Empower People in Mexico

By Daniel Tapia-Quintana

Goals and Work

Over the last six years as founder and Executive Director of Genera, a public policy consulting firm, I have developed an approach which includes providing different services and activities with the common goal of enabling ordinary people (public servants, academics, social entrepreneurs, activists, among others) to play an active and influential role in decisions which affect their lives, with the collaboration of different agents. In the last years, we have been involved in different projects related to empowering individuals, such as indigenous peoples, to be agents of change, advancing educational opportunities for girls, improving accountability in low-income Mexican schools, and assessing the outcomes of public programs with different national and international partners.

"Change" and "impact" are words frequently used in our professional career but difficult to explain fully. Both words assume a framework from which we can assess outcomes, so that we can determine what has changed or had an impact. However, both words share a pattern: individuals, specifically a group of individuals, with a common vision can lead a social transformation and make both words useful and relevant for the common good.

José Saramago, Nobel Peace Prize in Literature, wrote a significant book entitled "Blindness," where he underlines the importance of observing and analyzing when nobody else stops to do so, and the virtue to perceiving and understanding reality and acting on it. In my view perceiving, understanding, and acting to transform reality are only possible with others, by collaborating together to change our reality and develop solutions based on a shared goal.

My consulting firm generates and uses data to support the improvement of education decision-making. As an example, in a project Examining Student Performance in Mexican Schools for the National Educational Evaluation Policy (NEEP), we learned that principals develop their

199

strategies based on perceptions and do not use data to ensure objectivity. In the Mexican context, there is a lack of consistency of assessment across schools, classes, principals, and teachers. Building a performance-based culture within institutions and individuals is one of our purposes to support better policy-making.

I believe in the power of collaboration. If we truly want to make a significant and positive change in our political, social, and economic environment, we need to work together, taking advantage of the power of networks and using alliances and partnerships to make an impact in our society. I embrace the idea that collaboration enables change, and eventually, might generate impact. Throughout this process, there is something particularly important that is developed in the transition from one phase (change) to another (impact): trust. Currently, we are a low-trust society where social participation is minimal compared to that of other countries. This lack of trust impedes collaboration.

I am certain that the set of values that we share on our team and the value that we permeate in our activities have influenced others. Our philosophy and our work are based on leading by example, to be congruent with the vision that we embrace. We are aware that the actions (projects) that we make are a reflection of our values and beliefs, and they are linked towards a specific purpose (vision).

Impact

It is difficult to measure the direct and indirect impact of our work in Mexico and countries where we have also developed social projects such as Haiti, Honduras, and Costa Rica. However, I believe that 150 individuals have been directly and indirectly influenced by *Genera's* work during the last year through the development of evaluations, trainings, and qualitative and quantitative reports. From 2010 to 2017, more than 500 individuals have been influenced by our work. However, impact has not been a one-way road, but it has been reciprocal. These individuals, also, have influenced and have helped us to enhance and improve our approach and our work.

Challenges

Probably, the most difficult challenge I faced was to inspire others to engage in changing the context of violence and impunity that we face in Mexico. For example, it has been very difficult to strengthen social capital and develop initiatives to collaborate and to generate positive outcomes. In Mexico, there is a deep-rooted tradition that sees leadership as an individual practice. Historically, our leaders have concentrated power and authority without a system of checks and balances. Currently, besides important policies regarding decentralization, there exists a culture of a top-down hierarchy from the national to the local level in different areas such as education. Our new generation of leaders just want to lead on their own and develop a vertical view without checks and balances.

Creating a culture that supports change in this state of affairs is a difficult task. It is challenging to state these purposes and to discuss them with key stakeholders. As a result, it becomes very difficult to know why the system must change, the causes of the challenges, and to eventually define how it would change. For that reason, collaborative leadership is relevant to guarantee a plural and holistic perspective/approach to undertake a change and generate positive impact.

Making changes in a collaborative perspective in the education systems is complex and might take time to value the outcomes. It will require patience and commitment. However, the need for improvement in our countries (emergent economies, such as Mexico) is necessary and urgent. To achieve this goal, we need to develop transformative alternatives, to think "out of the box," and to deliver creative alternatives. Today´s challenging educative issues cannot be solved in a traditional way, for that reason, I encourage new generations to be as creative as their resources, capabilities, and context allow them.

Bio

Daniel Tapia is the president of GC Genera, a public policy consulting firm based in Puebla, Mexico. Daniel graduated from the International Education Policy Program at the Harvard Graduate School of Education in 2009.

HIGHER
EDUCATION

Connecting Research and Practice: Networks to Improve the Distribution of Educational Opportunities

By Sergio Cárdenas Denham

Goals and work

I still remember one of my very first meetings with Fernando Reimers, when he asked: Where do you see yourself five years from now? At that time, my response was almost automatic: "I see myself working as a top public official in the Mexican Ministry of Education." This response was explained by a then very recent personal experience as a member of a team of public officials implementing a school-based management program in Mexico ("Quality Schools Program"). This experience allowed me to learn how our education system operated almost at every level, from decision-making processes in the Federal Ministry of Education, to the day to day administration issues resolved in isolated rural schools.

Almost 15 years after responding to Fernando's key question, I work as the Director-General of an international agency conducting research and organizing professional development activities focused on adult education in Latin America (CREFAL). This is the closest I have been to becoming a public official, given that until very recently, my professional role was as a professor at a public research center in Mexico. I became a researcher instead of a public official because of what I learned and experienced the years I studied at the Harvard Graduate School of Education (HGSE), particularly about the importance of generating and using sound evidence to improve the design and implementation of educational policies and programs.

Since graduating from HGSE, my main goal has been to conduct relevant research that contributes to the identification of effective ways and interventions to address the unfair distribution of educational opportunities in Mexico. This personal goal is directly related to Fernando's own vision and concern about this problem and to the education I received at Harvard. The courses Fernando designed and supervised not only raised awareness about the urgency of improving the distribution of educational opportunities in our countries, but also provided conceptual models for academic purposes and practical tools to conduct useful research. Every class was a good example of how intellectual reflection should be linked to practical issues in education.

During all these years after HGSE, I have been very fortunate to conduct research as part of formal and informal networks comprised by public officials and scholars. I have learned to interact, communicate, and identify problems, all aimed at increasing the effectiveness of education agencies in addressing social inequalities. This is still my main goal, and the experience and learning I have gained over the last years is now supporting my decisions at the agency I currently lead.

Impact

During the years I have worked as a professor my impact includes: a) professional development activities and b) research projects.

I have led professional development programs for graduate and undergraduates, as well as short term workshops, seminars, and conferences, which have impacted a total of around 4,500 students and participants. In terms of research, a key characteristic of the research projects I conduct is the ongoing collaboration with public officials and education agencies. I have led 14 different research projects funded by governments, as well as national and international grants. Each of these projects has resulted in publications or reports presented to public officials and decision-makers. An example of the impact of these studies can be seen in public debates about the recent curriculum reform in Mexico, where research conducted in collaboration with the Global Education Innovation Initiative was one of the references in the design of the national education reform. Another example of the impact of these research projects can be observed with the first large-scale impact evaluation of an early childhood education program implemented in rural communities in Mexico, funded by the International Initiative for Impact Evaluation, an evaluation presented to Federal authorities to support the redesign of a national program

Challenges

In leading these initiatives to advance educational opportunities I have faced two main challenges:

A) **Effective policy-research networks are difficult to sustain over time.** Although intuitive, stable collaborations between scholars, public officials, and other political actors interested in improving the implementation of educational policies demands a lot of effort, time, and resources. However, once these networks are created, the benefits or effects surpass any costs related to their initial organization. Unfortunately these networks are still uncommon, at least when considering the number of actors involved in the administration of the national and local educational systems. Creating and managing networks formed by practitioners and scholars is still one of the main challenges to conducting applied research in Mexico.

B) **Lack of qualified researchers.** Finding specialized researchers or colleagues interested in similar topics or methodological approaches to applied research is another challenge in Mexico. Although the number of young professionals and scholars in Mexico is rapidly increasing, it is still difficult to identify groups of scholars large enough to create research networks around specific topics, such as finance or economics of education. This certainly represents a challenge, given the difficulty in creating academic groups to address key educational questions and provide solid evidence to decision-makers.

Lessons Learned

A) **Collaboration.** A key aspect to effectively address education inequalities in Mexico is to increase the number of scholars and public officials informed and interested in the topic of inequality. To achieve this goal, it is necessary to include this topic in every professional development activity, to raise awareness across different educational actors. In addition, it is necessary to consider the importance of addressing inequalities as a guiding principle or focus when accepting or initiating research projects, with the aim of creating opportunities to increase available evidence on this issue, as well as promoting involvement of young scholars and practitioners.

B) **International networks.** A key aspect related to positive experiences in the implementation of research and professional development activities is the participation of international institutions and colleagues from other countries. This is one of the contributions graduates from the IEP program make, which has resulted in the positive evaluations of the projects they have contributed to implement. In addition, monitoring international educational projects and activities also presents an area with many opportunities for scholars in Mexico.

C) **Innovation.** Given the extensive demand for relevant and useful research on education in Mexico, there is a significant window of opportunity to conduct innovative projects. Innovation is well regarded (either when it is reflected by addressed topics or research questions, methods, or how evidence is utilized or disseminated), usually resulting in a positive perception about scholars and the results of research projects, thus opening opportunities to participate in new initiatives.

Bio

Sergio Cárdenas is the Director-General of CREFAL, and associate professor at the Center for Economics Research and Teaching (CIDE). A lawyer by training, he holds an Ed. M. and an Ed. D. from HGSE. He is the Editor of the journal "Reformas y Políticas Educativas", published by Fondo de Cultura Económica.
Note: Sergio did not formally petition to receive a degree from the International Education Policy Program, even though he took all the courses that would have allowed him to do so. He served as teaching fellow to various cohorts of IEP students while he completed doctoral studies at HGSE as my academic advisee. Fernando Reimers

Implementing Educational Technology at a Scale

By Eugenia Garduño

Goals and work

About fifteen years ago, in southern Oaxaca (ranked as the third most marginalized state in Mexico by the National Population Council of Mexico),[42] the principal of an indigenous multi-grade school asked me if I could help him get computers for his students. He was one of three teachers in the school, which had three small classrooms, no running water, no adequate classroom furniture, and no reliable electricity ·supply. Why would he want computers instead of running water or better sanitary conditions for his students? Why would he want computers when power was usually unavailable at his school?

The principal's request challenged my previous views on equality of opportunity and how decisions are made regarding educational interventions. What if access to computers could provide marginalized indigenous students a better opportunity to develop skills for the job market, rather than focusing on providing running water or better floors for their school? I had worked with educational technology and distance education initiatives in Mexico; however, the focus of most of these initiatives had been to increase access to educational services. And though I became interested in the potential of new technologies to help students develop the skills they needed for better jobs and to break the intergenerational cycle of poverty, I also realized that I did not have the tools to understand the complex nature of inequality, nor how to address the educational challenges that underserved populations such as the students in Oaxaca experienced. Given my challenges, I decided to pursue graduate studies at the Harvard Graduate School of Education.

---

[42] CONAPO (2016). *Índice de Marginación por Entidad Federativa y Municipio 2015*. Retrieved from: https://www.gob.mx/conapo/documentos/indice-de-marginacion-por-entidad-federativa-y-municipio-2015

My experience at HGSE helped me understand a diversity of theoretical frameworks, and provided me with instrumental experiences in research and practice that allowed me to return to Mexico better equipped to help implement educational initiatives that were more tailored for students and teachers in my country. For instance, in 2006, working with Dr. Ilona Holland and under the guidance of Professor Reimers, I participated in the evaluation of *Enciclomedia*, the first large-scale educational technology program in Mexico, providing digital equipment directly to public school 5th and 6th grade classrooms, including smart-boards and computers with digitized versions of the national textbooks.

From 2010 to 2013, I continued to work with technology in education. I collaborated with Mexican colleagues I met at HGSE on a number of projects: adapting a multiuser virtual environment program delivering a curriculum on scientific inquiry for Mexican schools; evaluating a learning objects repository for higher education institutions, developed by the National Distance Education System; and, conducting a study on distance higher education in Mexico.

In 2013, I was appointed as the Head of the OECD Center in Mexico for Latin America. As the representative of the Organization in Mexico, I participated in activities aimed at supporting the Mexican Government in implementing a diversity of structural reforms in the country, including a wide-ranging education reform establishing access to quality education as a constitutional right for all Mexican citizens.

In 2015, I was invited by the then Secretary of Education to head the Digital Inclusion and Literacy Program of the Mexican government (with an annual budget of 2.5 billion pesos and a staff of 70), where I oversaw the procurement process for the acquisition of 960,000 tablets and their distribution to 32,000 public primary schools in the country. However, the focus of this program was not limited to distributing devices. I was also responsible for professional development of 65,000 5th and 6th grade teachers on the pedagogical use of tablets, and developed 100 new digital resources (applications) for the tablets, aligned with the national curriculum for language, math and science.

In 2017, I have worked on teacher professional development using hybrid (combining online and Face to Face) models, training facilitators, and also taught a master's level course at the University of Texas in Arlington on how to design online learning experiences with teachers. I was recently appointed Provost at CREFAL, an international organization focused on adult education. An example of some of the activities I'm currently developing at CREFAL is designing and implementing a professional learning course for 1,200 public school teachers on effective teaching, math, science, and literacy.

Impact

In 2016, as a public official, my work had directly benefited around 2 million students. More than one million 5th grade students had gained access to new mobile devices and digitized educational materials, and around one million 6th and 7th grade students benefitted from access to new digitized educational resources. Additionally, more than 65,000 teachers benefited directly from training provided on the use of mobile devices in the classroom, and three thousand facilitators participated in professional development sessions. In addition, as students were allowed to take their devices home, this program also indirectly benefited families of primary school students.

Challenges

The most difficult leadership challenges I faced have been in managing people and creating a space that supports teamwork and collaboration. In a society like Mexico's, where power distance relations prevail, there are a number of obstacles to engendering collaboration. In my view, collaboration allows all individuals to feel as though they have contributed to a goal that no one person could accomplish alone, and that their participation was valued and integral to the success of all. In every leadership position I have held, I have focused on empowering people and developing a context where trust and transparency can create a solid foundation for group cohesion and cooperation.

Lessons learned

I believe in teamwork, because large goals require the efforts and skills of many individuals, and my time at HGSE allowed me to meet colleagues with similar interests and values, with whom I continued to collaborate in developing and implementing innovative educational initiatives. The relationships I developed at Harvard, particularly with alumni that returned to Mexico, were key in advancing many of the projects, ideas and values I cultivated under the intellectual guidance and encouragement of Professor Reimers in the International Education Policy Program. In my perspective, advancing educational opportunity can only be achieved by building a critical mass of individuals working together to achieve the same goal, or are ready to work together to shape the right set of goals to meet the needs of an emerging country. Therefore, continuing to strengthen the network of HGSE and IEP alumni is critical not only in furthering specific projects, but also in maintaining the motivation to continue working in contexts that are not necessarily friendly to equality of opportunity and social justice.

Bio

Eugenia Garduño graduated from the International Education Policy Program at the Harvard Graduate School of Education (HGSE) in 2006, and holds a doctorate in Educational Policy, Leadership and Instructional Practice, also from HGSE. She has worked at the Mexican Ministry of Public Education as General Coordinator of @prende.mx, and as the Head of the OECD Center in Mexico for Latin America. She has been a lecturer at the University of Texas, Arlington, and is currently the Provost at CREFAL.

Advancing Educational Opportunity in Colombia, a Multi-sector Challenge

By Luis Felipe Martínez-Gómez

Goals and Work

My interest in education began from personal experience; my mother has been a teacher for most of her career. After teaching in a low-income school in Bogotá, Colombia's capital, I decided that education in Colombia needed to be addressed urgently, and that it should be addressed by adequately prepared leaders with personal and professional motivation to advance educational opportunities for all children in the country.

That decision led me to Harvard's International Education Policy Program. I wanted to become one of those adequately prepared professionals, who besides having the best preparation possible, also had a direct connection with schools, classrooms, and children in low-income contexts in Colombia. Since finishing my master's program at Harvard, I have had several different opportunities to address educational challenges in Colombia from different sectors.

From my experience as a teacher, I learned that teachers play a key role in the learning process of students; teachers can clearly explain topics and provide academic skills, but also inspire students to fall in love with learning and with the different subjects taught. That was my main motivation to start working with Universidad Externado as a teacher of teachers and as a member of the team that developed a new teacher assessment tool for the whole country.

Until 2015, the teacher evaluation process, a high impact assessment that determined teachers' salaries, was done with a "paper and pencil" test, focusing on teachers' knowledge. After a long discussion between the Ministry of Education (MEN), and teacher unions in Colombia, they agreed on changing teachers' evaluations into an assessment of what was happening inside the classrooms. I worked with a team of professionals to design this assessment, pilot it, and train teachers from other universities on how to implement this assessment. During the

213

pilot and training process, we received input from each of the actors involved, as well as from the Ministry, and gave the Colombian Evaluation of Education Institute (ICFES) the assessment instrument.

My second experience was leading the English language department and teacher training programs at a privately administered public school network of five schools, serving low income populations in Bogotá, called Alianza Educativa (AAE). Approximately 6,000 students attend these schools. During my time there, I developed a teacher training curriculum where teachers learned about their subject areas, cooperative learning, teaching for understanding, action research, neuroscience, and group management. On the other hand, as the English department leader I revised the English language curriculum, observed teachers and gave them feedback, and had the chance to lead a 10th grade group on their English language learning.

I am currently working with the World Bank Group (WBG) in Colombia. I liked the direct experience in a school network, but felt that I could have a larger impact in Colombia working with an organization that advises the national and local governments. During the year that I have been working with the WBG, I have worked on improving the autonomy of schools through increasing the management skills of principals, developing socioemotional skills of students, and evaluating successful experiences in order to generate rigorous and useful evidence on successful interventions in education.

All of these programs are still in the design and early implementation phase, so at the time of writing this, no one outside of MEN has been in direct contact with them. However, once the pilot phase is over, all the public schools in Colombia must register their information in a system, and that system will be replaced with the management tool we are working on. Hopefully if MEN uses an adequate communication strategy about this tool, and does not use it as a high stakes assessment or school ranking, it will promote evidence-based decision-making in schools and for regional authorities. On the socioemotional skill front, we have intensely studied a very successful model in Manizales, Colombia, and are working on generating rigorous evidence on how and why it works. This model, inspired by *Escuela Nueva*, is bolstering students' learning, as evidenced on the assessments administered by the Organization for Economic Cooperation and Development, as part of the Programme for International Student Assessment (PISA) and by national assessments of students' knowledge and skills. It is also giving many of its students leadership skills, resilience, and other essential skills needed to have a successful life.

Finally, I have the fortune of participating in the Global Education Innovation Initiative (GEII), a Harvard based research consortium working on fostering 21st century competencies for all children. Thanks to GEII, I have had the chance of collaborating with a relatively large network of private organizations in Colombia who are working on developing 21st century competencies in the children of Colombia. Among the main strengths of the GEII is the support of Harvard and the network of countries all around the world working on the same agenda.

Impact

As of the writing of this paper, about 32,000 teachers have taken the teacher assessment tool I worked on, and have received feedback in the areas of planning, pedagogical praxis, classroom environment, and reflection. This should help them improve. Hopefully, each student of these teachers will be impacted with this work since their teachers will improve their own practice and teach them better skills, while creating a better classroom environment.

Working with AAE gave me the opportunity to have a broader perspective of a small educational system. I was able to directly impact a group of students in the classroom and indirectly promote the learning of English language in all the students of the participants in my teachers' team and improve students' experiences in all the schools of AAE by organizing teacher training that prioritizes topics that would improve their experiences.

From this experience, I have had the chance, hopefully, to have a huge impact on a specific student from AAE. While in class, one student asked me to speak with me during recess. When we talked, she wanted to know how the process to study in the United States worked. I arranged a meeting with her mother and discussed the application process. We have been working on preparing the student for the SAT and giving her additional training in English since March 2016. I am financially supporting her English lessons in a formal English teaching institution, and we are studying by meeting for coaching every weekend through video conference. The main challenges we face are her lack of knowledge and money. However, she has well developed socioemotional skills that she uses to ask for help and works really hard for her dreams.

From the rest of my work, there is an important potential for impact. The teams I am working with are hoping that we will improve school management, principals' leadership skills, and students' socioemotional and 21st century skills.

Challenges

While the use of the new teacher assessment has had a beneficial impact on students' experiences, it has not happened without challenges. There are two main sources of problems with generating impact from this evaluation. The first one is, that given the high impact of the evaluation, some teachers have hired script makers or have performed the class they will be recording several times to make sure that they will succeed on the assessment. These actions lead to invalidating the assessment, rendering the feedback received by teachers completely useless since it is not based on their daily experiences and trumps students' learning as they repeat a lesson several times. The second source of difficulties is related to its implementation. The videos are assessed by teachers, who are not necessarily trained in the same area at the same level. This means that teachers' knowledge of the topics taught are not receiving the best feedback possible.

Among the main challenges I faced in my role at AAE were the high teacher rotation and the heavy workload of teachers. I worked very hard trying to develop a close, peer, trust-based relationship with all the teachers on my team. I believe that I succeeded in creating collegiality and that some teachers remained in the schools because they felt they were learning from working with me; however, it was very difficult to prevent them from looking for more stable and better paying opportunities. Also, it was very difficult to assess teachers' learning since they did not have much time to work on reflections related to their courses.

There are several general challenges that Colombia faces in order to advance educational opportunities for all children. Among these challenges are a deep sense of inequity and anger ingrained in Colombian society. Inequity has led to a segregation of opportunities that destroys the will of low income students to work hard, as well as their hopes of having a good future. When I have been a teacher I have had at least one brilliant student each year who decides to stop caring about their education because they feel there is no point to it; they will end up in their same neighborhood anyway, working the same bad jobs their parents had access to.

On another topic, Colombia is facing a historic moment where it could end a 60 year-old internal conflict. The actors in the conflict deeply damaged many people, and this has led to the feelings of anger and revenge that I mentioned previously. The implementation of the peace agreements has not happened easily. There is a large political and population sector opposing them, because according to them, the peace process is leading to impunity for those involved.

Finally, a consequence of inequity and anger, as well as institutional weakness, is the huge problem of mistrust in Colombian society. This problem is seen all over society, but is also visible in education-related processes. Negotiations between MEN and teacher unions are very complicated because of a mutual lack of trust, the existence of close relationships between teachers and students, honest relationships between bosses and workers, and collaborations among different organizations.

Lessons Learned

During this whole process I have also learned several lessons. First, only through humility is it possible to make changes that benefit most children. If in a dialogue one part sees itself as the owner of truth, knowledge, and will of doing things right, there is no possible middle point. Second, education is the key to changing society.

Through education we can give the population the skills needed to make a more generous, less judgmental, and more tolerant society. Third, collaboration leads to longer lasting programs. The public sector has the power to scale programs, but is also tied to regulations that lead to the rotation of personnel and programs. Through partnerships, it is more likely that programs have a longer life; most results in education take several years to happen.

Bio

Luis Felipe graduated from the International Education Policy Program in 2015 at the Harvard Graduate School of Education. His experiences before Harvard include teaching mathematics in an elementary school in a low income neighborhood in Bogotá, in the Teach for Colombia program, and doing research to inform teaching in the Colombian Institute of Evaluation (Icfes). After graduation he worked with Universidad Externado, a network of privately managed public schools called Alianza Educativa, and with the World Bank in Colombia.

Promoting Multicultural Education and Improving Educational Outcomes for Marginalized Students in the United States

By Eliana Carvalho Mukherjee

Goals and Work

My journey as an educator has its roots in my own experience as a student. My family and I emigrated from Brazil to the United States in January of 1979, and I have distinct memories of my first day of kindergarten. I spoke only Portuguese, so when I entered that classroom in Toledo, Ohio, I was lost. I did not understand anything the teacher or my classmates were saying. The school was culturally homogenous, so they did not have much experience with immigrant students like me. The principal convened a meeting with my parents, and the solution the school offered was for my parents to stop speaking with me in Portuguese and placing me in a special education class for part of the day. The consequences of those decisions were long-lasting, but as I entered adulthood I was determined to do what I could to improve educational opportunities for all children, especially those who have been marginalized.

I began my career as an elementary school teacher in San Diego, California, where the majority of my students were children of immigrants from Central and South America. Those students, and their families, had a profound impact on my understanding of oppression and determination. After graduating from the Harvard Graduate School of Education, I worked as a principal and director of an international school in Costa Rica, which served elite Costa Ricans and U.S. expatriates. The juxtaposition between the marginalized students I had in prosperous California and the wealthy students in the developing country of Costa Rica gave me a more global understanding of inequality and privilege.

In Costa Rica, I then worked as an assistant professor at the United Nations mandated University for Peace (UPEACE) in the M.A. program in Peace Education. My students were educators from across the world who wanted to develop and deliver peace-oriented curricula. The courses I took while at the Harvard Graduate School of Education provided resources and ideas for the courses I taught at UPEACE. Graduates from that program are now doing incredible work in various fields of education. For example, one alumnus is the deputy director of an organization that establishes community libraries and resource centers in rural parts of South Asia. Another alumnus from Cyprus has developed and implemented peace education curriculum and projects in his divided island. The breadth of work currently being done by the peace education graduates is remarkable and inspiring. As part of my work at UPEACE, I was also involved in projects where we worked with partner universities in India, Sri Lanka, and Canada, on developing curricula for courses in peace and conflict studies, and with partner organizations in Honduras and Angola on integrating conflict sensitivity and human rights in the work they do. Although I resigned from my faculty position at the University for Peace after six years, I continue to teach short courses and advise students' master's thesis projects periodically.

My career has evolved from teaching to teacher education. I currently work as a faculty member at Palm Beach State College, a community college serving over 45,000 students. I teach introductory courses in education, which are required for those seeking a teaching certification in Florida. The work I do mostly focuses on improving the quality of education and the relevance of what is taught in the classroom. Many of my students are first generation college students and are from low-income families, so they will be able to relate to many of the students they will eventually teach. One out of every five children in the area lives in poverty, and they need teachers who understand their circumstances. Central to my classes are issues of multicultural understanding, social justice, and culturally relevant pedagogy. I try to instill in my students the value of diversity and the responsibility teachers must have to ensure all students experience educational success. I save notes my students have written to me, and on a recent message, one student wrote, "My resolve to teach for social justice has never been stronger and I feel excited and prepared to move onto the next phase of my teacher education." I try to inspire and prepare my students to be exceptional teachers to *all* students. I also try to empower my students to have the moral courage to stand up for what they believe is right for their students and for public education in general. I require my students to follow news on education, and we discuss ways in which they may impact policy and curricular decisions, such as attending and speaking in board meetings, contacting their representatives, becoming involved in decision-making committees, etc. In other words, I strive for my students not only to be capable and caring teachers, but also knowledgeable on how they can have a broader impact on decisions that affect their students.

Impact

When asked how many learners have been influenced by my work in a year, I feel overcome. In the past year, I have directly influenced about 250 learners who are students in my education courses at the community college. In my work at the University for Peace, I impact about 15 students in a year through the short courses I facilitate and through the theses that I advise. It is difficult to calculate the number of learners I have indirectly influenced over the last year, but I estimate it being around 5,000. Scores of my previous students are working as teachers in classrooms and educators in organizations, so their learners have been impacted by my influence in terms of the quality of education they receive and the relevance of what they learn. In a decade, I estimate the number of learners that I will influence to be in the thousands, from the students I will have in my own teacher education courses to their future students. I estimate that directly, I will impact 2,650 learners, and indirectly about 35,000 learners. I am overwhelmed with this thought, and it reinforces my commitment to help develop the most skillful, compassionate and committed teachers that I can.

Challenges

The most difficult challenges I face in my work have to do with policy and ideological differences. In terms of policy, decisions are sometimes made which I believe run counter to what is good for children and teachers. For example, Florida recently eliminated the required courses on diversity for teacher certification. I teach some of those courses, and I believe in a multicultural setting such as Florida, it is a disservice to teachers and students to not equip teachers with the skills and knowledge to better prepare them to work with our diverse learners. The rationale is that topics of diversity will be integrated into other courses, and the change will allow for more content-area courses, but I fear the focus on multicultural education will be lost. The current political climate in education makes it challenging at times to motivate my students to remain in the teaching career. This worries me tremendously because without good, dedicated teachers, the future of public education is at risk. My other area of work continues to be in peace education, and a major challenge is the struggle to get recognition and acceptance for peace work. Peace education is often perceived as unimportant, irrelevant, or a threat to the status quo, making it difficult to implement and grow. Most people are unsure of what peace education entails, so it remains in the fringes of education reform. I would like to see a growing movement of peace educators around the world; it is something desperately needed in these times.

Lessons learned

Addressing these challenges has made me more aware of my power as an individual educator. I have learned that I need to be an active citizen in changing policy. That means I must get involved in the policy arena, whether it is volunteering to join working groups looking at an issue, joining political organizations, or vocally advocating for policy change by speaking at board meetings and contacting legislators and other decision makers. I have learned that I have a sphere of influence within my work, and I can encourage and motivate others to become politically active citizens. In my work as a peace educator, I have learned that sometimes I must 'rebrand' the work that I do. Instead of referring to my work as peace education, depending on the context, I may refer to it as global education, conflict resolution education, environmental education, etc., in order to garner more support, acceptance, and understanding. I also appreciate the capacity of networks in addressing challenges. There is incredible power in joining forces with others who are like-minded and who share my interests. I am an active member of several associations and informal groups dedicated to advancing the interests of teacher education, multicultural education, and peace education. Maintaining those connections validates the work that I do and provides resources for support.

I have come a long way in my career, and a pivotal point was my education at Harvard. It provided me with a foundation of knowledge about complex educational issues, and has launched me into a career dedicated to teacher education and improving educational outcomes for all students.

Bio

Eliana Carvalho Mukherjee graduated from the Harvard Graduate School of Education in 2002. Afterwards, she worked as the director of an international school in Costa Rica, then as a professor of Peace Education in the United Nations mandated University for Peace. She currently is a professor of teacher education at Palm Beach State College, and she is completing her Ph.D. in Curriculum and Instruction from Florida Atlantic University, where her focus is on global education and teacher preparation.

Reshaping Educational Measurement to make Education Relevant in Canada

By Elyse Katherine Watkins

"Measurement matters. While reason and imagination also advance knowledge, only measurement makes it possible to observe patterns and to experiment—to put one's guesses about what is and is not true to the test" (Duckworth and Yeager, 2015).[43]

Goals and Work: Advancing Skills Measurement in Ontario

Measurement is a daunting word in education. During my time at the Harvard Graduate School of Education (HGSE), I realized that my three passions—Canada, skills, and innovation—converged on the extent to which student and system performance could be captured (a.k.a. measured). My focus on assessing student learning and system success evoked a variety of responses from my peers that ranged from recoil to support. However, in spite of these polarized reactions, one thing was clear – measurement matters *a lot*. These experiences at HGSE informed and solidified the goals for the next steps in my journey: to commit myself to maintaining the quality of the Canadian education system, as well as to improve it by challenging existing structures and policies around measurement.

Impact: Measuring Skills from Kindergarten to Postsecondary

Following HGSE, I returned home to Toronto, Ontario to join the *Measuring What Matters* project. The *Measuring What Matters* project was the brainchild of People for Education, an education non-profit in Toronto, whose mission was to ensure that public education in Ontario was living up to its promise for students in the kindergarten to grade 12 (K-12) system. Through this project, I had the opportunity to engage with education stakeholders, from the classroom level to the Ministry

---

[43] Duckworth, A. L., & Yeager, D. S. (2015). Measurement matters: Assessing personal qualities other than cognitive ability for educational purposes. *Educational Researcher, 44*(4), 237-251.

level, to unpack how broader areas of success—creativity, citizenship, social-emotional learning, health, and quality learning environments—could be captured and explored in Ontario. Our study included 80 educators in 26 publicly funded schools and seven district school boards. While the number of students varied in each setting, having the opportunity to directly impact classroom-level curriculum and pedagogy, was a great achievement for the project as well as for the conversation around what *really* matters. This work reaffirmed my commitment to measurement, as well as illuminated the challenges and opportunities inherent in broadening the proxies for success of our education system.

After my work on the *Measuring What Matters* project, I transitioned to my current role as a Researcher in the Centre for Learning Outcomes at the Higher Education Quality Council of Ontario. Today, I work with Ontario's colleges and universities to understand the diverse ways in which they are assessing higher-order cognitive skills (e.g. critical thinking) and transferable skills (e.g. collaboration). One of the projects I co-manage is the Learning Outcomes Assessment Consortium. The Consortium consists of several colleges and universities committed to creating, validating, and implementing assessment tools for skills, such as critical thinking, communication, and lifelong learning to inform broader change at the postsecondary level. As I continue this research, I reflect on what I have learned from my experiences in K-12, and work to not only change conversations around skills in higher education, but also to build a bridge between the elementary and postsecondary sectors on these discussions of measurement.

In the province of Ontario, there are almost 3,000,000 students from the kindergarten to postsecondary level. Through my work at People for Education and the Higher Education Quality Council of Ontario, I have had the opportunity to be involved in initiatives that impact approximately 60,000 students. My goal over the next ten years is to be a part of policies and partnerships that will transform education for all three million students in Ontario by changing the way we all see and use measurement of learning.

Challenges & Lessons Learned: The Inextricable Link Between Failure and Success

My nascent journey into capturing students' achievement of skills has presented a variety of challenges and opportunities. Given the current focus on 21st century learning and connecting education with the labor market, the climate is ideal for having difficult conversations around what students need to be successful in today's world and how to capture it. To date, my work in measurement has revealed three key challenges and associated lessons:

1. **The devil is in in the details** – Before you can start to measure skills, it is important to know *what* they are. While this seems simplistic, taking a step back to define and refine what is being measured will help to prevent confusion and miscommunication amongst stakeholders about what skill is being captured.

2. **There is no silver bullet** – It is easy to think of the differences between regions, provinces, and countries. However, there is also a great deal of variation within and between institutions in the same geographic region (i.e. the province of Ontario). Given this diversity, there is no one way to measure broader areas of success. While there can be commonalities across goals, definitions, and assessments, there are a multitude of avenues to elucidate the extent to which a student, class, or institution is performing on skill development.

3. **Your ethos is important** – A lot of the time, I see the work I do from a content-heavy lens where I am only focusing on the message and not how I am acting as the vehicle for the message. I engage with the world using a specific identity, series of perspectives, and set of biases from which I cannot separate my work. This has been a powerful lesson, because it has informed the way I see equity in measurement, as well as giving a voice to student experiences that are not always represented in education. It is important in my work to own my ethos and use it to help more students and ideologies be represented and heard in the measurement debate.

Bio

Elyse Watkins is a Researcher at the Higher Education Quality Council of Ontario (HEQCO) in Toronto, Ontario (Canada). She graduated from the International Education Policy Program at the Harvard Graduate School of Education in 2015.

Reimaging the School of Education of Tomorrow: A Theory of Impact for Children in Pakistan

By Mariam Chughtai

Goals and Work

Growing up in an impoverished country exposed me to the considerable turmoil faced by distressed people throughout the world. The political repression and economic marginalization in Pakistan often left me wondering "What forces perpetuate such oppression?" *The Colonizer and the Colonized* (Memmi, 1990) would have characterized me as the young colonizer who realizes that her choice is not between good and evil, but rather between evil and uneasiness.

Education empowered me immensely. I internalized the attitude that knowledge and learning are never-ending critical conversations with scholars, books, and oneself. Deeper questions about inequality in society prompted me to pursue knowledge at a graduate level in the United States, where I could study current scholarly perspectives on complex questions of equity and equality in education. I came to see education as *the* tool for empowerment and sustainable social change.

It was clear to me that the spheres of research, policy, and practice had long been operating in isolation, or at best with two spheres coming together and the third one missing. We had the best research but limited it to peer-review journals that much of the developing world could not access, well-informed policies with no implementation in practice, and ground-breaking ideas without scale. I committed to a theory of change which I had read on the walls of Longfellow Hall at the Harvard Graduate School of Education; in my work for education reform, I would only operate at the nexus of research, policy, and practice.

After graduating with a Doctorate in Education from Harvard, I made the bold move to return to Pakistan. But it was only after I was on ground zero that I realized the magnitude of the education crisis I was facing. Every tenth child in the world who is illiterate is Pakistani. Education statistics from Pakistan are no longer on par with South Asian countries but rather rank amongst the lowest-performing countries from Sub-Saharan Africa. The difference is that Pakistan is also a high population country, and it has a nuclear bomb.

Impact

Upon returning, I took on the challenge of setting up a new kind of School of Education at a leading university in Pakistan called the Lahore University of Management Sciences (LUMS). It required a reimagining of education for tomorrow, embedding within it extensive field engagement as part of the curriculum and a constant engagement with leading researchers.

In January 2017, the LUMS School of Education was announced with the agenda of leading public discourse on education reform in the country. A robust network of partnerships in the public, private, non-profit, and donor spheres of education was underway. It is now coupled with a global network of faculty at top schools of education, keen to make their research accessible to practitioners and policymakers in the developing country landscape.

In the upcoming decade, the LUMS School of Education is well positioned to produce a new class of hundreds of educational leaders, knowledgeable and globally connected, to provide strategic direction to education reform in Pakistan. Thus, I will play a part in steering the burgeoning education ecosystem of Pakistan towards sustainable and positive social change.

I also began my scholarly career as a post-doctoral research fellow at the same university. My current book project, based on my doctoral research, illustrates the power of history textbooks and the politics of hate in modern times. It shows explicitly the extent to which a state can use the student's mind as its canvas for ideological brainwashing. Once published, this book will contribute to our understanding of the widespread phenomenon of identity politics fostered through education, the teaching of history to inform a student's sense of self and the 'other,' and the power of education in the creation or possible prevention of violent conflict in communities.

Challenges

<u>Dependency, Distractions, and the Saviors Within</u>

It is difficult to be the voice of criticism in education reform, especially when there are immediate, short-term gains to be realized. It is especially hard when large sums of money are exchanging hands.

I am a firm believer in the power of non-profit organizations and the strategic advantage they bring to the education ecosystem. Frequently, they are the drivers of innovation in education. Similarly, donor agencies in developing countries play a tremendous role in supporting governments where capacity falls short.

However, when a pervasive culture of non-government actors doing the work of the government takes hold, it absolves the government of fulfilling its constitutional responsibility of ensuring free education for every child. Such dynamics nurture an inefficient system dependent on a perpetual need for external funds, thus distracting from long-term, systemic solutions. Well-intentioned citizens motivated to do something in the face of abysmal education conditions do what is most simple. They write checks to support non-profit organizations and feel they have performed their civic, moral, and patriotic duty. However, this is a distraction from real change.

The same dynamic is operational at a global level, where development aid has created an entire ecosystem of consultants and top-down interventions in Pakistan, designed such that despite millions in foreign aid very little reform has come about. Donor money has similarly excused the Pakistani government from taking ownership of the educational crisis in the country. Once the aid dries up, Pakistan will be left with a severe dependency on external funds, revealing gaping holes in local capacity. Relying on external funding for short-term reform only creates an illusion of change. It is akin to moving people from the bottom deck to the top deck without accepting that they are all on a sinking ship.

Finally, even when we know that our collective strength is our greatest asset, it is difficult to resist the savior mentality within. Perhaps strongest in education reformers, with an impatient drive to see change, we are comfortable being lone warriors both in our efforts and in keeping the resultant spotlight on ourselves. Research and reflection on configuring the right model takes collaboration. Yet, politically popular quick fixes championed by individuals are rampant in the education sector. For example, despite findings of limited success in the MIT One Laptop Per Child program, countries like Pakistan continue to hand out technology products without a focus on learning. Such interventions achieve little except a false sense of heroism for a few. In the end, it is the school-going child who is shortchanged.

Lessons Learned

Education reform is not a popularity contest: I take inspiration from Stanford University Professor Linda Darling-Hammond, whose work I read when I was an International Education Policy (IEP) master's student. At a time when Teach For America (TFA) was a national sensation that everyone was rushing to fund and scale, Linda Darling-Hammond exemplified for me scholarly courage and an unfaltering commitment to education, as she critiqued the TFA teacher training model for being inadequate. In doing so, not only did she ignore popular sentiment and pushback against her, but she made sure that the ultimate winner was the student. Some years later, TFA updated its teacher professional development method to include both pre- and in-service support for its teachers.

Take time to admire the problem.[44] To go fast, sometimes one must go slow. For these moments, I think back to the final assignment in Fernando Reimers' core course for IEP master's students. There was structured time in the course devoted to getting a deep understanding of the education reform issue at hand, the complexity of why it had not yet been resolved, and a full command over the gaps in literature and current research. It gave us an immense advantage, in clarity of thought

---

[44] Thank you, Brittany Emal Hurd, my colleague from HGSE Ed. M. 2007, for this brilliant term.

and focus, for when we were at the stage of devising policy solutions. Thus, spending the time to gain a deep understanding of the issue and the varying perspectives of stakeholders in the ecosystem is a considerable step forward in the trajectory of reform.

Bio

Mariam Chughtai has a Doctorate in Education (EdD, 2015) from Harvard University specializing in Education Policy, Leadership and Instructional Practice. Mariam has two Masters degrees from Harvard University, in International Education Policy (2007) and in Education Policy and Management (2011), and a Bachelors in Political Science from Rice University (2005). She is now based in Pakistan, working as Director Pakistan Programs for Harvard University South Asia Institute and as Associate Director, School of Education at Lahore University of Management Sciences (LUMS).

Increasing Access to Technical and Vocational Education in Thailand

By Jomphong Mongkhonvanit

Goals and Work

My time at the Harvard Graduate School of Education's International Education Policy Program equipped me with the knowledge, skills and network to work and live towards my career in education. Looking back on my work over the last decade, I find my career both rewarding and challenging.

I believe in the principle that education needs to prepare people to become good citizens and part of an effective workforce. Increasing educational relevancy to social and economic demands has been central to my career in education. Like many other countries, technical and vocational education in Thailand is highly demanded by society and the economy, but seems to have a lesser value for students and parents. In Thailand, major challenges of technical and vocational education have included students' violence, negative image, lack of competencies demanded in the new economy, lack of qualified teachers, and ineffective quality assurance of technical and vocational education. As the Chair of Federation of Colleges of Technology and Vocational Education of Thailand Under Patronage of HRH Princess Maha Chakri Sirindhorn, I have attempted to address these issues in the country's technical and vocational education. Courage and a sense of purpose are very important in working towards changing systems and changing public attitudes. I sometimes feel discouraged to continue my work, but I look at the challenges as a big opportunity to work in the national policy arena and change the system. I sometimes feel that the problems are bigger than my capacity to achieve. The challenges and problems, however, have given me ways to improve myself and provided for me to tackle problems from different angles.

Impact

I was very pleased to eventually initiate the Dual Excellence Initiative that has promoted work-integrated learning where workplaces and

235

colleges co-deliver technical and vocational education based on competency development. HRH Princess Maha Chakri Sirindhorn of Thailand presided over the opening of the Dual Excellence Initiative and Conference in October 2014. With the support of the Royal Government of Thailand that has put dual education as one of its priorities in educational development, more than 300,000 students have benefited from this program each year through their competency development, apprenticeship, and compensation. In addition, thousands of companies have benefited through apprenticeships and human resource development, while hundreds of colleges have benefited through up-to-date instruments and trainers in companies. The Dual Excellence Initiative has been documented in many research papers and publications. This program has also resulted in the drafting of new laws that require companies to participate in dual education, which can help prepare youth to be a part of an effective workforce for the country.

Challenges

During the past few years, I have had opportunities to visit and observe schools in both cities and rural areas as part of the trail in improving technical education for the country. Access to relevant education is still a major issue in many areas. This is something I would like to tackle in the years to come. It is always a privilege to work with a purpose that is larger than myself. Linkages between educational institutes and companies are very essential factors to equip students with the necessary tools to become an effective workforce. Mutual trust between educational institutes and companies is instrumental to enhance cooperation. A working platform of educational institutes and companies needs to be developed, while an exchange of staff is important to co-create the culture of cooperation for mutual benefit.

Lessons Learned

During my journey of work, I feel that clear purpose and determination are essential to keeping things moving in the determined direction. It is important to find time for reflection and being re-energized. Even though I have been very fortunate to travel around the world, my most favorite destination is Harvard University and Cambridge, Massachusetts. This place and the city reminds me of the time that I learned a great deal with dreams and passion.

Bio

Jomphong Mongkhonvanit is Councilor of Thailand's National Education Council, Chair of Federation of Colleges of Technology and Vocational Education of Thailand, and Associate Professor in Educational Policy at Siam University. He was advisor to Thailand's deputy prime minister. He has been a policy consultant, researcher, and author. He graduated from Harvard Graduate School of Education's International Education Policy Program in 2004 and obtained a doctorate from the University of Bath in 2008.

Promoting Understanding of Muslim Heritages and Culture

By Razia Velji

Goals and Work

Having worked in Pakistan at the Aga Khan University's (AKU) Institute for Educational Development for several years prior to attending the Harvard Graduate School of Education (HGSE), I wanted youth in my home country (Canada) to understand the challenges of development. Thus after graduating, I joined the Aga Khan Foundation (AKF) Canada to lead their development education initiatives. With exhibitions and speakers from South Asia, we travelled across the country, speaking to 500+ university students and interested individuals about development challenges and the work of the Foundation in East Africa and South Asia. We also developed resource packs for primary school teachers to support teaching about international development; this was coupled with an invitation to schools across six cities in Canada to be part of a fundraising walk to raise money for international development. Today this walk has grown and in 2016 was held in ten cities, raising over 7 million dollars for projects in Africa and South and Central Asia.

Continuing at AKF, I then managed a grant for the Foundations' education work in Tajikistan. With a million dollar plus grant from the Canadian International Development Agency, it was important to ensure that project delivery was of highest quality; funding supported school development programs in numerous districts in the mountainous region of Gorno-Badakshan as well as teacher development. The engagement offered an opportunity to learn about the educational challenges of the region while also enabling me to dialogue with local education leaders about ways to improve the effectiveness of delivery. The efforts of AKF in education were supported by other entities of the Aga Khan Development Network (AKDN)[45] working in the region; this enabled a multi-pronged

---

[45] AKDN brings together a number of development agencies, institutions, and programmes that work primarily in the poorest parts

approach comprising infrastructure, economic, and social development in communities that supported the more concrete teacher training and provision of educational materials.

In 2003, I returned to AKU, this time in London, UK and at the Institute for the Study of Muslim Civilisations (AKU-ISMC). While at AKU-ISMC I have had an opportunity to step back into higher education planning and administration and work alongside scholars and researchers who through a study of historical and contemporary Muslim societies seek to improve the understanding of Muslim heritages and cultures and address challenges of society today.

AKU-ISMC is a small private higher education institution that has been in existence for fifteen years. It seeks to make an impact through research, publications, and educational programs. Its two-year master's program has attracted students from countries around the world such as Armenia, Austria, Canada, Egypt, France, Germany, India, Indonesia, Iran, Iraq, Nigeria, Pakistan, South Africa, Syria, Taiwan, Tajikistan, Tunisia, the United Kingdom, and the United States. Students from the aforementioned countries have gone on to undertake PhD's or work in a range of sectors, from education and development to architecture and media.

As I joined AKU-ISMC when it was only a year old, our challenges were many-fold. These ranged from developing quality educational offerings to becoming known in the UK context, as well in wider Muslim contexts from where our students would come and where our research needed to remain relevant. Beyond the development of educational products, there arose the issues of administration and operations, quality assurance, and alignment with both the UK higher education

---

of Asia and Africa. A central feature of the AKDN's approach to development is to design and implement strategies in which its different agencies participate in particular settings to help those in need achieve a level of self-reliance and improve the quality of life. (www.akdn.org)

institutions as well as our University which was headquartered in Pakistan.

For a variety of reasons, between the time I joined AKU-ISMC and today, I have had the privilege of undertaking a range of roles. This has meant gaining a broad understanding of the opportunities and challenges of the institution as a whole. These roles have included: Head of Administration, with oversight of finance, operations, human resources, and communications; Student Affairs Officer; and now, Manager for Academic Planning and Research Development. In these roles, I have had the opportunity to assist in the development of the institutional strategy, support the shaping of policies and procedures, and engage in program implementation.

The Impact

Working with scholars from Morocco, Tunisia, Germany, Iran, Pakistan, and beyond, I had the opportunity to contribute to the development of the Institute's MA program that supports students, both academically and if necessary, financially, to understand Muslim cultures and heritages, as well as contemporary challenges in Muslim contexts, through the tools of the social sciences and humanities. The MA program has now seen its approximately 90 graduates either undertaking doctoral programs at top universities in the UK, Europe, and North America or working in a range of sectors including education (primary to post-secondary), architecture, law, and media. Access to a UK-based MA program would likely have not been within the reach of most of our students; however, it has become a reality because of AKU's commitment to the provision of education for any individual who is admitted to one of its programs.

Supporting faculty to pursue their research through acquisition of grants has been a particularly fulfilling role. In the last few years, two of our faculty members have acquired British Academy Rising Star Engagement Awards (BARSEA) and one has received a British Academy Mid-Career Fellowship. BARSEA grants enable faculty to offer training for colleagues in areas of relevance. In one case, scholars used algorithms to compare and mine Arabic texts, to re-think history. In another case, scholars worked with media practitioners to explore how best to make their research relevant, impactful, and known.

These are just a few examples of ways in which I have contributed to a larger educational project that seeks to educate Muslims and non-Muslims about the rich and diverse histories and cultures of Muslims, through understanding Muslim cultures as part of world cultures, while recognizing the interconnectedness of culture, tradition, and religion.

Covering the span of my time since graduation, direct impact on learners has been made through my development education work, program development, and teaching (approximately 800 learners) while indirect influence has been through teacher training and institutional/systems development (impacting approximately 1000 learners).

Challenges

What has become apparent to me over the years, is that leadership is not about being in charge, but rather about being able to influence, shape, and bring about change – be that in individuals or organizational structures and initiatives.

Working in a relatively small entity with a staff of no more than 30 individuals has provided me an opportunity to have a wider breadth of experience and influence, however, the challenge in such an organization is finding the right balance between resources – human and financial – and growth. In this regard, I think one critical element is being able to prioritize and focus efforts on a few initiatives that will have the greatest impact, while still supporting growth.

Another sometimes frustrating, but also interesting, challenge has been the alignment of process and policies between an international university and the norms of higher education in the UK—the context in which AKU-ISMC operates. The expansion of the university into several countries has eased this challenge to some degree, as the recognition and role of the 'center' and perhaps the position of the 'center' is being reviewed and redefined as needed.

Being a small fish in the big sea of higher education institutions in the UK has been yet another challenge; it has meant that AKU-ISMC has had to clearly define its competitive advantage and niche, recognizing the importance of remaining relevant to the learners and other stakeholders it serves. A useful tool has been the building of partnerships which enables the Institute to bring its expertise, while at the same time, having partners who bring credibility and marketing reach. Partnerships also serve as an opportunity for institutional learning and development.

Lessons Learned

Having had the honor to work with four incredible but very different directors at AKU-ISMC over the last 14 years, as well as other leaders within the wider University and the AKDN, I have learned that each individual has their strengths and weaknesses. This is true for those who lead and those whom one leads. Along with personalities and personal histories and experiences comes one common link – *purpose*. What the AKDN has is a very clear vision and purpose. It is this vision that serves to motivate people. It is the ability to get beyond the power, personalities, and bureaucracy and to build a community of purpose, one that invites and values different voices and views, that leads institutions to propel forward and succeed.

At the Harvard commencement address in May 2017, Mark Zuckerberg said "Let's give everyone the freedom to pursue their purpose—not only because it's the right thing to do, but because when more people can turn their dreams into something great, we're all better for it." Mark Zuckerberg was right in saying, 'It is the right thing to do.'

But it is not always easy. It requires you to reflect on your own leadership style, to re-think your way of speaking or listening, to reconsider how your email or words might be understood (no matter how good your intentions), to try and understand others' points of view even when rushing full speed ahead seems to make more sense. Freedom to pursue ones' purpose means being heard; as a leader, this means listening. It means changing. It means reflecting. It means having the humility to be critical of one's own self and being willing to improve and be better. And it means learning…for life.

Bio

Razia Velji graduated from the International Education Policy Program at the Harvard Graduate School of Education in 2001. She has worked in Canada, Pakistan, and the UK and has experience in primary, secondary, and tertiary education. Her roles have included teaching, grant management, institutional development, and research management. She is currently Manager, Academic Planning and Research Development at the Aga Khan University in London.

Promoting Empowerment through Education in Mexico

By Erin Esparza

Goals and Work

My journey to, through, and from the International Education Policy Program (IEP) has been accompanied by several major transitions. My belief in education as the fundamental engine, both for individual development and for the social, economic and civic development of our larger communities prompted me to leave a long career in business. With this came transitions from a for-profit lens to a non-profit lens, and from large, corporate environments to smaller, grass-roots organizations. In addition, I chose to begin my work in education in a culture and a language that were new to me.

Since graduating, I have had the opportunity and the honor to work on initiatives focused on empowerment through education, including entrepreneurship and economic empowerment, as well as citizenship empowerment, mostly focused on youth from middle school to university. I work with two universities in Mexico whose core missions are to provide low-income populations access to quality high school and college programs. I also work with Vía Educación, a nonprofit whose programs develop democratic citizenship and community participation skills, working both within schools and with groups throughout the community. In addition, I continue to work remotely with Journeys Within Our Community (JWOC) in Cambodia, providing college scholarships for students whose volunteer hours, in turn, enable free English and technology classes for local residents, as well as community programs in areas such as personal finance, parenting, health, and hygiene.

Based on the experience from my business career, much of my work provides support at the organizational level through the development of strategies, organizational structures, financial models, budgets, fundraising, and leadership team coaching. However, what I find most rewarding for me is the work on programs interacting directly with the young people we reach. I regularly serve as a coach/judge for business plan competitions at the university, and am developing programs to teach entrepreneurship and software development, while taking advantage of economic trends and opportunities to provide new pathways to social mobility for our students. As part of a team at Vía, we launched a program aimed at reducing dropouts and ensuring students' success in entering the world of work and exercising effective citizenship. As with our programs at JWOC, the program is centered on the concept of co-responsibility, in this case, with high school student "mentors" trained to lead groups of middle school students in activities designed to develop 21st century skills, culminating in projects that give them an opportunity to shape their own futures and those of their communities.

Impact

Paraphrasing Vía Educación's mission statement, my aspiration for this work is to be a catalyst that enables individuals to transform themselves and their society. During the last year, Vía's programs worked directly with more than 25,000 participants, sharing tools and processes for community participation that enabled these groups to touch the lives of more than 60,000 additional members of their own communities. The universities' operational strategies are helping to sustain and grow a higher education option each year for more than 20,000 students (who previously had none), while the business plan competition program arms several hundred graduates with hands-on experience to further expand their options for social mobility in the world of business and entrepreneurship. Over our 12-year history, JWOC has graduated nearly 150 students who are rapidly growing into leaders for the re-building of Cambodia's future in education, in business, and in social impact organizations – and the pipeline continues with 75 college students enrolled and providing education for more than 3,000 community members each year. For me, the most important thing is that the impact of almost every one of these individuals will continue to multiply, as they come away, not with a single accomplishment, but armed with the tools, the direct experience, and the confidence to know that they can change their lives for the better – as well as a sense of co-responsibility that leads them to become catalysts for others.

Challenges

My most significant challenges have come in figuring out how to be effective in new venues. These challenges loosely organize themselves into three areas, usually *after* you already have a fairly clear idea of the vision and mission you are involved in pursuing. They are not about *what*; they are all about *how*. The first is learning to effectively navigate anew within each new environment. To effectively move initiatives forward, you need to understand the unique roles (yours and others'), working norms and practices, communication loops, and decision-making processes. The second challenge is identifying where your highest and best value is for the organization and for yourself. If you bring past experience, you need to find the balance between what *you* may perceive as contributing the most value (concrete deliverables) vs. what the organization may benefit more from (coaching and capacity-building), while still gaining new experiences that will allow you to have a more significant impact in the long run. Third is recognizing and being willing to follow unexpected paths. While it goes without saying that in any new environment, many (most!) things will not progress along the path you expect, it can still be a challenge to know when to persist in the path you have in mind, and when to have the confidence that you will ultimately make better progress to the vision if you let go and try a new approach.

Lessons Learned

The most important lessons I have learned center around change. While these may have been brought into sharper relief by the number of simultaneous transitions in my case, I believe this dynamic of constant change is inherent in the work that each of us does. By the very nature of who we are and what we have decided is important in the world, we consistently seek out new venues where we can both contribute and learn.

The first lesson is that among the strengths and skills that we may bring to this work, the most important is the ability to communicate effectively. Successful change requires, of course, a clear vision and thoughtful planning, as well as the knowledge and skills needed to make

247

a positive impact. However, while you can bring all of these *together*, without the ability to bring them *alive* and mobilize others, you will likely accomplish little. This requires effective communication. By that, I do not mean the ability to talk. I mean the ability to listen, observe, understand reactions and messages conveyed in indirect ways and interpret relationships among people. This is critical to ensuring that together you are creating the right vision in the first place, and that you can make it real. Of course, this is doubly (or more!) challenging when working in a new language. There, you must not only pursue excellence in the communication basics, but also prioritize your effort to master the nuances of the language as quickly as possible. In the meantime, listen well and do not be too proud to communicate by whatever means works: draw pictures, sign, speak "Spanglish," smile, laugh, but find a way! Somehow, genuine human feelings always seem to communicate the best.

Another lesson has been to err more often on the side of action than on waiting for clarity. While I have had the good fortune to work with amazing, smart, and talented people, I have also come to find that it is more rare than I expected that any one of us is the super-knowledgeable, super-experienced person we need for any specific topic. In addition, as was true in my business career, it is rare that the steps in the path to the vision are obvious. Waiting for that level of clarity to materialize (or for someone else to give it to you) before you grab hold and move ahead is not a good use of time. We all come armed with the ability to research, to learn, to seek out help from our networks, and to think creatively and pragmatically. I have found that it is better to act. Be thoughtful in identifying what you think has the most potential, but then go. Push ahead with confidence – tempered with humility and ensuring you are including and engaging all stakeholders – but push ahead.

Lastly, as we do this work, each of us should recognize the need for "change management" at the personal level. We need to stay aware of the presence and impact of change in our lives – not to avoid it or rail against it, or somehow "fix" it, but to be conscious of the energy it requires and perhaps, be a bit kinder in our self-judgment. While showing the preference for action I mention above, we must also recognize the need for patience, realizing that the occasional bit of inertia can be okay as you go slow now to go faster later, once necessary changes have been made. We must also value the flexibility that change demands of us, knowing that things rarely go in a straight line, but that we often reach a better version of the original vision than we intended. Through it all, remember to reach out to this community of which we are a part to find the encouragement and the fun and the kindred spirits who help us keep moving toward a better quality of life for all.

Bio

Erin Esparza graduated from the International Education Policy Program at the Harvard Graduate School of Education in 2015 and from Harvard College (Economics) in 1985. Following a business career focused on product development and new business creation, she works in Monterrey, México on projects focused on youth, entrepreneurship and participatory citizenship.

Advancing Educational Opportunity through the Advancement of Knowledge

By Ernesto Treviño

Goals and Work

Currently I am commited to advancing educational opportunity by providing empirical evidence of the challenges that Chile and Latin American countries face in their sinuous roads to more inclusive educational development.

More specifically, I have been studying different ways in which the education system provides opportunities to children and young people from disadvantaged backgrounds. One line of these studies is related to access to higher education; it investigates the main economic and academic barriers that students from low socioeconomic status (SES) have to deal with in order to access and succeed in higher education. Another line of studies focuses on issues of quality of education.

Within this line there are three types of studies. First, several studies have focused on the school, teacher, and family factors that explain student achievement in Latin America. Second, other studies have focused on the way in which schools distribute students across classrooms, unveiling a strong belief among principals and teachers that academic segregation within schools improves educational opportunity while my findings demonstrate that segregation has a negative impact on disadvantaged students' outcomes. The third line of studies concentrates on the way in which teachers implement their classes using observational tools of teacher practices, research on the ways in which they differentially serve students of different SES, and providing feedback to teachers so they can improve their own practices. The aim of these studies has been to provide input that helps to understand the challenges of educational systems at different levels in order to design measures which are more likely to improve educational opportunity.

Impact

During the last year I have been able to work with approximately 10 young researchers that are following academic careers relating to educational opportunity, and through the research projects I have been collaborating on, improving the opportunities of nearly 600 students from Pre-K to grade 12, who participate in my research projects. During the past decade I was fortunate to: influence nearly 40 young researchers that have followed different academic and practice paths related to improving educational opportunity; I have worked on projects that involved approximately 4000 students in the Chilean school system; and have worked on international evaluations that involved the participation of nearly 100,000 students in Latin America.

Challenges

There are three main interrelated challenges in working to better understand the educational phenomenons that are related to educational opportunity. First, doing research in this area requires an interdisciplinary perspective, which entails working with people from different academic backgrounds, who have to enter into productive dialogues in order to better understand educational challenges. Second, the richness of such academic work is sometimes limited by a lack of humillity as researchers can impede a fluent and productive communication. The latter applies both to the work in the research teams and to our capacity as researchers to collaborativelly work with practitioners in order to create evidence relevant for the improvement of educational opportunities, so these can be incorporated into the daily lives and practices of educational institutions. Third, effectively influencing educational change requires that a leader combine a solid empirical base with an in-depth understanding of the pressures, conditions, and expectations that policy makers and practitioners face. Any proposed solution, to be viable, must take into account these two elements.

Lessons Learned

I have learned that one of the most important messages to others interested in educational opportunity, is to model that every instance is a chance to learn, and as in any learning process, we will inevitably make mistakes that can represent excellent opportunities to improve both our learning and educational opportunities. Such an approach has been very fruitful in working both with teachers and educators, as well as with young researchers and practitioners in the policy realm.

Bio

Ernesto Trevino is the director of the Center UC for the Transformation of Education and associate professor at the Faculty of Education of the Catholic University of Chile. He has been principal investigator of the Second and Third Regional Comparative Studies of UNESCO Latin America, and a researcher in projects funded by the National Council for Science in Chile and Mexico, UNESCO, UNICEF, UNDP, and the ministries of education from Chile, Colombia, Mexico, and Nicaragua. He graduated from the International Education Policy Program at the Harvard Graduate School of Education in 2001, and subsequently obtained a doctorate in education also from Harvard University.

GOVERNMENT

Rethinking Brazil's Basic Education Curriculum

By Teresa Cozetti Pontual Pereira

Goals and Work

I have the privilege of working at the Ministry of Education at a time of great relevance for Brazil's education system. I joined the Ministry in September of 2016, right after my maternity leave and a few months after President Dilma's impeachment. Amidst great political turmoil (it is still unclear whether President Temer will finish his term and as a direct result, whether I will complete a full year in my current role), the Ministry of Education is implementing reforms that are crucial to improving the quality of education, including bringing more flexibility to high school curricula and implementing Brazil's version of the common core (in Portuguese, Base Nacional Comum Curricular or BNCC, which literally translates to National Curricular Common Base). As Director of Curricula, it is my responsibility to lead the implementation of these reforms.

The high school reform was passed through a Presidential Provisional Measure, which has the force of law only during the 120-day-period during which Congress must decide whether it is passed into law or not. The fact that this was the instrument used to pass the reform was extremely controversial. Even those who supported the reform were against the means through which it was passed. Nonetheless, Congress passed the bill into law, albeit with some changes, on February 16th, 2017. The New Secondary Education, as the law has been referenced, establishes that high school curricula will have at most 1.800 hours of "common core" and the remainder of the 2.400 hours (4 hours per day) will vary according to what the schools can offer and the students have an interest in studying. The law organizes the flexible part of the curriculum between four knowledge areas: languages, mathematics, biological sciences, and human sciences. There is also a professional and vocational track, which can now fit into students' regular high school course load, whereas previously any vocational training had to be pursued separately.

Currently, secondary education in Brazil is focused primarily on college entrance, even though only 11% (Instituto Unibanco/Censo-INEP, 2015) of these graduates enroll in higher education. Its curriculum is considered a mile wide, with 13 subject matters taught all three years, but only an inch deep. According to the latest national exams, only 27.5% of students finishing high school had reached the adequate level of proficiency in Portuguese and barely 7.3% in Mathematics (Todos Pela Educação using INEP data, 2015). Only about 51% of those who enter primary education make it to high school (Instituto Unibanco/Censo-INEP, 2015). In 2015, only about 46% of 18-year-olds in Brazil had finished high school (Instituto Unibanco/Censo-INEP, 2015). In short, about half the students never make it to high school and those who finish are not well prepared for entering college or for joining the workforce. The New Secondary Education Law pushes states, which are responsible for public high school in Brazil, to make high school curricula more attractive to students and to rethink the purpose of high school, as it embraces professional and technical training as an important pathway for young people.

But diversifying high school curricula in a country with such unequal education outcomes as ours would not be possible if we were not simultaneously clarifying what all students need to accomplish at each stage of their basic education, including high school. Brazil began the process of developing a curricular common core in 2014. The documents' first version was published in 2015 and submitted for public scrutiny. Through an online platform, the Ministry of Education received more than 12 million contributions. A second version that took those inputs into consideration was published in 2016. The Ministry then helped states and municipalities organize local seminars to discuss and contribute to the document. Over 9,000 teachers participated. Their contributions, and those of international and national specialists, were then taken into account to produce the third and final version of the BNCC for early childhood and primary education only (the New Secondary Education Law has affected the BNCC calendar), which the Ministry sent to the National Education Council for consideration in April of 2017. The Council has scheduled public hearings in all five regions of the country to discuss the final version and is committed to voting the BNCC by September for the Minister of Education to

258

sanction. We are confident that the third version is an improvement on the first two, especially in that it sets ten general competencies for Basic Education, which involve empathy, self-knowledge, the ability to cooperate with others and to act ethically. These permeate and inform the skills and competencies that students are expected to develop at each grade and for each subject matter.

Considering these very ambitious reforms, my main focus is to ensure their successful implementation in a country as diverse and unequal as ours. Both of these reforms are extremely complex and require identifying and coordinating multiple stakeholders, especially since the Ministry itself is not responsible for running public schools, which is constitutionally the job of cities and states. We are currently in the process of designing the programs that will support states and cities in implementing the BNCC and help the states to implement the New Secondary Education Law.

There are five elements we are taking into consideration for planning the BNCC's implementation: communication and engagement, adaptation of local curricula by cities and states, adaptation of textbooks and other curricular resources, adaptation of initial and ongoing teacher training, and adaptation of student evaluations. For many of these, such as textbooks, initial teacher training and student evaluations, the Ministry plays a major role. In others, the leadership falls to cities and states, as is the case with local adaptation of their curricula and ongoing professional development for their workforce.

The first and probably biggest challenge is communication, both internally within the Ministry, and externally with each of the stakeholders of the process. It has been my experience in the almost 10 years I have worked in public education that communication is always an important challenge. In large, complex systems, there are many stakeholders to consider and communication usually needs to be customized to each one. Most governments focus their communication staff solely on the press and not on this internal ministerial communication or external communication to stakeholders. With the advent of social media, this issue has only been made worse, as news takes on a life of its own and everyone is a potential media outlet. Governments have been slow to adapt to this new information age. This is a crucial element of implementation and the one to which we are worse equipped to address. Thankfully, Brazil has built a coalition around the BNCC that is a civil society movement: the "Movement for the Common Core" (movimentopelabase.org.br), made up of education NGOs, foundations, and education specialists from all sides of the political spectrum. This movement has been crucial to the BNCC's process thus far and will continue to be through its implementation. Their communication efforts have been more effective and farther reaching than the government's.

To help states and cities adapt their curricula according to the BNCC, we are developing courses and providing financial and technical assistance to help build their internal capacity around issues of curriculum development. We are also working on building our own internal capacity so we can provide better technical assistance.

To adapt our materials, the Ministry is making changes to the National Textbook Program, which has given public school students access to textbooks since 1929 (making it the Ministry's oldest program). We are focused on bringing the BNCC into the public bidding process to ensure book publishers will incorporate these changes into their production. Buying and distributing textbooks to about 50 million students is a herculean task that costs the federal government about R$2 billion (about US$600 million) a year. Therefore, the program has run in cycles of three years: in the first year, books are purchased for 1st through 5th grades; the second year for 6th through 9th grades; and the third year for all high school grades. In 2017, we are in the process of buying the books that 1st through 5th graders will be using in the 2019 school year. Next year we will purchase the ones that 6th through 9th graders will be using in 2020 and the year after that the books high school students will be using starting in 2021. This means the 9th graders of today, for example, will never use national textbooks aligned with the BNCC. The high school textbooks pose an even greater challenge in that they will need to take into consideration the flexibility introduced by the New Secondary Education Law.

It is my goal in life to help make sure that all children in Brazil have access to the kind of education that helps them fulfill their own goals. I am confident that successful implementation of the reforms I just described will contribute to improving the quality of education for all children in Brazil, especially those who face the greatest adversities.

Impact

Over the last year, my work in the Ministry of Education has indirectly influenced the 47.8 million students enrolled in public (82%) and private (8%) Basic Education, nationally. More immediately and directly, my work has affected the four million primary school students in schools that are implementing the program *Novo Mais Educação - NME* (literally, New More Education) and the three million high school students in schools that are implementing the program *Ensino Médio Inovador – ProEMI* (literally, Innovative High School). Through these programs we have transferred R$1.3 billion (about US$409 million) directly to schools for after-school programs with a focus on Portuguese and Math in the case of *NME,* and for rethinking their curriculum with more elective classes in line with student interests in the case of *ProEMI*.

In the past decade, my work has directly impacted one million students in about 1500 schools in the state of Rio de Janeiro's public education system, where I worked as undersecretary of education from 2008-2010; 600 thousand students in over 1000 schools in the city of Rio de Janeiro's public education system, where I worked as project manager from 2010-2012; and 140 thousand students in over 400 schools in Salvador's public education system, where I worked as undersecretary of education from 2013-2016.

Challenges

I've faced many challenges working with public education at the city, state and now federal level in Brazil. The main one has been political discontinuity. Most of the time, a change at the top of the political chain dismantles the work done thus far, and begins anew, many times in a completely different direction. Long-term planning, which is critical to the success of most education policies, is at odds with Brazil's political culture, placing a great barrier to the success of education reforms.

The challenge of political discontinuity is closely related to another great challenge: motivating the civil servants who are the heart of these bureaucracies and are the only ones who can ensure the continuity of policies. This challenge is exacerbated by the apathy that sets in once these civil servants have endured many changes in leadership. Influencing, motivating, and building their capacity is the biggest challenge that people who are nominated to positions in government face, if they want their reforms to have long-term impact.

Another great challenge I have already mentioned is communication. Without effective communication and support from key stakeholders, successfully implementing education reform will be almost impossible. Especially since to reform an education system, one will most certainly need to cause disruption and question the status quo.

Lessons learned

In the almost ten years since graduating from the Harvard Graduate School of Education, I have learned that resilience is the most important skill needed to endure the challenges affecting long-term change in public education. Setbacks are constant, but keeping a focus on the children, whose education one is working to improve, and on the importance of the mission to build the kind of society one wants to live in and wants to leave for our own children, helps to bounce back ready to take on the next challenge.

Bio

Teresa Cozetti Pontual Pereira is Director of Curricula in Brazil's Ministry of Education. She graduated from the International Education Policy Program in 2008. Upon graduation, she worked as Undersecretary of Education for the State of Rio de Janeiro. She later worked as Project Manager for the City of Rio de Janeiro's Education Department and as Undersecretary of Education for the City of Salvador.

Increasing the Value of the Teaching Profession in Peru

By José La Rosa

Goals and Work

Teacher policies, especially those that influence and regulate how teachers are educated, have been proven to be a key component for educational reform around the world. Paradoxically, while one out of every two Peruvians believes that teachers perform poorly in school, three out of every five Peruvians would not want their children to become school teachers in order to help change this statistic.[46] As a country, we have the urgent challenge of increasing the value of the teaching profession, as it has an important effect on improving the quality of learning for students. Therefore, the Ministry of Education has recently established this as one of the four priority pillars for educational reform. The goal is to make the profession more attractive, focusing on teacher training, professional development, and the improvement of working conditions for teachers.

As a former researcher at the Ministry of Education, I had the opportunity to travel to some of the most distant rural schools over several years. There, I talked with teachers working in the most complex and difficult conditions. Those years gave me the chance to understand the many factors that influence educational institutions in Peru. When I returned to the Ministry after Harvard, I had never worked directly on the design or implementation of a large scale education policy, but I had developed a set of new technical and analytical skills that prepared me for the task. Most importantly, I returned with the conviction that improving the teaching career would be a key contribution to improving the quality of education in Peru.

After spending a few months as a policy advisor for the Teacher Development Department at the Ministry, I decided it was time to dive in and contribute directly as part of one of the many teams designing policy interventions for teachers. Soon, I was given the opportunity to start working in the Pre-service Teacher Training Department on the

---

[46] IPSOS 2014. Encuesta de Percepción Docente

design of a new curriculum for teacher training, which will be implemented nationwide during the next couple of years. This new curriculum is part of a huge reform of Public Education Institutes (Institutos Pedagogicos) in Peru. We are focused on developing, not only pedagogical and subject knowledge skills in teachers, but also a new set of competencies similar to the 21st Century Skills framework. We aim to prepare teachers to think critically, communicate effectively, assume leadership, solve problems, innovate, and use technology, among other abilities. This will become the trademark of future Peruvian teachers.

In addition, our team is also responsible for designing the implementation plan for the new curriculum. We have to develop materials and guidelines, as well as train, monitor, and evaluate teacher trainers. We are also working with other teams at the Ministry in order to assure that the basic conditions for the proper implementation of the curriculum are met in the next few years. For instance, some of our main priorities are the hiring of new teacher trainers, changes in infrastructure required for technology use, and a general shift of the institutional management model.

Impact

The implementation of the new curriculum will directly impact all teacher candidates attending Public Education Institutes, which represent about 70% percent of the total number of teacher candidates attending Education Institutes in Peru. In 2016, 20,000 teacher candidates were enrolled at public institutes and only 9,793 were enrolled at private institutes.[47] In that sense, the work we are currently doing will have a huge impact as new generations of teacher candidates enroll at Public Education Institutes, graduate, and go on to work in schools across the country.

---

[47] Ministerio de Educación del Perú 2017. Estadística de la Calidad Educativa

Challenges

I have encountered many challenges throughout this experience. The first one is that I was not trained as a teacher. As a researcher, my experience comes from observing classes and interacting with teachers and students in order to analyze their behaviors and performance. However, teaching experience is only one of many skills required for this type of work. In fact, the ability that I have to use multidisciplinary evidence to inform large scale policy decisions has been a great way to contribute to the team. This has also been an amazing opportunity to learn from the many teachers who have been involved in the curriculum design process, and to gain a deeper understanding of how teaching works. Regardless, I do believe educational policy makers should be required to do classroom work at some point, in some capacity, as it gives us important insight into the many factors involved in effective teaching, and the many barriers to improving the quality of education.

Another important challenge is based on the fact that this policy intervention will take a very long time to cause any impact in classrooms. It will take at least five years after the implementation for the first group of teachers trained under the new curriculum to begin working in schools. In fact, we still have a couple of more years to go before implementing, which means that the first group of teachers will not begin working until seven years from now. This is why, as policymakers, we need to see the big picture and realize that a well done and significant reform takes time and patience. We must also be prepared for political changes, which usually affect and guide policy interventions in terms of budget, deadlines, and priorities.

Lessons Learned

Our contribution as a new generation of policy-makers must be focused on improving what has been done before us, while identifying mistakes and treating them as opportunities to do a better job. For instance, prior to designing the new curriculum, we evaluated the previous one, identified its major issues, as well as its many strengths. We learned that the old curriculum failed to elaborate guidelines and provide an efficient support system for teachers, which is why we are focused on filling those gaps and designing a monitoring and evaluation system that can assure the best implementation possible.

Furthermore, the new teacher training curriculum is part of a bigger reform that aims to improve the overall status and quality of the teaching career, which includes increasing teacher salaries and providing better opportunities for professional development. This is why it is important to focus on what our specific team is doing, but also to find ways to collaborate with other teams, as the success of our intervention also depends on the success of the whole reform.

Finally we must never lose our focus and always remind ourselves that we are working for the children, many of whom are living and learning under very difficult conditions. At a personal level, the teachers and students I met in rural schools during my fieldwork days and those that I continue to meet and learn from, constantly guide my work and remind me of my main goal, which is to improve the lives of people just like them.

Bio

Jose La Rosa is a Curriculum Management Specialist at the Pre-service Teacher Training Department in the Ministry of Education of Peru. He is currently a Professor of Education Policy at Universidad Nacional Mayor de San Marcos. He has an undergraduate degree in Social Anthropology from Pontificia Universidad Catolica del Peru and graduated from the International Education Policy Program at the Harvard Graduate School of Education in 2016. His prior work includes being a researcher and program evaluator for the Ministry of Education of Peru and UNICEF.

Advancing the Educational Opportunities of Rural Indigenous Youth in Guatemala

By Juan de Dios Simón

Goals and Work

Rural indigenous youth in Guatemala face multiple challenges that include: lack of educational opportunities, diminished prospects for employment, sexual and reproductive health challenges, violence, and constrains to full participation in the civic life of their communities. Most indigenous children in rural areas of Guatemala, from 0 to 5 years old, are considered Deprived, Excluded and Vulnerable (DEV) due to the low level of access to health, nutrition, and educational services available in their local communities. Indigenous children from 6 to 12 years old should be in school and ready to succeed in mathematics and reading but curricular relevance, the preparation of bilingual teachers, and the quality of educational materials are not totally adapted to their reality and cultural context. Youth from 13 to 18 years old should be studying in high school, responsible for sexual and reproductive health, ready to work, and exercise their multicultural citizenship but most of them already have children. Too many youth are young parents, drop out of school, and seek job opportunities but without the qualifications.

I am currently the National Director of the non-formal schooling system of the Ministry of Education of Guatemala working to implement three strategic lines: 1. Coverage, 2. Quality, Equity and Inclusion; 3. Diverse modalities to deliver educational opportunities, formal schooling, and no formal schooling.

In terms of coverage, Guatemala failed to achieve education for all for year 2015, therefore the new goal for 2021 is to increase the coverage of primary universal school from the current 82% to 90%; in low secondary school (7th to 9th grades) the goal is to increase coverage from the current 46% to 54%; and for high secondary (10th to 12th grades) the goal is to increase coverage from 24% to 28%. The Ministry of Education has historically invested in primary education but needs to invest more in low secondary schools and high schools. The investment in the current administration will focus on infrastructure, hiring new

267

teachers, printing more textbooks, and producing more alternative programs to reduce barriers for rural indigenous youth to come back to school and complete schooling.

Youth Out of School (YOS). A recent study conducted by USAID Guatemala shows that 3,087,000 Guatemalan youth from 15 to 24 years old are out of school. Approximately 1, 670, 000 of them never finished nine years of schooling, as most of them obtained only primary education and are now out of school. sixty percent of YOS are indigenous and from the Central and Western Highland of Guatemala.

To increase diverse opportunities, I am involved in the creation of the National Institute of Distance Learning. This institute will provide opportunities to study in diverse education modalities: online, full e-learning, by radio, and mixed methodologies with books and intranet training. The main idea of distance learning with the modality online is to provide opportunities to youth and adults to study anytime, anywhere, and from any device. If they do not have the technology, then they will use mixed methodologies between traditional books and tutors. Distance learning will provide flexibility in schedules, curricula organization, and adaptation to diverse methodology.

I am responsible for overseeing the implementation of alternative educational programs with linguistic and cultural relevance. 1) Provide primary school for excluded youth and adults. Instead of studying six years, they study two years in an accelerated modality. They have to be older than 13 years old to be qualified for this type of education. The main idea is to provide second opportunities for youth and adults who did not finish primary school to come back and get their certification. 2) Provide flexible modality for low and high secondary school. Instead of studying three years from 7th grade to 9th grade, students study only two years and have to be older than 15 years old. To finish high school (10th to 12th grade) students will also study two years and need to be older than 17 years old. In summary, students with an alternative education can study six years to finish primary school, low secondary school and high school, instead of 12 years as regular programs do.

My Directorate is also promoting the technical preparation for occupational areas. Many youth and adults do not want or need academic credentials, but are getting a certification for occupational areas such as electricity, food industry, mechanics, hotel and restaurants, construction, tourism, and agriculture. It is similar to a community technical college in Guatemala, but at the high school level.

My work addresses access as well as quality and relevance of education. First, through a participatory assessment, we identified barriers that influence children and youth to drop out and leave schools. The reasons to leave schools are mainly low income or financial limitations, school distances, lack of linguistic and cultural relevance in contents, and family issues, such as youth becoming fathers or mothers at early ages. Twenty-five percent of youth between 15 to 24 years old already have children.

Illustrative factors

Low income: Most indigenous youth and adults work in informal agricultural settings. Since most of them do not have secondary education, they do not obtain professional jobs with benefits. Most of them do not have contracts and are not making even the monthly minimum wage in the country (US$350). Many of them are seeking new educational opportunities.

School distance: Most indigenous families live in rural zones that are geographically isolated and therefore far away from educational centers. It is harder for them to come to high school when they must walk many kilometers to a learning center. National tests in mathematics and reading comprehension show that children and youth in rural areas score lower than children that attend schools in urban areas. They need reinforcement and alternative ways of learning.

Relevance of educational materials: Despite advancements in the intentions of creating diverse curricula to develop competencies and create bilingual and intercultural focus, there is a necessity to revise and analyze the texts and cultural images in textbooks. The content, discourse, and images in educational materials are often not relevant to the local realities of students, and without local input it is hard to relate intercultural learnings. Topics about the conquest, colonization, and republic life are portrayed in Eurocentric ways that are biased against the vision and dignity of indigenous peoples. Correcting the content and cultural images in educational materials is therefore important.

Impact

Approximately 83,000 students have benefitted directly from my work in 2016. They are distributed in the following ways: primary education for youth and adults, 6,700 students; basic or low secondary education, 31,000 students; technical training for employment and self-employment, 40,000 students; and high secondary education, 5,300 students. For the last ten years approximately 450,000 students have benefitted from my work.

The technical proposals or academic analyses provide evidence and data, but it is necessary to understand the political agendas of people in Congress, Mayors, and other elected officials. We often plan the technical part very well, we enjoy seminars with hard and heavy data, but political timing is not always the timing of technical processes. Another challenge is dealing with promises and good intentions without budgets. If a budget is not there in our annual operational plan, anybody can say anything but it will be hard to deliver that promise.

The institutional culture matters. Behavior and attitudes of employees are not written. Learning about institutional structure and adapting yourself to new roles, before trying to change from within, is probably a key. Then preparation and good communication about change is important to decrease resistance to change. For example, some people have worked in public institutions for 10 or 15 years and they have a network and understand the levels of hierarchy, which can make it harder to make changes without understanding the institutional culture.

Lessons Learned

It is important to combine academic preparation, networks, work experience, and personal commitment. In the professional area, besides the technical and academic preparation, it is fundamental to understand policies, administrative, and financial procedures. Most good ideas cannot be implemented without knowing the processes, bureaucracy, and financial management. Most important is to know about the person in charge of making the final decisions.

In the Personal area: Be focused on your expertise, do your homework, never give up, besides your salary and work environment, the real test is how much are you committed to transformation. How much do you believe in adding the extra mile in favor of the most disadvantaged and excluded people? Are you willing to talk to your wife and children to let them know that you are doing something for the country? And perhaps you will fail to pay full attention to them?

Bio

Juan Simón graduated from the International Education Policy program at the Harvard Graduate School of Education in 2005. He is currently working for the Ministry of Education of Guatemala, and has worked at UNICEF Perú, the Interamerican Development Bank, IDB (Washington DC), and ChildFund International (Guatemala).

Supporting Teacher Education in Argentina

By Mariana Clucellas

Goals and Work

I currently work at the National Teacher Training Institute (INFD) in the National Ministry of Education in Argentina. As Planning Coordinator, I lead a team of professionals in four main specific tasks:

i. Design of a policy for strengthening initial teacher training, which includes planning the implementation of a global plan at the provincial level in order to attend to their specific needs with the ultimate goal of improving public education at the early childhood, primary, and secondary levels in the whole country;

ii. Development and improvement of a virtual system that will help us identify the need of specific teacher profiles (in certain subjects, especially for secondary education) in order to promote young graduates to choose teaching in those fields, providing the educational system with qualified teachers in all areas of knowledge;

iii. Development of a planning tool that helps local Ministries of Education plan their educational policies and build synergies in an articulated way. This is contrary to how it has been until now, with each local area planning their policies with no regard for the planning of other areas (e.g. secondary develops their own programs separately from primary).

iv. Design of short educational policy training programs for the local higher education teams in charge of teacher training, so as to empower them in a mixed top-down/bottom-up strategy for design, planning, and implementation of teacher training policies. This can assure that teacher training really improves public mandatory education throughout the country and not only in the most important cities.

In addition to this work, since I love teaching, I have been a coordinator of the Regional Annual Course developed by UNESCO's International Institute for Educational Planning (IIEP), Regional Chapter Buenos

Aires, for Latin American officials from Ministries of Education. For the last few years, I have taught a course on planning and evaluating educational programs and projects. I also assist Latin American countries sporadically on how to plan effective interventions to improve and enhance educational opportunity (Guatemala, Mexico, Bolivia, Uruguay, Dominican Republic, Peru, and Colombia, among others).

Impact

If I had to specify a number of learners influenced directly by my work in the last year, I would mention approximately 200 education professionals: 25 participants in the Annual Regional Course given by IIEP in Buenos Aires; another 30 people through a course given by The Latin America Faculty of Social Sciences (FLACSO); 100 people in four different provinces of the country; and 50 people in Guatemala, all the aforementioned people, through on-site intensive courses. It is hard to come up with a number of people indirectly influenced by my work, since I have only taken into consideration participants of courses I have been in charge of. I would have to add those influenced by these 200 students of the different courses and include people working with me in the National Ministry as well as in the places where I travelled during 2016, visiting at least 18 Argentinean provinces for workshops attended by 20 people each.

In the last decade I have probably directly reached 1,000 education professionals through different courses, even at universities, all related to planning in education and with a strong focus on public education for all and ways in which to improve equal opportunities for children and adolescents, not only in Argentina, but in Latin America as well.

Challenges

While doing my job, I believe I did not encounter difficult challenges until I started at the National Ministry of Education. Until that moment, my team and I at UNESCO did a great job reaching and opening people's minds to new ways of doing things so as to make education that incredible driving force in enhancing educational opportunity. I would read new bibliographies on public policy planning to be able to teach them and that seemed to be enough: "Just do what the text says." But when I started at the National Ministry of Education, almost all, or at least a great part of what I had been trying to teach to officials in other countries or even in my country, seemed to be of no use. It was hard to bring a team from the previous administration on board with the new one and to maintain the focus on the policies and goals. Most of the time was devoted to coming up with solutions for emergencies and setting aside the important, the substance of my work. Actually, it was (and it sometimes still is) quite frustrating by the end of the day, when I find I have devoted up to ten or twelve hours working, and cannot see any "finished" substantial product. Challenges range in difficulty from opposition of the unions to any new policy of teacher training (even when I invite them to discuss possibilities so as to negotiate), to dissatisfaction with people on my team because they are not motivated to complete the tasks they perform (many times a legitimate request, other times not so much). At those times, books do not seem to help but they finally do, as does a commitment to educational enhancement and passion for what one does and pursues.

Lessons Learned

While there have been times with tremendous challenges, there have also been times of incredible learning. The most important ones I can share with you today: educational policy results cannot be measured in short periods of time, they are processes and as such, they take time. Actually from the moment they are designed (thought of, dreamed about) until they reach students, they change many times in many ways. Does this mean you do planning to achieve any result? No, you do not. You just have to maintain focus and admit that the same good result - to enhance educational opportunity – can be achieved in ways you had not even imagined. Another great lesson is that actual policies in education – and in almost any area of public administration – require strong negotiation skills. Planning sounds great when defined in theoretical terms, but when it comes to reality and to actual planning, more than the theory about the phases public policies linearly undergo (educational planning included), negotiation and "good reading" of real interests held by stake holders is key. As Carlos Matus has put it (a Harvard graduate too in the last century), in order to plan effectively planners need theory, method, and personal skills. Planners need to have be technicians and politicians as well. Academic knowledge is not enough to plan and achieve results. As planners we need to know about what we are planning, but we also have to know how power is distributed among stakeholders. Watch this video and listen to Carlos Matus speak about the public questioning of democracy. I've learned a lot from him and his writings.[48]

The goal is clear: we want all children to get a good education so as to develop their life project. Keep that in mind and think of at least five or six ways to achieve it. And then think outside the box of other alternatives and bear in mind that as important as knowledge in the matter is, to stay honest (both intellectually and towards the people you work with and those you work for); committed, passionate, and above all, keep a peaceful state of mind even if the road gets insurmountable. If you stay focused, there is a high probability that you will meet the goals you dreamed about. You just have to give it a try all the time and never give up.

Bio

Mariana Clucellas obtained an undergraduate degree in Political Science at the University of Buenos Aires in Argentina and graduated from the International Education Policy Program at the Harvard Graduate School of Education in 2000. She then worked at the United Nations Development Program (UNDP) Argentina until 2003. Afterwards she coordinated educational programs at a local NGO until 2005 when she became a full time consultant for the Institute for International Educational Planning from UNESCO. In 2015 she joined the National Ministry of Education in Argentina. In the meantime she was a professor at two national public universities (FLACSO and UNLA), always working on issues related to planning of educational policies.

---

[48] Matus, Carlos (1987) Adiós Señor Presidente, UNLA. Argentina; Matus, Carlos (1987); La Teoría del Juego Social, UNLA, Agentina.

Levers for Change: System Strengthening in the Gulf and Levant Countries

By Tara Mahtafar

I was very fortunate to begin my career after graduating from Harvard's program in International Education Policy (IEP) exactly where I had dreamed of working to improve education—in the Middle East, the region where I had gone to school, for a major system reform at the scale of effort that originally inspired me to get into education development. An IEP alumna who had served in this role made introductions to 'bypass the impasse' of automated applications to get to a live person and an interview – this was the first of many instances of seeing IEP alumnae generously support one another across cohorts and geography, making us a truly global family.

My role in policy and planning, within the K-12 division of the Education Council in Abu Dhabi, United Arab Emirates (UAE), focused on formulating and implementing policies and programs across a wide range of topics within the emirate's system-wide reform of public education. All Gulf states have invested commendable political will and significant resources into re-engineering their education systems over the past decade. The UAE has often led the way in setting up levers for change from the institutional, such as establishing the region's first inspectorate (a success spotlighted in the World Bank's The Road Travelled MENA series[49]) in 2007 and rolling out national licensure in 2017, another first for the region; to testbeds for innovation, such as the virtual labs initiative by Dubai's Future Accelerators; and Abu Dhabi's annual Innovation Week which gives students hands-on exposure to future-focused industries and an incubator for schools to carry out research projects. This progress-minded, can-do environment has felt both inspiring and empowering. My supervisors at the Abu

---

[49] Cuadra, Ernesto P.; Thacker, Simon. 2014. *The road traveled : Dubai's journey towards improving private education - a World Bank review.* MENA development report. Washington, DC ; World Bank Group. http://documents.worldbank.org/curated/en/578491468172474244/The-road-traveled-Dubais-journey-towards-improving-private-education-a-World-Bank-review

Dhabi Education Council (ADEC) always had an open-door policy, not only in their management style, but also in their welcoming of ideas. Throughout my four years there, I was able to propose and implement new protocols for our division's work to expand scope and increase efficacy. This was usually in small incremental steps, and always took a fair bit of time to advocate for and secure buy-in from stakeholders we worked with, but the salient points remain that a) the culture at ADEC was receptive to bottom-up change and that b) the impact of policies were visible due to the size and accessibility of the system (about 250 schools mostly within a 2-hour drive radius).

The most significant work I supported at ADEC, within the past year (2016), was a year-long 'policy refresh.' In this project, we redesigned the policy development framework itself to include better use of data, a broader consultative process, rigorous implementation planning (previously often the 'missing link' between policy on paper and in schools), and a new monitoring and evaluation system to track progress, identify gaps, and feed into revision cycles. Secondly, we reformulated the entire body of policies for public schools to align them with the updated government strategy, as well as make them clearer, focused, more reflective of the context and readiness of schools, and therefore more 'implementable.' The new policies shape every aspect of the reform, from learner-centered curriculum and assessment, to establishing an architecture for self-improving schools, and will impact 130,000 students and 15,000 staff across Abu Dhabi's public schools.

During the past year I moved to a new organization. Education Development Trust is a UK charity which provides education consultancy services and invests earnings in publicly available research. My role is leading business development for the Middle East and North Africa (MENA) region, by building client relationships, identifying opportunities, developing bids, and mobilizing in-country project teams. With the shift to a regional focus, the learning curve has been challenging yet exciting. In the past six months, I have led and mobilized bids for large-scale programs for:

- The Design and implementation of UAE's newly established Moral Education (Ethics) curriculum;

- National school inspections to incentivize quality improvement in public schools across the UAE;
- Assisting the UK Department for Education (DfE) in creating an area-based ecosystem for developing school leaders in underserved districts of England;
- Embedded support for system strengthening to the government of Lebanon's Reach All Children through Education (RACE) strategy on behalf of the UK Department for Foreign Aid (DFID);
- Developing a system-wide school improvement model for Saudi Arabia's Ministry of Education (MoE) in line with the country's Vision 2030 education sector goals; and
- Capacity building of teachers working with refugee children in Jordan, in partnership with the Queen Rania Teachers Academy.

Collectively these projects represent a direct and indirect impact on the learning of all public school students in these systems. I love my work, and enjoy being part of an organization that is research-led and committed to evidence-based solutions.

A key lesson I learned at both at the ADEC and EDT has been the tendency for teams to get caught up in the day to day challenges and slow the pace of reform, which can lead to cynicism. Part of effective leadership is therefore helping teams keep sight of the big picture, recognize incremental progress toward end goals, and realize that results are never overnight and even the best-planned efforts (whether a policy or a technical solution for a program) are often an iterative effort open to re-evaluation and revision.

IEP was the catalyst for and start of a journey that I never want to stop. I am grateful to the program and to the faculty for instilling the mindset and skillsets in us to go forth in our areas of interest across the globe and contribute in our myriad ways to the good fight for education.

Bio

Tara Mahtafar is a senior development consultant at Education Development Trust, a UK charity, leading EDT's work in the Middle East North Africa region

279

through building strategic partnerships and designing and mobilising scalable, sustainable solutions for government and donor clients. Previously, she served as a policy specialist at Abu Dhabi Education Council, focusing on the formulation and implementation of policies for public schools in Abu Dhabi, UAE in support of the emirate's education sector reform.

INTERNATIONAL DEVELOPMENT

The Partnership Approach to Systems Strengthening: A Promising Model for Improving Educational Opportunity Around the World

By Wilson Aiwuyor

Goals and Work

With over 263 million school-aged children not in school and many more who attend school but are not learning, the world is facing a global education crisis. Without ambitious and sustained large-scale action, more than half of 1.6 billion young people by 2030 – including over 90% of youth in low-income countries – will lack the basic education skills that they need for employment.[50] Since 2014, I have had the great opportunity to work for the Global Partnership for Education (GPE), the only global compact devoted to getting all children into school for a quality education. GPE's mission is to "mobilize global and national efforts to contribute to the achievement of equitable, quality education and learning for all, through inclusive partnership, a focus on effective and efficient education systems and increased financing."[51]

Founded in 2002 and hosted at the World Bank, GPE brings together developing countries (currently 65 countries), bilateral donors, multilateral institutions, civil society organizations, teacher organizations, private foundations, and the private sector to improve education systems. The partnership strengthens education systems of its developing country partners by providing them with financial and technical support to design quality education sector plans (ESPs), and by mobilizing financing to provide large-scale grants in support of the implementation of ESPs. It uses its influence to promote education in the global development agenda and drive mutual accountability among

---

[50] See the report published by the International Commission on Financing Global Education Opportunity, titled: *A Learning Generation: Investing in Education for a Changing World*, available at http://report.educationcommission.org/report/.
[51] See GPE mission at http://www.globalpartnership.org/about-us.

stakeholders, while incentivizing developing country's governments to prioritize education in national planning and budgeting.

I have worked with colleagues at GPE to assess education sector plans, review grant portfolios, and support stakeholder engagement as part of a broad consultative process for the development of the partnership's new strategic plan (GPE 2020).[52] I have also been a part of the working group developing a methodology for the monitoring of developing country governments' education financing targets ahead of the next GPE education funding campaign or replenishment.[53]

Assessing Education Sector Plans

The development of a strong and credible sector plan is a core eligibility requirement for developing countries to receive support from the partnership. As a member of the monitoring and evaluation team in 2014, I helped assess the soundness, credibility, and feasibility of some of the sector plans using a set of criteria. This exercise requires an examination of whether the plan includes an overall vision, clear priorities, and clearly defined strategies – such as human, financial, and technical capacities – for achieving the vision. It also involves an examination of how holistic the plan is in terms of its coverage of the country's education subsectors, from early childhood to higher education, non-formal education, and adult literacy. The extent to which the plan is informed by evidence is also considered by assessing if the plan contains a robust sector analysis that provides relevant data analysis to inform proposed strategies and policy interventions.

The criteria also include how well the plan addresses certain country-specific contexts. For example, an ESP for a country affected by

---

[52] See "GPE 2020" at
http://www.globalpartnership.org/content/gpe-2020-strategic-plan
See "GPE 2020" at http://www.globalpartnership.org/content/gpe-2020-strategic-plan.
[53] The next replenishment will take place in early 2018. For additional information, visit
http://replenishment.globalpartnership.org/en/home/.

vulnerabilities such as disaster, economic crises, or conflict is expected to address preparedness, prevention, and risk mitigation for improving the resilience of the education system at all levels. Another key element in this exercise is the extent to which the plan recognizes and addresses significant gender differences and inequalities, such as physical disabilities, socio-economic disparities, and regional/geographical disparities that may affect access to quality education.[54]

Grants Portfolio Review

GPE provides up to $100 million in Education Sector Program Implementation Grants (ESPIG) to eligible developing countries to fund certain programs in their education sector plans.[55]

The ESPIGs are designed to strengthen national systems by ensuring that the funded programs are aligned with a country's ESP, and whenever possible, use the country's core systems, including domestic budgeting, treasury, procurement, accounting, audits, and reporting mechanisms.

As part of the team that conducts the annual portfolio review of the grants, I helped examine to what extent some of the grants are meeting their performance objectives. My contribution to this project included data aggregation and analysis of indicators such as number of teachers trained, schools built, learning materials and textbooks supplied, education management information system (EMIS) development supported, etc. It also included an analysis of the implementation modalities employed for each grant, to ascertain how these modalities are contributing to the strengthening of national systems.

---

[54] Guidelines for ESP preparation can be found here: http://www.globalpartnership.org/content/guidelines-education-sector-plan-preparation

[55] Information on the different grants awarded by GPE is available at: http://www.globalpartnership.org/funding/gpe-grants.

<u>Stakeholder Consultation for GPE 2020 Strategy</u>
In 2015, GPE adopted a new 5-year strategic plan (GPE 2020),[56] which aligns the partnership's vision with the post-2015 Sustainable Development Goal for education (SDG4) – calling for inclusive, equitable, quality education for all by 2030.[57] The process for the development of GPE 2020 included consultations with partners to solicit comments and contributions on the initial concept note. I worked with colleagues to organize the consultations and articulate the views of all stakeholders that were then used to inform the final plan.

<u>The Next GPE Replenishment to Mobilize Funding for Education</u>
Increased funding for education is critical to resolving the global education challenge, and one of the strategic objectives of GPE is to "mobilize more and better financing."[58] GPE periodically embarks on a global campaign (or replenishment) to raise additional funds for education financing and systems strengthening. The next replenishment will take place in early 2018, with the goal of GPE becoming a $2 billion a year organization by 2020.[59]

With increased funding during this period, GPE plans to support 89 developing countries to improve quality and access to education for 870 million children and youth. It will also be able to provide ESP implementation grants to 67 developing countries and encourage governments to increase domestic spending on education; as well as drive quality improvements through learning assessment support, and data improvements through strengthened education management systems. During this period, the partnership also plans to train 1.7 million teachers, build 23,800 classrooms, and distribute 204 million textbooks.

---

[56] Visit http://www.globalpartnership.org/content/gpe-2020-strategic-plan.
[57] See https://sustainabledevelopment.un.org/sdg4.
[58] GPE Strategy, http://www.globalpartnership.org/about-us/strategy.
[59] The next Replenishment will take place in late 2017 or early 2018. For additional information, visit http://replenishment.globalpartnership.org/en/home/.

Plans for the replenishment include a pledging event at which it is expected that developing country governments will announce their commitments to progressively increase domestic spending on education up to at least 20% of total public expenditure. I have had a great opportunity to work with colleagues to develop and roll out an approach that will be used for tracking and monitoring the progress that would be made by developing country governments towards the fulfillment of their replenishment pledges from 2018-2020.

Impact

Over the past decade, GPE has allocated more than $4.7 billion in financial support and technical assistance to strengthen education systems in 65 developing countries, with about half of its funds going to fragile and conflict affected countries in 2015. It has built classrooms and provided learning materials in the most vulnerable communities, supported teacher training, helped improve education management information systems (EMIS), and supported interventions to improve learning outcomes. In 2016, 29% of developing countries that receive GPE's support had a ratio of fewer than 40 students per trained teacher, up from 25% in just one year. In these countries, 64 million more children were in primary school in 2014 compared with 2002, and 73% completed primary school in 2014 compared with 63% about a decade earlier. The primary completion rates for girls increased from 56% in 2002 to 71% in 2014, while lower secondary completion rates increased from 38% to 50% during that period.[60]

Challenges

My work with GPE has given me a better appreciation of the scale of the global education challenge and a practical understanding of the centrality of systems strengthening to tackling the challenge. Some of the challenges militating against the expansion of quality educational opportunity are inadequate funding, lack of prioritization of education

---

[60] "GPE Replenishment Case for Investment," available at: http://www.globalpartnership.org/content/gpe-replenishment-2020-case-investment.

(especially for the poorest groups) in national planning and international development, and the unavailability of sound education management systems, including quality data for evidence-based planning, policy intervention, and monitoring.

Lessons Learned

Education funding is understandably accompanied by demands for results that are in some cases attributable to specific interventions. However, the process of building and strengthening education systems requires an understanding that the desired impacts will be achieved only if there is a sustained long-term engagement, unlike in other sectors such as agriculture where returns for investment may be visible within a one or two-year period.

Yet, there is a need to design effective tools to monitor progress. GPE has responded to this challenge by accompanying its strategic plan with a results framework for tracking progress on all of its goals and objectives.[61] Similarly, to address the dearth of quality country-level education data, GPE is not only providing funding for capacity building to develop data systems through its grants, it also requires countries applying for grants to meet certain data requirements. The organization also partners with other stakeholders, for example the UNESCO Institute for Statistics, to improve data collection.

Furthermore, the existence of internationally agreed-upon minimum standards for systems strengthening activities such as the preparation of credible sector plans is important. In the absence of minimum standards, countries tend to set subjective standards through the limited lens of their own contexts and needs, making it difficult to have an effective quality assessment mechanism that can be applied across the board. To resolve this challenge, GPE collaborated with UNESCO's International Institute for Education Planning (IIEP) in 2015 to

---

[61] See "GPE Results Framework for 2016-2020," available at http://www.globalpartnership.org/content/gpe-results-framework-2016-2020.

develop the *Guidelines for Education Sector Plan Preparation.*[62] These guidelines are now being used to assist countries in preparing credible sector plans that are not only adaptable to country contexts and needs, but also based on common denominators.

In conclusion, the complexity and scale of the global education challenge requires the kind of partnership that engenders cooperation and collaboration, mutual accountability, and openness to innovation at the global and national levels, all geared towards a holistic, not piecemeal, approach to improve systems and deliver results. Efforts to tackle this crisis have yielded some results, but much more needs to be done. Organizations like GPE that bring together multiple partners and stakeholders to improve systems and expand access to quality education, especially for the most vulnerable children, should be further empowered to do more.

Bio

Wilson Aiwuyor graduated from the International Education Policy program at the Harvard Graduate School of Education in 2012. He has worked for the Global Partnership for Education in Washington DC since 2014. He previously worked as education consultant for various organizations, including the Center for Universal Education at the Brookings Institution. From 2016 to January 2017, Wilson was a political appointee in the Obama Administration, where he served as a Special Assistant in the Office of Postsecondary Education at the U.S. Department of Education.

---

[62] http://www.globalpartnership.org/content/guidelines-education-sector-plan-preparation.

Advancing the Sustainable Development Goals: a Path to Meaningful Learning for All

By Lily Neyestani-Hailu

Goals and Work

Raised as a Baha'i with the notion that service to others is a primary source of fulfilment, I chose to study and work in the field of educational development in the hopes to contribute to more equitable and meaningful learning opportunities for all.

In my current capacity, serving as the education policy and planning cluster lead at the UNESCO Regional Office based in Dakar, Senegal, my work focuses on working with countries on integrating Sustainable Development Goal (SDG) 4 – Education 2030 into their national education planning. The new vision of quality education and equal learning opportunities for all, and throughout life, calls upon education systems to leverage all means and modes of learning to meet the diverse needs of all children, youth, and adults, including the millions of out of school children and youth, and those at risk of dropping out. This requires multiple and open learning systems with flexible pathways between them, and is accompanied with qualifications frameworks that also recognize all types of learning. The 2030 education vision, which expands beyond a focus on schooling towards learning for all, requires education reforms and planning that moves away from business as usual.

My work and that of my team revolves around three modalities, centered on the strengthening of national capacities in education planning and management in the context of SDG4-Education 2030: 1) analytical work and tools development; 2) knowledge production, management, and exchange; and 3) country support. In addition, I am actively involved in strengthening and facilitating inclusive and participatory sector dialogue, bringing together the diversity of national and regional actors and stakeholders involved in education planning, management, implementation, and monitoring. This includes governments at state and local levels, civil society, development partners, private sector, youth organizations, and researchers. The policy dialogue I have been involved in focuses on systems strengthening towards learning and skills that are meaningful for individuals and societies, and integrating them into life and work.

Our team's focus on skills development for life and work pushes for innovative approaches to facilitating the acquisition and certification of foundational and transversal skills and competencies from an early stage and throughout life. Our focus on equity and inclusion calls for targeted policies, strategies, and resource allocation within education sector plans focusing on girls and disadvantaged populations. The quality and relevance of learning and learning outcomes, with a renewed focus within the 2030 vision for education, is central to our work. Moreover, beyond promoting the cultivation of a broad range of knowledge and skills, our programs around Learning to Live Together (LTLT) include developing tools and materials for the teaching of global citizenship and education for sustainable development, providing learners the opportunity to contribute to more peaceful and resilient societies, and to foster values that promote unity in diversity.

Impact

Since graduating from the International Education Policy Program (IEP) program in 2001, I have supported policy work in 26 countries throughout Latin America and sub-Saharan Africa. The work I have been involved in, revolves around developing national capacities in the preparation of education sector plans and setting policy priorities and has directly and indirectly influenced millions of children, youth, and adults.

Challenges

In this context, the present-day challenges in education sector planning are 1) going beyond purely mechanical and technical planning processes, and 2) shifting away from the primary aim of getting everyone into formal schooling, to getting every child, youth, and adult to learn. Using the SDG4-Education 2030 framework for action as an opportunity to push the reflection to the country level, we work towards building national consensus around a change theory and working collectively towards reaching it. What kind of world do we want to live in? What citizens do we want for our country that will in turn contribute to global citizenship and to sustainable social and economic advancement for all? What knowledge, skills, and values will our learners thus need to acquire? What types of learning spaces should be offered? What alternative learning modes could be proposed? Formal, non-formal, and informal? How should entry and re-entry be possible at all ages and levels? How can learning systems include recognition and certification of all types of acquisition of knowledge, skills, and values, valid across nations?

Education planning and governance are therefore taking on a new spectrum. Among the challenges: inciting a rethinking and new construct of education around lifelong learning. In sub-Saharan Africa where I currently work, education systems are, for the most part, inherited from a colonial era with scarce efforts to seriously rethink education and to render it more relevant and meaningful, thus not allowing it to fully release its transformative power.

Furthermore, policy reforms and the resulting change in the education sector are long term. Unlike those who teach in a classroom or who work at the grass roots or community-level—who may witness the results and impact of their work—working at the macro/systems level, one learns to accept that change takes time to observe and that tireless efforts often lead to results that are less palpable. The distance between innovation/policy and impact/change is long.

This protracted sense of change has often been accompanied by political turmoil and interference. In addition to high turnover within ministry teams (challenges for capacity development), and high turnover of high-level officials (challenges of ownership and continuity), SDG4-related data and information challenges and national capacity gaps can also be testing.

Lessons Learned

Leading and coordinating the work of UNESCO in sub-Saharan Africa, in the area of sector-wide education policy and planning, has required me to seek a balance between the strengthening of national capacities in technical planning skills and techniques, with stimulating more profound dialogue at each stage of the policy and planning cycle. I find myself going beyond econometric analytical tools, financial simulation models, logical frameworks, and results matrices, to dialoguing and building consensus around the purpose and potential of education in transforming individuals and societies and creating global citizens who, beyond bearing a sense of responsibility, feel gratification in rendering service to others.

Leadership is not only individual but is also collective, requiring a shared vision for change and the collective conviction that we can reach it. It also requires being in constant learning mode, and building strategic partnerships. Education is transformational and is key to achieving all the Sustainable Development Goals. We therefore, cannot work in silos but must join forces across sectors (health, labor, energy, environment, justice…) in an integrated manner.

When facing challenges, we must look for opportunities: working with ministries of education across a number of countries opens the possibility for an exchange of experience and learning between countries, for better resource mutualization and greater cooperation, and ultimately cutting across superficial national barriers and borders towards greater and mutual understanding and appreciation.

Bio

Serving as UNESCO regional planning specialist for sub-Saharan Africa, Lily Neyestani-Hailu has extensive field experience working with education ministries on sector-wide policy and planning, including formerly in Latin America. Her work has primarily focused on systems strengthening, policy dialogue, and education planning and management capacity development. She graduated from the International Education Policy Program in 2001.

Advancing Educational Opportunity with the United States Agency for International Development (USAID)

By Kevin Roberts

Goals and Work

As an Education Development Foreign Service Officer with the United States Agency for International Development (USAID), my resources and goals often shift with changes in presidential administrations, US foreign policy, congressional budgets, agency priorities, mission strategies, mission leadership, host country relationships, and host-country priorities. By August 2017 I will have begun work in my fifth country in just over seven years (USA, Dominican Republic, Malawi, Pakistan, and South Africa). One needs to quickly adapt to ever-changing situations to promote sustainable education development – which includes access, quality, and relevance – amid a changing political and geographic landscape.

Soon after I started, USAID released a Global Education Strategy that further refined the funding earmarks allocated for international education development from Congress. Using basic education funding, we focus almost exclusively on early grade reading; with higher education funding, we focus on generating workforce skills relevant to a host country's development goals. We use either type of funding for education access in crisis and conflict environments. The Strategy keeps us from being overwhelmed by all the challenges and lets us focus on one thing and doing it well. It keeps us from endlessly discussing "what" to do and lets us instead talk in-depth about "how" to do it, which is often a much more interesting and productive conversation.

Obviously, access, quality, and relevance are intertwined in the same ways that improving pedagogy and materials, for example, can lead to better educational outcomes, a higher demand for education, and motivate those who otherwise would have left school to persist. This is the essence to USAID's Education Strategy.

I've found that in many countries where we work, almost every child will attend school at some point; however, the overwhelmed systems with overcrowded classrooms, lack of reading materials, poor management, and too few trained teachers no longer have an access problem as much as they have a "how the heck do we teach all these kids?" problem. So, on the whole, I would say that the majority of my efforts are toward quality and relevance as opposed to gross access.

To me, quality and relevance are the more interesting topics in which to spend my day. Access programs certainly have some advantages, since it is far easier to solve and for the most part we do so through school construction/improvement and scholarship programs. Also, 'access' issues are relatively easy to obtain political buy-in, show progress, and results. However, on the whole, they are resource intensive and one is easily bogged down by the operational elements of managing a USAID program such as impact evaluations, combating fraud, and investigating why a certain student did not receive their scholarship payment. While these are not the reasons why I entered into education development, in my experience, our access activities are linked with our quality/relevance so to me, the balance is very much worthwhile.

Working on quality and relevance is often more complex and difficult politically than access issues, but once established quickly grow to scale. Certainly we all know that improving reading is not as simple as creating a new set of textbooks for teachers to use -- it is showing the government the current reading levels and offering policy solutions for improvement, establishing national standards and benchmarks, creating new materials and teaching pedagogies, proving the concept, training in-service teachers, incorporating new pedagogies and materials into pre-service curriculum, training administrators, finding time in the school schedule, working with the teacher unions, assessing progress, and mobilizing the parents and communities. Each step has its own ministry staff and department(s), proponents and opponents, competing priorities, and varying levels of interest. Add in elections, coups, deaths, and the need for broad participation and incremental progress becomes piecemeal to great victories. I still believe that once these collective challenges are overcome; there is the possibility of making systematic impact on a large scale, especially if the improved materials and practices are integrated into the regional and national education systems.

Impact

Over the past year my work has directly impacted about 2.5 million children; over the next 10 years, it could impact an additional 13 million children.

Challenges

The most difficult leadership challenge that I face is creating the space for education to happen.

Creating that space comes in many forms. Internally, it seems that I am constantly defending the validity of education as a tool for development. While I have yet to meet a person who disagrees, I live in an environment of limited resources and competing development priorities. As new strategies are formulated or the latest congressional budget is built and tough decisions need to be made, the utility of education is scrutinized in comparison with other possible uses of US Government resources. This can be especially difficult as the time and effort it takes to improve the education system and see results is much longer than, for example, the results from a vaccination campaign. So I need to make sure that education remains a priority, or at least not left behind, as part of a comprehensive development package.

I also need to create space for our projects to respond to unforeseen circumstances they will encounter in the future. When I write an intervention, it may be for 3, 5, or even 7 years in the future. US Government contracting has not evolved to procure education outcome interventions, focusing instead on more tangible and measurable things like tables or airplanes. So I need to work with our contracting office to make sure they are comfortable and understand what USAID is buying while at the same allowing our future intervention the room to grow and react to the world it will be living in.

I create space for our implementers to do their work while they follow and adhere to the terms and conditions of their contracts at the same time. I have to be their advocate to USAID and USAID's advocate to them.

Last, I create space with host country governments to allow the interventions to be implemented. Sometimes that means working with them to create a policy and then supporting them in its realization. Sometimes it is working with them to create space in the school day, or even add time to the school day, so our interventions have the space to function.

Lessons Learned

I have learned that it is extremely important to try and understand the perspectives of the local people with whom you work. Understand their perspectives and goals and you will better understand what they want and how you can work toward mutual benefit.

A government official might want to show results toward a policy. A contracting officer needs something "real" to contract. A program officer might need a way to show progress toward strategic results.

If you can deliver on these things, give them an answer, find the place where we can satisfy all our binding rules, regulations, and policies, and help them be successful in their jobs, you will be able to create even more space for education to happen.

The views expressed in this essay are the author's own, and do not necessarily reflect the views of the United States Agency for International Development or the United States Government.

Bio

Kevin Roberts graduated from the International Education Policy Program at the Harvard Graduate School of Education in 2009. He has lived and worked in the education sector in seven different countries. He joined the USAID Foreign Service as an Education Development Officer in 2010. More importantly, he is the husband to Emilia and father to Kian, Elyse, and Estella.

Raising Literacy Levels in Latin America and the Caribbean

By Michael Lisman

Goals and Work

I began working for the US Agency for International Development (USAID) at its Washington, DC-based Bureau for Latin America and the Caribbean (LAC) in 2011. This followed a 5-year stint at a think-tank, also in DC, called the Inter-American Dialogue, which was one of my first jobs after graduating from International Education Policy (IEP) in 2005. That experience helped cement my professional focus on the LAC region and my career in education development assistance.

As a Peace Corps Volunteer in the Dominican Republic from 2000-2002, I forged personal connections to this work and to young individuals seeking to improve their educational opportunities. Today, I still feel a strong sense of connection to the field and the advancement of educational opportunities, though working from a systemic level.

Impact

From DC, and with frequent travel to the region, the work I do today is meant to improve educational outcomes at the primary and post-secondary levels in the poorest countries of the LAC region. A great deal of this is devoted to improving early-grade reading outcomes for children in the first years of primary school. This work has helped shape the teacher training, support systems, assessment practices, and national literacy policies in more than 10 countries. While this work sometimes lacks the direct personal connection to students that teachers enjoy, it has helped me in some way affect the educational opportunity and reading ability of over 5 million children.

Challenges

Working at a place like USAID is not without its unique and daunting challenges. A federal bureaucracy has its own language, culture, and limitations that take years to learn. Finding your place in such a system can be difficult and rarely offers immediate gratification. Learning where you can add the most value to the organization and to the real lives of the people you hope to impact is also an important challenge worth pursuing in order to maintain your passion for the work.

Lessons Learned

I have found that certain core principles and practices—some that were recommended to me during and after my time at HGSE—have helped me meet these and other challenges, and ultimately to be a more strategic leader. Here are a few simple yet extremely valuable ones that I have come to appreciate.

Situate yourself strategically. A career in international education development is cobbled together, and not always a straight line. In some cases we need to move opportunistically and based on timing, but being purposeful about our choices, we should ask ourselves key questions along the way. Do I want to work with people, or with ideas? Do I want to see short-term impacts on real people, or am I interested in systemic change that takes time, patience, and involves more uncertainty? Do I want to be on the grant making side, or am I comfortable fundraising? The answers to these questions may change, so it helps to ask them routinely. In just under 20 years of international development experience, I have worked for NGOs, private businesses, universities, and now in the public sector. It has been useful, not only to gain different experiences in this field, but it has helped me to map the overall development of the world in which we operate. Diverse experiences help you to instinctively know when to explain (or leave out) jargon or acronyms, when to go big picture and when to get into details, who to contact when and if expertise out of your circle is called for, and generally staying aware of what particular value you are adding to any given enterprise.

Be mindful of others. Just as we plot our own careers and experiences, we must be particularly understanding of the perspectives, interests and motivations of key actors in the field in which we work. Different individuals at ministries of education, political actors, NGO leaders, scholars, journalists, teachers, and union representatives each play an incredibly important role in their respective education systems, and in the success of any given education program funded by international donors. It is important to remember that they each have a particular job to do, probably care as much as if not more about children learning as you do, though it is not always clear to us what pressures or contexts they face. Being an effective leader in this field means being respectful, creating spaces for "informed dialogue," and creating strong working relationships based on human connections. These are efforts that should never be overlooked before pressing ahead with any donor-driven objectives. In fact, looking back on what I have seen work and what I have seen fail, I have come to believe that trusting relationships matter every bit as much as powerful ideas.

Do good work, and sleep well. In development assistance, we have come to understand that it is no longer enough to "do good," but rather, we must "do good well." This implies a commitment to efficiency, results, and measuring outcomes that can justify our efforts and investments. Indeed, we have a responsibility to be accountable to both our beneficiaries and the tax payers or others that fund our work. That said, there is a balance that we should seek to find. One certainly needs a passion for and commitment to advancing educational opportunity to choose this line of work, but I firmly believe that one should not have to be a martyr to do it, even as circumstances can become extremely demanding of time and resources. I feel strongly that the measure of our productivity should not be blood and sweat, but rather efficiency and accomplishment. If we can find the ways to keep life balanced, both our work and personal lives will be the better for it.

The views expressed in this essay are the author's own, and do not necessarily reflect the views of the United States Agency for International Development or the United States Government

---

Bio

Michael C. Lisman (IEP, 2005) is an Education Advisor with the US Agency for International Development (USAID), and an Ed.D. candidate at the Johns Hopkins University School of Education.

Improving Education in Myanmar by Enhancing Teacher Competency

By Jamie Vinson

Goals and Work

Yangon, Myanmar is a city of over 5.5 million, but when my husband and I moved there in July 2011, it felt like a small town. The wide streets were nearly empty, save for the occasional careening WWII-era bus and a few dilapidated taxis, almost as old. There was a sense of quiet and of time standing still – no cell phones, no corporate restaurant chains or mega shopping malls. When our first son was born within a year of our move, it didn't seem odd for strangers to ask to hold him because, in a small town, isn't everyone your neighbor?

But, of course, that small town charm veneered the restricted reality of life under military control. In terms of national education, that sense of going back in time was, at least in part, the result of an isolated and underfunded system. In most cases, the school buildings were there, but the policies and directives they operated under seemed designed to obstruct meaningful learning and to keep the country from joining the global community.

What we couldn't have predicted at that time was how quickly things would change. Within a year or two, shiny imported cars choked the streets, cranes dotted a rapidly developing skyline, and teenagers stared at smartphone screens while waiting at bus stops. "Small town" Yangon had developed into a complex and messy adolescent, struggling to establish its identity in the wider, more modern world. These changes carried significant implications for the kinds of skills, knowledge, and aptitudes young people needed to thrive and positively participate in a new global economy.

Acknowledging the pressing need to upgrade its education system, the Myanmar government committed to an ambitious reform agenda in 2012 through a Comprehensive Education Sector Review (CESR), designed to provide a foundational evidence base on which to plan and implement improvements in educational access and quality. These ongoing reforms, initiated under President U Thein Sein and now carried forward by the National League for Democracy (NLD) government – who came to power in 2015 through the first free and fair election in over 50 years – have achieved some important milestones, with much still remaining to be done. There is a new National Education Law, the Ministry of Education (MoE) has been restructured, education funding has increased significantly, and still-nascent, but long overdue curriculum reforms in basic education and teacher education are being put in place.

As an education specialist with the UNESCO Yangon office, my initial role was to coordinate the organization's support for the CESR, providing comparative analyses, capacity building, and technical advice in the areas of education policy, management and legislation, and liaising with other Development Partners to ensure complementary and coordinated support. Participating in this intensive national education reform process repeatedly fleshed out theoretical-sounding issues I had studied about at HGSE into a multi-dimensional, complex reality.

I learned first-hand about the foundational importance of stakeholder engagement, participatory consultation, and capacity-building. I experienced for myself how education policy development is equal parts a technical science and a diplomatic art. For the first time, I understood the compromises required in prioritizing how best to provide inclusive, quality education in a system that needs to reach almost 11 million school-aged children and employs over 380,000 teachers in more than 40,000 basic education schools, spread across a geographically, ethnically, and linguistically diverse country. It was exciting; it was, at times, maddening; it was hard work.

In 2014, while I was still with UNESCO Yangon, I narrowed my focus to pre-service teacher education – a sub-sector in Myanmar in urgent need of reform, given the estimated 25% of the teaching workforce lacking qualifications and the state of the country's Education Colleges, which struggle to address teacher trainee needs in the face of extremely limited budgets, outdated curriculum and textbooks, and inadequate teaching and learning resources. To address these critical challenges,

UNESCO, in partnership with the Government of Australia and the Ministry of Education, initiated the "Strengthening Pre-service Teacher Education in Myanmar" (STEM) project with a focus on developing key teacher policy frameworks, restructuring and redesigning the pre-service teacher education curriculum, and strengthening EC management practices and ICT capacity.

Impact

Now two and a half years into implementation, the STEM project is making significant impact at the central-level and across all 25 Education Colleges in Myanmar; it is raising momentum and awareness around the importance of teacher education and laying the groundwork for full realization of curriculum and management reforms to improve the quality of pre-service training in Myanmar.

When my family moved from Myanmar to Northern India in mid-2016, over 150 stakeholders had been involved in the Education College curriculum review and development process, and the continued implementation of the program will eventually impact the 15,000 teachers each year who pass through Myanmar's teacher education system.

Challenges

Implementing a project like STEM is certainly not without significant challenges, most of them related to the nature of working in a context like Myanmar during such a critical time of transition, from military rule to democracy and from relative global isolation to a commitment to join the international community. In my tenure with UNESCO Yangon, I worked with four different Ministers of Education, requiring constant consultation, as well as patience, in allowing for new structures to be put in place; there is no shortcut to reform. There remains a great need to strengthen capacity within the MoE in Myanmar to take on evidence-based reforms and to build understanding of the fundamentals of teacher education and curriculum development at all levels, making up for years of limited exposure to new strategies and techniques.

My team's response to these challenges focused on a redoubling of efforts and time to ensure authentic government ownership, quality products, and inclusive processes. The only way for the pre-service teacher education system in Myanmar – and, indeed, the education system as a whole – to be strengthened in a sustainable and meaningful way is if organizations such as UNESCO whole-heartedly commit to local ownership, doing whatever it takes to build the capacity required to produce quality products – and in an inclusive way that involves all stakeholders. I was honoured to be able to work toward this goal in Myanmar, where we were beginning to see the fruits of this approach in milestones such as the development of the first national teacher competency standards framework and the prioritization of teachers by the MoE, resulting in increased salaries and a commitment to reforming the way teachers are trained and supported.

Lessons Learned

Now working from our new home in the foothills of the Himalayas, where my husband is the Vice- Principal at Woodstock School, I am still involved with the STEM project in a consultant capacity and also take on freelance international education assignments for other organizations. A few months ago, I completed a Progress Report for the STEM project, which – in conjunction with my family's recent relocation, the shift to freelance consulting, and a new baby thrown in the mix – has led to reflection on the challenges and triumphs of working with a program like STEM and, on a more personal level, how I can best use what I've been given to impact the world in pursuit of inclusive, quality education for all.

It's been seven years since I graduated from HGSE and transitioned from teaching in a high school classroom to working in education development with the goal of improving equity and educational quality for underserved populations. In that time, I've worked for public and private organizations, including the Inter-Agency Network for Education in Emergencies (INEE), international schools, UNESCO, and Altamont Group, a private consulting firm.

However, in all my roles, from program management to curriculum development to program evaluation, I realize that I consider my contributions embedded within the greater global whole. I take my cues from standard-setting instruments and targets such as the Sustainable Development Goals, from the work of true thought leaders in international education, and from the guidance of local counterparts who are the true duty-bearers of education reform in their countries. From there, I get to work. I am an implementer and a foot soldier who, I sincerely hope, can set a positive and proactive tone and with enthusiasm, technical skill, and cross-cultural understanding get things done so that all children and youth can learn and contribute to their local and global communities.

Bio

Jamie is an education specialist with experience working for UNESCO, the Inter-agency Network for Education in Emergencies (INEE), and UNICEF as well as schools in Mozambique, India, Serbia and Myanmar. Her areas of expertise include education policy development, teacher education, education in emergencies, curriculum development, and monitoring and evaluation. Jamie holds a master's degree in International Education Policy from the Harvard Graduate School of Education and is a member of the UNICEF Education Global Talent Pool.

Ensuring Equal Access to Education in Myanmar

By Annika Lawrence

Goals and Work

A little over a year ago I took on a role for which I had been preparing myself since I became interested in education and international development. I joined UNESCO Myanmar's Capacity Development for Education (CapED) team as an education analyst. Working at a UN agency came with expectations of its bureaucracy as well as its strength in a network of leading experts and having influence at a large scale. I jumped into this role open-eyed, excited to take advantage of the good and work in intrapreneurial ways to mitigate the bad.

Our team supports the Myanmar Ministry of Education and the National Education Policy Commission in sector-wide education planning and management, and the promotion of the United Nations Sustainable Development Goal 4. This involves hosting workshops on these topics for ministry officials at the central and subnational levels, developing the country's first electronic education management information system, managing policy research projects, supporting the government in applying for global funding, and writing policy research briefs as needed.

Impact

In this type of work, we are so far removed from the student, and similarly from the timeline, when our work begins to have an effect, that it is difficult to assess how many students we affect through the system. There is also the fear that our work could be erased should there be a new administration. This distance between what we do on a daily basis and our purpose can be dangerous for losing a shared vision, but it also allows us to handle a different set of challenges that comes with policy and central government level work.

Challenges

The most common discussion around the research and design of our programmes is equitable access, pushing to ensure that all students have the same opportunity to get an education and also to succeed in it. But what does this look like in Myanmar? It could be temporary schools in Internally Displaced People camps, or students understanding what the teacher is saying on their first day of school because they are speaking the same language. It could also be that all students are receiving the necessary level of instruction to pass the test instead of having to pay extra private tuition fees, or ensuring there are paved roads to schools in remote areas.

I question what my role (as an outsider, at the invitation of the government) is in making sure this is prioritised. Education in Myanmar has become very politicized. It is one of the government's most important tools to create economic development and prosperity, and it is also a right that disadvantaged communities demand. Quality and equity often seem to be in competition for resources, when really they should be looked at as complementary. These two perspectives can shape very different ideas of education. Then, there are additional layers of challenges in reaching the most disadvantaged populations, many of whom are in areas of ongoing civil war, such as making the curricula relevant for them.

On the issue of relevance, I question who is the best education service provider for these diverse groups of children, and how more of them can benefit from the public system. Who will create the least amount of harm? NGOs? The government? Ethnic education organizations? Which organization has the mandate, capacity, and funding to achieve and sustain this? Working at the invitation of the government means navigating this fine line of working with their policies to be able to carry out the work you know is important, and still pushing important issues that may cause tension.

This long list of questions which I have been privileged to engage in discussion with my colleagues, other development partners, and government too often never leaves the room. On one level, consensus can be reached, but maybe the timing is not right, or approval needs to be requested from the highest levels of government. When our work is about planning what will help other people in the ministry set out their own plans for the education system, we can start to feel very far removed. The conviction of technical discussions make way for longer ones on logistics, but I know the importance of balancing the two to actually make a change.

Political constraints mean that people in the Ministry are pressured to show results quickly and fairly. Why children from disadvantaged communities should be prioritized is sadly sometimes a difficult thing to sell in this context. This is where the international conventions and treaties step in. I see reminding people of these external tools and how they can be used locally as one of our clear roles as outsiders. A power of the Sustainable Development Goals is that they provide an overarching commitment that pushes departments and ministries to collaborate with each other, pool statistics efforts, and justify decisions to their constituents. I've seen these Goals and other external forces, such as the Global Partnership for Education, move conversations forward that have been stuck in circles because of people having their hands tied.

The other challenge I face is on a more personal level. While I know I have the training, and experience to take command of what I do, I do not always have the confidence that should match these skills. This stems from needing to figure out many work challenges in silo through my own research, and by trial and error as a last resort. In attempts to avoid failure, I sometimes overly seek consensus rather than backing my opinions, even when I know they are strongly evidence-based. As I advance in my career, I am working to break this habit because I know others look to depend on me for advice. I remember to use the very strategies from the youth development programs that I designed for others: encouraging myself to learn from failure rather than shying away from it, setting realistic goals, and using my own management style instead of imitating others.

Lessons Learned

I've found it important to remember that education is a special field where there is an abundance of opportunities with which you can engage. This may be through work, but getting out of these circles, to zoom out and reflect on why you're passionate about education, is not to be underestimated. Over the last year, volunteering with a non-formal school teaching English and global citizenship has helped me to stay motivated and started to fill in the big picture of what education in Myanmar looks like. Connecting directly with six students to support their plans for their small communities' future is just as meaningful as influencing policy that will shape the central education system for millions. Both processes are slow and the full impact in a decade is unknown.

Bio

Annika Lawrence graduated from the International Education Policy program at the Harvard Graduate School of Education in 2016. She has worked in private international education in China, as an education analyst with UNESCO Myanmar, and is starting as a Young Professional at the Asian Development Bank in the Southeast Asia department and Human and Social Development division.

Using Evidence to Advance Educational Opportunity

By Nicholas Moffa

Goals and Work

As part of the Education Division at the Inter-American Development Bank (IDB), I have the opportunity to advance educational opportunity throughout Latin America and the Caribbean (LAC) as an analyst on the *Centro de Información para la Mejora de los Aprendizajes* (CIMA) team. The goal of CIMA, as a joint initiative of the Education Division and regional governments, is to fill the data gap in the region and promote comprehensive and evidence-based analysis in order to guide the design and implementation of education policies and programs. The initiative consists of four distinct components: an online statistics portal, a series of publications, regional work groups, and an institutional strengthening strategy.

In my specific role, I have the chance to contribute to all four components of the CIMA initiative. My work on the online statistics portal consists of compiling spreadsheets of disaggregated data (i.e., by gender, socioeconomic status, year, etc.) for use by Ministries of Education, National Institutes of Statistics and Evaluation, education specialists, think tanks, and researchers. I analyzed and wrote a series of one-pagers entitled "Did You Know?" meant to introduce the online portal to a broader audience, touching on topics ranging from learning assessment results to early childhood education access. I continue to author a variety of short analytical brochures on the current state of educational opportunity in LAC using PISA results and other indicators available in CIMA. Additionally, I help coordinate the regional work groups and work together with my colleagues at the IDB to encourage countries to: a) strengthen their systems of data collection and analysis; b) participate in regional and international learning assessments; and c) evaluate the impact of education reforms at all levels.

Impact

I firmly believe that in my role at the Inter-American Development Bank, I am helping to expand access to education, improve education

313

quality and increase the relevance of what is taught both inside and outside the classroom throughout the LAC region. While the direct influence of my work on learners may be minimal, the indirect impact is exponentially larger. While the online portal highlights many different indicators for which a large amount of data is available (e.g. access and descriptive indicators like number of schools, total school-age population, and net and gross attendance rates across various age groups and education levels), it also underscores the substantial number of indicators where the data pool becomes noticeably thinner. While the current impact of the statistics portal and the current publications may be limited (the portal only officially launched in early 2017), their potential only grows as the regional work groups gain traction and the institutional strengthening strategy takes root. Though it may sound extreme, I believe the work the IDB's Education Division does has the potential to impact the lives and learning experiences of millions of children throughout Latin America and the Caribbean.

Challenges

One of the most difficult leadership challenges I have faced during my time at the Inter-American Development Bank has been attempting to generate consensus around how best to organize and streamline efforts to improve access to education and education quality throughout Latin America and the Caribbean. While it is clear that the vast majority of people who work in international education policy are deeply engaged in the work in order to improve the educational opportunities of children and learners, I have learned that the intelligent, passionate people in the field frequently disagree about how best to do so. One clear example of this manifested itself in the planning and organizing of a meeting of national evaluation agencies throughout the region, surrounding the implementation and future of the IDB's CIMA initiative. While the planning initially appeared straightforward, critical questions quickly arose. What should be the role of a regional intergovernmental organization like the IDB in the development of education policy? Should it serve as a neutral convening body or an experienced research organization with a nuanced policy perspective? How should future iterations of the statistics portal be determined (i.e., which indicators should be continued, which should be dropped, which should be added)? Should the first meeting of the regional work group on education quality continue the work of previous networks, or begin anew?

While at first blush these questions may appear unrelated to the intricacies of impact evaluations, randomized control trials, and contextualized policy transfer, the answers to questions of this sort can determine the effectiveness of policymaking at the national and regional level. Multilateral organizations like the IDB can offer extraordinary support to national governments when it comes to financing innovative new projects and reforms, offering expertise on the effectiveness of distinct education interventions, and/or convening diverse work groups from across the region. Nevertheless, the aforementioned leadership challenge clearly demonstrated the importance of the IDB remaining constantly alert to the ever-shifting nature of policy goals and map of policymakers and influencers across the region.

Lessons Learned

In conclusion, I learned two key lessons from my work generating interest and organizing work groups around the IDB's CIMA initiative. First, I learned the immense value of mapping out all of the actors involved in policymaking in a particular context, nation, or region prior to acting. An in-depth understanding of the roles and interests of the different people, organizations, and governments that can effect policy change in a given context proves invaluable in the generation and continued cultivation of consensus surrounding improving education quality. Not only does this ensure that your organization places itself in the best possible position to effect true change; it also provides each actor with an empowering space where they can maximize their strengths. Second, I learned the value of defined flexibility. International education policy is a dynamic field, especially when it comes to the sometimes-high levels of turnover in governments, organizations, and agencies (many of which frequently have competing, if not incompatible, agendas). This requires a base level of flexibility in order to adapt to changing contexts and environments. Nevertheless, the one constant on which the vast majority of those in the field can agree is that the end goal should be the advancement of educational opportunity for learners everywhere. While one should not compromise that point, debate and disagreement should be welcomed, almost everywhere else, in order to ensure the highest levels of access to and quality of education for all.

Bio

Nicholas Moffa graduated from the International Education Policy Program at the Harvard Graduate School of Education in 2016. He currently works as an Analyst in the Education Division at the Inter-American Development Bank (IDB). Prior to joining the IDB, he worked as a research assistant with the International Commission on Financing Global Education Opportunity at the United Nations and as a consultant for UNICEF coding early childhood education standards.

Rethinking Assessment to Focus Governments' Attention on what Matters

By Manuel Cardoso

Goals and Work

My work for the past twenty years has revolved mainly around the large-scale assessment of learning outcomes in developing countries. It has not focused on access, quality, or relevance, but on equity, a concept often erroneously reduced to differences across groups in access to schooling. Equity entails including everyone in the educational process, but also making sure that everybody, regardless of their background, learns.

From 1996 to 1999 I helped establish the national assessment system in Uruguay, my home country. I resumed this work from 2000 to 2004 after obtaining my Ed.M. as part of HGSE's first cohort of students in the International Education Policy program. Our work helped dispel the myth that Uruguayan private schools, which charge a fee, outperformed their public counterparts, which are free, by showing that controlling for socio-economic status of the student body explained the difference away. But how could policy ameliorate these inequities? Although Uruguay performs relatively well as compared to its region in international large-scale assessments such as LLECE[63] and PISA,[64] revealed two challenges: academic performance is strongly associated with socio-economic status, and the school day is shorter than in other countries. "Full-time" public schools had been created to address this issue. In 2004, I showed that from 1996 to 1999, full-time schools had improved their performance both in terms of quality and equity as compared to other urban public schools (Cardoso 2004). Since then, the number of these schools has increased substantially.

---

[63] Laboratorio Latinoamericano de Evaluación de la Calidad Educativa, conducted with support from UNESCO.

[64] Program for International Student Assessment, conducted by OECD (Organisation for Economic Co-operation and Development)

In 2005 I joined the UNESCO Institute for Statistics (UIS) in Montreal, where I worked until 2014 as Program Specialist. During my first two years there I did not work on assessments, as UIS's focus was still on access to education. However, I worked mostly on areas that deviated from the relatively narrow focus on mainstream formal programs for children, adolescents and youth.

In 2006, I led UIS's first ever data release on participation in Technical and Vocational Education and Training (UNEVOC 2006; Cardoso 2009a; Cardoso 2009b). TVET is a traditionally overlooked stream that may do a better job at reaching underprivileged adolescents and retaining them in the system, as compared to general education. At the same time, it can equip adolescents and youth with marketable skills to enter the labor force in accordance with their life goals. A functioning TVET system, based on robust data, has important equity repercussions.

In 2007 I led UIS's first ever release of educational attainment data on adults, developing the relevant indicators (Bruneforth et al. 2006; UIS 2008). Education data on adults is another area that receives less attention than it should. As schooling systems in developing countries have now been expanding for decades, children and youth are more likely to attend school than their parents and grandparents. In addition, among those older generations, there are bigger divides along gender, location, and socio-economic status lines. Therefore, once again, good data on educational attainment may help shed light on inequities in schooling and on the need to ameliorate these. This applies not just to the "school-age population," but to entire nations, including the people who have already become, or are in the process of becoming, active citizens and contributors to the economy and the community.

By 2007, my work on the educational attainment of adults, combined with my background in large-scale assessment in Uruguay, led to my involvement in the Literacy Assessment and Monitoring Program (LAMP). This was a household-based assessment of the literacy and numeracy skills of adults in developing countries. Initially conceived as an adaptation of IALS (International Adult Literacy Survey) and spell out what this stands for ALL (Adult Literacy and Life Skills), it also added new elements that better met the needs of this new group of countries, notably a new data collection tool called "Reading Components." This new instrument, which elicited oral answers from the respondents, focused on the reading abilities of those adults that are still unable to read fluently and with comprehension. Precisely because the responses were oral, this instrument could accurately assess adults' reading skills, even if these adults had not yet learnt to write. This was a significant advantage over traditional "paper and pencil" assessments. It reached underprivileged adults, which again had important consequences in terms of equity.

By 2014, my experience with LAMP led to a new project that attempted to build consensus among the practitioners and funders of an emerging class of measurements: the oral assessment of early reading skills in developing countries. By bringing together the likes of RTI (the ones behind EGRA and EGMA) and Save the Children (the creators of Literacy and Numeracy Boost) with citizen-led assessments such as ASER (Annual Status of Education Report) and Uwezo, among many others, we were able to compile a number of experiences across a wide range of regions, and draw on some important lessons learnt. This effort lent credence to the feasibility of assessing reading in early grades in a globally comparative manner. This may have contributed to the adoption of SDG indicator 4.1.1, which entails the assessment of children's reading and mathematics proficiency not only at the end of primary and lower secondary, but also in grades 2 or 3. The focus on early grades and oral assessment has obvious equity implications as well: it reaches children at an early stage when they are less likely to have dropped out of school, and once again it assesses their reading skills although they may not have yet learnt to write. The output of this project was the e-book *Understanding What Works in Oral Reading Assessments* (UIS 2016).

That volume also includes an article that I co-wrote as part of my new position as Learning Specialist at UNICEF, where I started in 2014. The article explores the possibility of developing a new module for UNICEF's Multiple Indicator Cluster Survey (MICS) that would assess foundational reading and mathematical skills among 7-14 year-olds. This module was developed with inputs from other agencies that focus on oral reading assessments, including the PAL Network, RTI and Save the Children (Cardoso and Dowd 2016).

After being validated through field trials in Belize, Costa Rica, Ghana and Kenya in 2015-16, the module is now starting to be implemented in a small number of countries as part of MCIS 6. This module departs from school-based assessments in two ways: since it is household-based, it can reach students who are not enrolled in school or do not attend regularly; additionally, it benefits from all the household background information collected by this survey. Once more, this increases the availability of information for analyses that focus on equity concerns.

Impact

Given the global nature of my work, I might be tempted to overestimate its impact in terms of the number of learners affected by it. I must admit, however, that whatever impact it may have is indirect and therefore cannot readily be compared to the much deeper ways in which learners are shaped by those educators who work in direct contact with them.

Challenges

First, not all sources of data on learning outcomes enjoy the same level of credibility among the global community. This perception may occasionally be justified, but prejudice may also exist against data produced by developing countries. This poses a conundrum: the countries with the most room for improvement in education systems are perceived, sometimes erroneously, as lacking the required data to monitor their own progress.

Second, and perhaps more importantly, we should not take a simplistic or naïve approach to comparability. We must be aware that the comparability of education systems does not precede our methodological devices, but is created by them (Cardoso and Steiner Khamsi 2017); the development of these devices cannot be entirely reduced to pure technical rationality.

Lessons Learned

As academics, we sometimes tend to associate a higher degree of technical complexity with a more sophisticated understanding of educational phenomena. But in my view, the more general lesson to be learnt is that technocracy will always have great limitations. Only an approach that integrates political, cultural and historical considerations can have any expectation of success.

References

Bruneforth, Michael, Manuel Cardoso, Albert Motivans, John Pacifico and Yanhong Zhang. 2006. *Education Counts. Benchmarking Progress in 19 WEI Countries. World education indicators-2006.* UNESCO Institute for Statistics. Montreal, Canada.

Cardoso, Manuel. 2004. Calidad y equidad en las escuelas de tiempo completo: un análisis de sus resultados en las evaluaciones estandarizadas de 1996 y 1999. *Prisma*, (19), 171-190. Montevideo, Uruguay.

Cardoso, Manuel. 2009. "The challenges of TVET global monitoring." *International Handbook of Education for the Changing World of Work*, 2053-2065.

Cardoso, Manuel. 2009. "Statistical Overview of TVET across Educational Levels." *International Handbook of Education for the Changing World of Work*, 2095-2161.

Cardoso, Manuel and Amy Jo Dowd. 2016. "Using Literacy Boost to inform a global, household-based measure of children's reading skills." In *Understanding what works in oral reading assessments*. UNESCO Institute for Statistics. Montreal, Canada.
http://uis.unesco.org/en/news/understanding-what-works-oral-reading-assessments

Cardoso, Manuel, and Gita Steiner-Khamsi. 2017. The making of comparability: education indicator research from Jullien de Paris to the 2030 sustainable development goals. *Compare: A Journal of Comparative and International Education*, 47(3), 388-405. London, UK.

Guadalupe, Cesar and Manuel Cardoso. 2011. Measuring the continuum of literacy skills among adults: educational testing and the LAMP experience. *International Review of Education*, *57*(1-2), 199-217.

Ravela, Pedro, Beatriz Picaroni, Manuel Cardoso, Tabare Fernandez, Dina Gonnet, Graciela Loureiro and Oscar Luaces. 1999. *Estudio de los factores institucionales y pedagógicos que inciden en los aprendizajes en escuelas primarias de contextos desfavorecidos en Uruguay*. MECAEP – ANEP/BIRF – UMRE. Montevideo, Uruguay.

UIS (Ed.). 2008. *Global Education Digest 2008: Comparing Education Statistics Across the World*. Institut de statistique de l'UNESCO. Montreal, Canada.

UNEVOC. 2006. *Participation in Formal Technical and Vocational Education and Training Programmes Worldwide*. Bonn, Germany.

The opinions expressed in this document are the author's own and do not necessarily reflect the policies of UNICEF or any other agency.

Bio

Manuel Cardoso joined the initial IEP cohort at HGSE (2000), after helping establish the national assessment system in his native Uruguay. He worked at UIS for ten years. He is currently a Learning Specialist at UNICEF in New York, and a Ph.D. student at Columbia University's Teachers College.

Shaping Global Education Policies with Ministries and Governments

By Myra M. Khan

Goals and Work

One of the main goals I have adopted since working at the World Bank is to ensure that the policies created in education are producing the outcomes we want. I currently work in the Educational Global Practice at the World Bank, more particularly in the Global Engagement and Knowledge team (we call ourselves GEAK). The GEAK team at the World Bank focuses on working across all the regions at the World Bank, through providing key research and different themes in education to our partner countries. Our aim is to do work that is relevant for policy and practice, and will be key in enabling the World Bank to meet its Education For All 2020 strategy.

All of our work is done in conjunction with countries' governments, so our teams always engages with the Education Ministries of the countries we work in, which is quite exciting. The potential for scale is enormous, as we usually support the government in designing and implementing system-wide policy changes.

What this research tangibly looks like, however, varies from country-to-country, but I will give two examples. First, a project I am currently working on is in Lao PDR. This project is focused on looking at how the education ministry, and more generally, the Government of Lao PDR, is delivering public education. We conducted an in-depth quantitative survey with dozens of indicators, gathering information on school facilities, teacher background and knowledge, school leadership, community participation in education, and many more.

This analysis was conducted as the first step in a three-year project the Government of Lao PDR is working on with the Global Partnership for Education, trying to improve the access to and quality of education in the whole country.

Second, another project I just finished working on was in the West African country of Guinea-Bissau. There, the focus was on improving school-based management practices, and how the government can work to improve on currently existing policies. Using qualitative methods, we conducted an analysis to see what the School Autonomy and Accountability policies in place were, and provided recommendations to the government about what areas to improve in order to have better school management.

The work I do focuses on ensuring that the high-level education systems are making the best possible choices for improving and advancing educational access, quality and equity, and working with the ministries of education in various countries in order to do so.

Impact

It is hard to estimate my impact given that the World Bank works with so many countries, and with the education ministries. Usually, when we have an engagement, the policies are being recommended for the entire student population of that country, or with a focus on primary or secondary education. Giving an estimate to say thousands of children have been affected by my work alone, would be unfair to say. We all work on teams and with teams that support us. Since I am not based in schools or directly have learners I work with, all my work indirectly affects students in the countries we work with. However, we do know that thousands, if not millions of children, are affected by the policies that the government eventually creates, which are in part aided by the advice of the World Bank.

Challenges

Given the nature of my role, which involves a lot of counterparts and stakeholders, there is always a certain amount of unpredictability. The challenges faced are not necessarily milestones that you can see, but rather what you do not see. There are times when projects have to be dropped – that have possibly been worked on for years – because governments change, or priorities change.

Further, I think management of time and resources is also challenging. Almost everything I work on at the World Bank has a big "ASAP" deadline stamped on it. Prioritizing and understanding how to manage multiple deadlines, as well as timelines that governments and other teams have is important. There are many pieces that need to fit together to get the work done.

Lessons Learned

The main thing I learned was to remember constantly that the reason we are all in this work is for children. This is why I started working in education, and have dedicated my life to it. Working at a big bureaucratic organization will sometimes make you forget that. There is a lot of red tape around the work we do, and moreover, even my own professional development and type of contract. Centering yourself, taking a deep breath, and remembering the mission behind all this work puts me in the right mindset to approach work.

There are some more practical approaches I now use, as well. First, I learned that it is just as important to have a 'balcony view' as it is to have a 'dancefloor view.' Getting caught up in technical details is good, but only if you are able to keep the big picture of the project in mind. Second, but connected to the first, is a tool that I came to learn from teachers that I worked with in my previous role at Teach For Pakistan, which came from the Teach For All teaching as a leadership model: backwards planning. While many teachers would say this works well with setting goals for your students over the year, I truly believe it can come into use in any professional or personal setting. Ensuring that you set a long-term goal, and have short terms that lead up to it, greatly helps with organization and planning, whether you are trying to enhance a project, or your own career and professional development.

The opinions expressed in this essay are the author's own and do not necessarily reflect the policies of the World Bank or any other agency.

Bio

Myra M. Khan is an international education specialist with 6 years' experience that spans over South Asia, Latin America, the Middle East, West Africa, Eastern Europe and South East Asia. She currently consults for the World Bank on education in numerous countries including Lao PDR, Guinea Bissau, Kosovo, Serbia, Libya, and the Philippines over various education themes. Myra completed her Ed. M. in International Education Policy in 2015 from HGSE, and holds a B.A. Hons. In Politics, Philosophy and Economics. Prior to that, she worked at Teach For Pakistan where she supported the CEO on a number of projects from business development to strategic planning.

Building Public-Private Partnerships to Improve Education Systems

By Juliana Guaqueta Ospina

Goals and Work

During one of our final classes while I was a student at the Harvard Graduate School of Education, Fernando Reimers asked a small group of us what we saw ourselves doing 10 years later. Without exactly knowing where I would end up after graduation, my answer was that I wanted to work at the intersection of public and private sectors to help improve education systems and expand opportunities. I firmly believed, and still do, that education systems have much to gain from systematically partnering with private sector players that can contribute expertise in innovation, as well as operational and financing capabilities. I have been fortunate to do exactly this since graduation. I work at the International Finance Corporation (IFC), the private sector arm of the World Bank Group, where we invest debt or equity in private education providers that complement the role of public institutions and help expand access to quality education opportunities. We support institutions that offer scalable education services at an affordable cost for the growing middle class in emerging markets, for whom education is a pathway to gainful employment and social mobility. Our clients use the growth capital we provide to accelerate their growth plans, improve quality, expand program offerings, and incorporate innovative practices and technology to expand their reach.

One reason that I am passionate about my work is because the global education gap is enormous and governments alone have not been able to address it effectively. At the same time, private provision in many emerging markets has grown dramatically and helped raise overall enrollment rates. This is partly due to the fact that too often the financial and operating capacity of public systems is constrained, but also because families are seeking higher quality education and are voting with their wallets. In Africa, for example, around 21 percent of children and youth are being educated in the private sector and this proportion is likely to increase by 2021.[65] In Latin America, the market share of private higher education institutions rose from 43 to 50 percent between the early 2000s and 2013.[66] Through our work, we want to help raise the bar for the private sector to make a meaningful and sustainable contribution to expand the portfolio of learning choices available to students. That said, the private sector is not a panacea and we need to engage collaboratively with governments to encourage them to create optimal regulatory environments for private providers to expand access, with accountability, and to ensure they deliver relevant, equitable, and quality educational experiences.

Impact

Over five million learners have been reached by IFC between 2005 and 2015. This number is a drop in the ocean when placed in the context of the number of children that are out of school (124 million),[67] are in school but cannot read or write (250 million),[68] or youth that are unemployed (80 million, or 40 percent of total unemployment).[69] While in many ways the point of these investments is to create a demonstration effect in education markets and raise standards for others to follow, we are aiming at doubling our portfolio (currently around $700 million in active commitments) in the next 5 years thus, hopefully raising in a significant way, the number of learners that will be impacted by our investments. We have also expanded our areas of focus from traditional schools and universities, to include models that reach students through education technologies, and shorter—more relevant—formats that enable lifelong learning experiences. I think these are powerful options

---

[65] Caerus, Oxford Analytica, Parthenon EY, 2017. The Business of Education in Africa.

[66] World Bank 2017. At a Crossroads: Higher Education in Latin America and the Caribbean

[67] UNESCO 2015. POLICY PAPER 22 / FACT SHEET 31

[68] UNESCO 2012. Technical Note Prepared for the Education For All Global Monitoring Report 2012

[69] World Economic Forum 2017. The Challenge of Youth Unemployment

for learners to pursue their interests, open new employment opportunities, and advance their careers. For example, we invested in Coursera, a global Massive Online Open Content (MOOC) platform that has pushed the boundaries of online education. We also invested in Andela, a coding boot-camp in Sub-Saharan Africa that helps develop technology talent. Models like these help us expand substantially the number of students reached directly and indirectly. When we invested in Coursera in 2013 their user base was 2.3 million students and they have grown tenfold to reach 24 million users by the end of 2016, half of which are in emerging markets. Andela, on the other hand, is training 400 developers already from a wider pool of 60,000 applicants.[70]

Challenges

As a specialist at IFC, I analyze education systems where the private sector has a meaningful role, help develop new investment opportunities, oversee new projects, articulate development impact, and highlight main risks and issues. This role allows me the opportunity to lead by providing essential contributions to investment decisions, and challenges me to remain at the top of my game. Even though education is seen as being a slow-moving sector, it attracts sharp minds and passionate souls that are constantly looking for ways to improve the status quo, develop new research to understand what works and how, and come up with entrepreneurial approaches to improve teacher effectiveness and learning outcomes. In this context, I am constantly challenged to be a life-long learner, keep up with developments in education research and practice, look outside of the industry for fresh ideas, be a strong communicator, and constantly hone my analytical skills.

In large organization like the World Bank Group, decision-making tends to be consensus-driven and it takes a significant amount of teamwork across different types of professions, seniority levels, personalities, and cultures. In this type of environment, I have been challenged to be an innovator from within and try to move the organization in new and promising directions and, at the same time, not be afraid to get 'no' for an answer. I have also been challenged to take

---

[70] Wired Magazine. May 2017

leadership roles in a relatively junior position. Prior to joining IFC, I worked at the World Bank where I co-authored a publication on the Role and Impact of Public-Private Partnerships in Education, which examines ways in which governments would leverage the non-state sector to meet education goals. I also participated in the development of the World Bank Education Strategy 2020 that shifted the overarching goal of our work from schooling to *learning*. These have been unique opportunities to help define priorities in the global education development agenda and parameters that guide our interactions with governments and private sector partners. Through these experiences, I was challenged to use my analytical skills and passion to develop expertise on-the-go, and contribute with fresh thinking to extend the frontiers of knowledge.

Lessons Learned

Reflecting on the opportunities that I have had and decisions that I have made since my graduation from Harvard, it is clear that the professional and leadership paths have not always been straightforward. I did know the general direction of work that I wanted to take, but I could not always find a job description that got me excited, nor I can predict accurately the evolution of my professional trajectory. This has pushed me to seize every moment and find creative ways to generate work prospects through which I can fulfill my vision to expand education opportunities in unique ways. In this sense, I have learned to trust my intuition and follow through. I have been extremely fortunate to find an incredible group of colleagues and friends who have nurtured and guided me in honing my skills, making smart choices, and encouraging me to compromise when needed. It is essential to help each other and enable individual and collective leadership to address the urgent task of improving education systems. Harvard gave me a passionate and articulate voice and I am using it to hopefully make the world a better place.

My professional experiences have also reinforced the notion that education is a complex sector, and while most people would agree that learning is central to the development of individuals and nations, there are heated disagreements about how to go about it. In this sense, it is essential to inform investment and policy decisions with the growing research base, in order to optimize the allocation of resources and prioritize evidence over hype, ideology, or political inclination. That said, it is important to follow one's passion and not let detractors discourage you too quickly.

Bio

Juliana Guaqueta Ospina is an Education Specialist at the International Finance Corporation of the World Bank Group where she advises on education investments in Latin America and the US. Prior to joining IFC, Juliana worked at the World Bank where she co-authored several publications on global education policy issues. Juliana has a master's degree in International Education Policy from Harvard University (2007) and a Bachelors in Finance and International Relations from Universidad Externado de Colombia.

CONSULTING

Improving Access, Quality, and Relevance of Education for Primary and Secondary Students in Middle and Low Income Countries

By Ana Florez

Goals and Work

I graduated from the International Education Policy (IEP) Program at the Harvard Graduate School of Education (HGSE) in 2004. A few weeks before commencement I received a job offer to work for an international nonprofit organization and decided to stay in the United States (US) to begin my international development career instead of my native Colombia. This unexpected opportunity to work in the US changed my life. Today, after many years of multiple immigrant visas, I am proud to be a new US citizen, leading a successful multimillion-dollar education portfolio at FHI 360, one of the largest human development organizations in the country.

For more than 12 years, I have managed education programs focused on expanding access to education and improving the quality of education for both primary and secondary students in more than ten low- and middle-income countries worldwide. These programs have been funded by government agencies and private corporations, including the US Agency for International Development (USAID), Hess Corporation, the International Initiative for Impact Evaluation (3ie), and the Millennium Challenge Corporation (MCC), among others. In my current role as Director of Post-Primary Education, I oversee a portfolio that includes secondary education projects in Equatorial Guinea and Guatemala; tertiary education projects in Guatemala, Honduras and Jamaica; and research activities in El Salvador, the Dominican Republic, and Colombia. My portfolio also includes post-primary education activities in Afghanistan, Malawi, Kosovo, and Brazil.

Today's youth face complex challenges as they transition through life's developmental stages and prepare to find gainful employment, navigate real-world obstacles and opportunities, and contribute to society. I aim to increase educational opportunities for students in the developing

335

world by strengthening connections across all stages of the education cycle—from primary education through higher education—and by emphasizing the importance of merging secondary education with the realities of youth development, including the physical, cognitive, social, emotional, and moral dimensions.

The main way I have worked to advance education opportunity is by partnering with ministries of education to implement country-wide reform efforts aimed at improving access, quality, and relevance of education and aligning education policies that meet students' needs, labor market requirements, and societal demands. While working closely with ministries, I have drawn from my previous experience as a senior official within Colombia's Ministry of Education, where I developed a keen understanding of the challenges and opportunities that policymakers face when trying to provide opportunities to all students, especially disadvantaged populations.

My experience has taught me that a key way to ensure opportunities for all is through education system strengthening, focusing on the classroom level, school level, and central system level. For example, in my current work in Equatorial Guinea, El Salvador, and Guatemala, our goal is to help ministries increase enrollment and graduation rates while reducing dropouts in lower secondary school. To do this, we strengthen education quality and relevance by working directly with teachers at the classroom level to build both content knowledge and pedagogy using the Active Schools Model, which is an adaptation of the *Escuela Nueva* model from Colombia.

At the school and system levels, we promote professional learning communities for teachers and engage ministry advisors as pedagogical coaches for teachers. In Jamaica, Honduras, and Guatemala, we work at the school level by building the capacity of local community colleges and universities to increase access for disadvantaged youth so they may complete degree programs that equip them with skills demanded by the labor market. In Colombia, El Salvador, and the Dominican Republic we advocate to bridge the skills gap between educators and employers by promoting a common language around socio-emotional, cognitive, and technical skills that secondary students must have to succeed in school and life. This work involves collaboration and strengthening across all levels of the education system.

Impact

Over the last year, the projects on which I have provided direct technical assistance have influenced an estimated 21,000 secondary education students in El Salvador and more than 100,000 primary education students in Equatorial Guinea. During my 12 years managing education programs, I have likely influenced over 400,000 students across multiple projects.

Challenges

I have faced two primary leadership challenges over the last 12 years: (1) navigating unexpected changes and (2) ensuring sustainability of interventions. Working closely with ministries of education is complex and involves balancing political timelines with activity timelines, not to mention competing demands and priorities within the ministry. Changes in ministry staff can lead to unexpected delays, or demands in activity implementation, and may result in a complete re-design of a capacity building approach or intervention. These unexpected changes, which are largely out of the control of project implementers, have direct implications on our ability to effectively partner with students, teachers, schools, and ministries.

In addition to adapting to unexpected changes, a continuous challenge I face is ensuring that program interventions are sustained and continued by local actors after projects officially end. This challenge is particularly difficult given the short life span of most projects (typically no more than five5 years) and the fact that building trust and buy-in among local stakeholders takes time. The ability to sustain program interventions is further complicated by the withdrawal of program resources at the close of a project, which highlights the importance of investing in capacity development of local actors and introducing cost-effective approaches to educational reform.

Lessons Learned

I have learned that passion, perseverance, and patience are three key assets needed to effectively deal with challenges that arise. Passion refers to my personal commitment to ensuring a quality education for as many students as possible around the world. This passion is the force that drives my day-to-day work and helps me weather unexpected challenges. My passion for education also fuels my ability to persevere through challenges until I have found solutions that meet the needs of ministries, funders, and most importantly, students and educators. Perseverance is not only the ability to keep working, but the ability to also be creative, innovative, and forward-thinking so that students and teachers receive the best possible outcome from a difficult or challenging situation.

Passion and perseverance alone cannot overcome the fact that educational strengthening takes time, and therefore, overcoming challenges requires patience. Unlike some fields, in which a new technology or breakthrough may solve a problem forever, changes in education typically do not happen overnight. Since education involves working with people, patience (and persistence!) is required to form relationships, change behaviors, and transform mindsets to allow education reforms to take root. Together, passion, perseverance, and patience will allow me (and perhaps others interested in international education) to keep confronting challenges head-on as I continue helping to improve education for students around the world.

Bio

Ana Florez is an international development leader with over 20 years' experience working closely with governments and donors to design and implement complex education projects worldwide. Ana is the Director of Post-Primary Education at FHI 360. In her role, she supports school systems, and tertiary education institutions to improve students' skills, their chances to find jobs, and their opportunities to become productive citizens. Her research and policy interests include addressing factors affecting access, quality, and achievement at the secondary and tertiary education level of at-risk youth. She graduated from the International Education Policy Program at the Harvard Graduate School of Education in 2004.

Advancing Educational Opportunities for Students with Disabilities and English Language Learners

By Leanne Trujillo

In my current role as a Research Associate for a major international organization that works across all 50 U.S. states and 25 countries, I work on the evaluation of transition programs for students with disabilities; contribute qualitative/quantitative data collection and analysis of special education districts across the U.S.; coordinate national special education conferences, particularly for leaders working in districts with predominantly students of color; and advance the initiatives of a network of special education leaders across the U.S. In my work, I focus mostly on students with disabilities and English Language Learners (ELL), two highly underserved groups in the United States, who mostly make up culturally and linguistically diverse students from the U.S. and from several different countries. My work focuses on improving the quality of education in communities with culturally and linguistically diverse students in the United States as well as students with disabilities. Half of my job focuses on how to improve the collaboration of a national network of special education leaders in addressing various challenges in special education such as: social-emotional well-being, disproportionality, restraint and seclusion, bullying, classification rates, students with disabilities who are ELL students and universally designed classrooms. The other half of my job focuses on evaluating special education and ELL programs, particularly in the areas of transition and programs serving new students, or students who recently arrived in the U.S. At times, we follow up with school districts and help provide technical assistance through professional development.

Impact

Over the last year, it is hard to pinpoint exactly how many learners have been influenced by my work, since it involves ongoing evaluation of an existing transition program and a focus on leadership in special education district across the U.S. According to recent data, the special education leaders I work with in our collaborative serve approximately 13% percent of the total number of students with disabilities in the U.S.

339

Depending on our findings from the transition program, the study may have the ability to be the first of its kind to reveal the outcomes of transition programs for students from a student-based lens. Over the past decade, I have a better idea of the direct number of students I have impacted since I served many years teaching in non-profit organizations as well as in two different school districts. In my work with various education non-profit organizations in Guatemala, Nicaragua, and Arizona, I had the opportunity to influence 90 students in these roles. In my work as a classroom teacher for four years, one in Arizona and three in New York City, I directly impacted approximately 400 students at the middle and high school level. In my career, two of my classes have graduated from high school and over 85% of the students who graduated are enrolled in an institution of higher education.

Challenges

In my work, I have learned from my supervisor the value of the four frames to conceptualize leadership as proposed by Lee Bolman and Terry Deal.[71] The four frames are structural, human resource, political, and symbolic. In thinking about my current role, the most challenging leadership challenges I have faced fall within the 'structural' and 'political' categories. Working with many districts, there are often conflicting interests when it comes to determining what is best for students, particularly students with disabilities, at a time where the Individuals with Disabilities Education Act (IDEA) is being threatened in many ways on a national level. Much of the research over the past thirty years in special education has focused on the topic of disproportionality, or the overrepresentation of students of color in special education and underrepresentation of students of color in gifted education programs. The research on disproportionality stems back to the Civil Rights Movement and often shows us that students of color are systematically placed in segregated settings. Particularly in this past year, with tensions regarding race and difference unveiling themselves at the forefront of national political conversations, it has been a challenge to lead districts into really addressing the issue of

---

[71] Bolman, Lee G. Reframing organizations : artistry, choice, and leadership San Francisco : Jossey-Bass, [2013] 5th edition.

disproportionality within their respective communities. Many are afraid of the repercussions of this or are fearful of not meeting "compliance standards" in special education. This has made it uniquely challenging to really incite change in many districts.

The second challenge, falls under the structural category. In many different aspects of my work on special education and ELL projects, I have found it challenging to work within the current structure because of several 'compliance' measures in these areas. Under the Every Student Succeeds Act (ESSA), many districts feel under scrutiny (and fear a potential loss of funding) to simply focus on compliance to standards and "keeping their heads above water." It is often times challenging to work collaboratively to implement culturally relevant curriculum, improve instructional practices, and plan collaborative time with district members because of an intense focus on compliance. This is not to place blame on district leaders and employees, however, it is to highlight that special education and English language learning are still working 'alongside' general education initiatives and not foundationally within them. This perpetuates the notion that special education and English language learning are seen as a "place" for these particular students to go and learn outside of the general setting, rather than a "service" to accommodate their unique needs in order to perform alongside their general education peers.

Lessons Learned

In my current role, I have learned a great deal about the need to reframe the way we think about special education and English language learning. Because students who may need these services are labeled in this way, education leaders have fallen into the trap of "othering" these students and, in effect, viewing special education and English language learning as a place and not a service. This idea is dangerous. It perpetuates segregated classrooms and can drastically hold back the academic and social-emotional achievement of our students as well as drastically alter their life trajectories. Research has shown the effects of this segregation, many times leading to increased suspensions, restraint, and seclusion while in school, has long-term negative effects leading to incarceration. The services and Universal Design for Learning (UDL) that benefit students with disabilities can also benefit all general education students.

By universally designing classrooms to be accessible to all students, we are improving education, choice, and opportunity for all. Students who need individual supports in addition to this, should be accommodated as appropriately as possible, but held to the same expectations as their general education peers. The inclusion of students with disabilities and English language learners has shown immense positive effects for these students, but also benefited their general education peers who have the opportunity to learn in an environment that mirrors the real world— one where all can learn to live and celebrate their differences and uniqueness. As a leader, if you are to look at a school district or school community and assess its special education and ELL department, you can learn a lot about how the leadership values diversity, inclusion, mutual respect, and universal learning. I believe it is a true window into the effectiveness of schools in educating students, not only to achieve in academics, but also achieve in their social-emotional life. I think viewing these requirements more holistically, rather than as a mere compliance to meet, will help us educate students more effectively overall—particularly culturally and linguistically diverse students. Schools in the United States have become increasingly diverse since 2014 and it is important, especially in the current political climate, to reflect on the type of communities we want our students to continue to build – ones that are fundamentally inclusive.

Trajectories

My personal career trajectory has mostly taken place within schools as a teacher, at the district level as a teacher coach with a brief transition to research and evaluation. I have recently transitioned back to school-based initiatives in my new role with Teach For America San Francisco. I feel that I have transitioned to impacting more students through my work as a Research Associate and now in my role working with teachers and school leaders through Teach For America. I will be helping transform teaching across several schools, inevitably reaching more students than I had while classroom teaching. I have not made a transition from the private to public sector, however, I have made one transition since graduating from the International Education Policy (IEP) program, particularly to work more directly within schools. Although I appreciated and valued my work for a research organization,

I found that my personal impact was more effective working directly with teachers and school leaders.

Bio

Leanne Trujillo graduated from the International Education Policy Program at the Harvard Graduate School of Education in 2016. She has recently transitioned from Boston to San Francisco where she will be working as the Director, Education Catalyst for Teach For America San Francisco. In this role, she will be working directly in teacher leadership development as well as with school leaders across San Francisco's highest needs schools. Previously, Leanne has worked for the Education Development Center, the New York City Department of Education, Tucson Unified School District, the International Rescue Committee and several education non-profits throughout the United States, Central America, and Mexico. She is particularly interested in identity as it relates to education, particularly of Newcomer students.

Working to Advance Educational Opportunities Around the World in Ways Big and Small

by Bettina Dembek

Goals and Work

Born into generations of educators on both sides of my family, lifelong learning and helping others to learn is ingrained in me. But as I grew up, I rebelled against becoming an educator.

Instead, I set my mind on a career in chemistry and the pharmaceutical industry. After high school graduation, I spent a year traveling the world getting by on a tiny budget spending most of my time in the cheaper countries of Southeast Asia and South America. This experience changed me. No longer was I interested in having a big career and making lots of money: I wanted to spend time meeting people from different cultures and helping them to lead better lives. So upon my return to Germany, I enrolled in a teacher's college to become a teacher, just like my father and his father, my mother and her father, brother, sister, and several of my cousins. My goal was to work for GTZ, the German development-aid agency, but once I had completed my teaching certificate, I was told that GTZ needed engineers and not teachers. Because of personal circumstances, I relocated to the United States for visa reasons, I decided to attend another university as a way of staying in the country. In my search for a good master's program, I heard about the International Education Policy Program at Harvard. At that time, I still planned to work at an international development agency like the United Nations or the World Bank.

Fast forward 15 years: I have gone back and forth between small-scale work on the ground, teaching in classrooms and providing mentorship for single school districts, and larger scale projects such as national programs that aim to change how science is taught in the 21st century. I helped with the implementation of Ghana's Education Management System and transformed Pakistan's learning and teaching practice from rogue learning to one that fosters critical thinking and problem solving. I have helped develop a digital authoring platform to digitize innovative inquiry-based curricula funded by the National Science Foundation. For

345

the Department of Defense, I developed an environmental high school science course that is taught on all American military bases around the world. I have organized student exchanges and advised on how to use open education resources to supplement curricula at alternative higher education institutions in countries such as Kenya and Rwanda. One day you might find me taking over a class in a remote school to model how to integrate 21st century skills into a science lesson. On another day, I might be leading a negotiation with the Australian Public School Authority to grant more local control over the core curriculum taught in remote aboriginal communities. What I have come to accept and finally to appreciate is that it is okay not to have one area of focus but to embrace my different interests. Working all those years globally also opened my eyes to what needs to be done locally. I decided to walk the talk wherever I am, including at home. Currently, I am helping USAID build a community of practice to increase more equitable access to education in areas affected by conflict and crisis. I also launched my own small business to promote sustainable agriculture and to protect pollinators at the Eastern Shore of Virginia. Reflecting on this rich experience, I am convinced that, regardless of the level at which we work or where we work, education paired with opportunity is transformative.

Impact

In fact, today, I see the meaningfulness of my work no longer associated with prestigious organizations or in the large numbers of people I reach, but in the individual lives I know I was able to touch first-hand and helped improve even if it was just a tiny bit. It is in keeping the beacon of hope for a better future alive where my deepest satisfaction stems from now. One person at a time from the ground up or from the top down, it really does not matter. It is all important work. I know that the power of numbers is that they can be quantified, compared, and reported. But in their aggregate, they often lose the story of the individual life that has been touched. When I look back at my work, the individual was my main motivation to carry on when conditions were tough, when change came about slowly if at all, and when hours were long. Often as I teach, I try to inspire, aware that I, too, learn and am inspired. In one of my implementation workshops in Pakistan, when I saw our goal of reforming the national curricula for student teachers slipping beyond reach, one of the university directors rekindled my hope by assuring me "We might not bring the rain that is needed, but we can bring the first drops that could start that rain."

Challenges

As we try to bring about systemic change on national and international levels, we must not lose sight of the individuals. One of the hardest decisions I faced was when I helped implement policies for refugees in Germany, where asylum rights made perfect sense in the aggregate on a national level. However, that same policy had detrimental consequences for some individual refugees who had the "wrong nationality" and found themselves on a list that denied them asylum status. I faced moral dilemmas because I had to help implement those painful policies in my community. I knew these people. I knew their story. I knew their dreams, and it was awful having to tell them they could not stay because of their "unacceptable" nationality. Knowing restrictions have a place means that we have to accept that some individuals are left out. But that makes me wonder what we mean by equal and equitable rights. Being in the position of having to make decisions over finite resource allocations is a heart-wrenching experience. To this day, I find myself bouncing back and forth between working at the grassroots level where my efforts can have more immediate impact, but where I directly face restrictions in policy frameworks and very limited resources, or working on a larger scale, where I have a respected input into policy frameworks and resource allocation. Yet, I still find the resources are not enough and change can be excruciatingly slow. However, I now have gained a deeper appreciation of the intricacy of the systems in place.

Lessons Learned

Though I have a superb education from Harvard, one that opens many doors and equipped me extraordinarily well, it is important to stay humble and open-minded. We must not make the mistake of assuming our values and life experiences are shared and appreciated everywhere. What is this about? Never judge a man unless you have walked in his shoes for two moons; and, when in Rome, do as the Romans do. At the tender age of 4, I encountered my first bidet on a trip to France. I told my mom that I couldn't use the bathroom because the toilet was "broken." Many years later on my trips across the world, I encountered many "broken toilets," and learned to adapt and even to appreciate them. I also learned to eat with my fingers as well as with chopsticks; and now I find it hard to justify why I consider sticking a sharp object like a fork in my mouth as the superior way of enjoying a meal.

Some experiences made me ponder both my core values and my beliefs. When I taught on an Aboriginal Reservation in Australia, the elders dismissed my initial curriculum as "Whitemen stuff." They introduced me to the deeper meaning of multiculturalism. It requires a very open mind, a lot of open dialogue, and learning objectives that go way beyond bilingualism or the mastery of reading and math. This is where I began to learn how people can thrive without numbers outside one, two, and many, and without a written language. I began to consider how educational values might have to be defined by the people they are meant to serve. I will always remember how my so-called "illiterate students" read the signs of nature and saved me from being eaten by a crocodile during what would have been a very short-lived swim! And how time can be seen as circular and maps can depict Songlines. My educational system is clearly different. Who is to say it is superior?

Now, when I see HGSE's banner "Learn to Change the World," it reminds me that my studies did not end at HGSE – *they began there*. The people I encounter through my work and from whom I continue to learn so much have replaced my professors. First-hand experiences have augmented textbooks. Changing the world requires leadership. When something is amiss, seeing a need, having a vision, and taking appropriate actions are the way I have learned to go. Being agile is striving to learn from everyone and everything while working hard to inspire others, to support their singular dreams, and to work jointly towards a shared vision using the skills and experiences of each individual. "To lead" requires passion and perseverance, self-confidence, and a collective humility that we can sustain *only* if we are our authentic selves and if we continue to believe and to dream. Success often comes solely through struggle and sometimes setbacks. Knowing when to stop and when to push through is a developed instinct and not as much a science one can learn. It comes from experience and walking the walk, not just talking the talk. Above all, leadership means having the courage to make decisions, to take action, and to commit to positive change along with others. Sounds easy. Yet, too often we feel the pressure to keep our organizations competitive and to focus on what divides us instead of trying to find common ground.

When I look at the worldwide network of IEP alumni, currently represented in so many organizations, governments, and institutions, I wonder what we could achieve collectively. Can the IEP values connect us across our 18 classes and multiply our impact? We have about 1,000 IEP alumni now. Could we reach across geographic and institutional barriers where others before us might have failed? I think we can. More so than ever, I believe we need to stand united behind IEP's core principles to learn, to lead, and to change the world.

Bio

Bettina Dembek has worked for the public and private sector; for international agencies, and for grassroots organizations and start-ups on five continents bringing her vast experience in learning and teaching, information communication technologies, and project management to bear. She graduated from the International Education Policy Program at the Harvard Graduate School of Education in 2001.

Advancing Educational Opportunities for Refugees and Disadvantaged Children from Afghanistan

By Zohal Atif

Goals and Work

The experience that drove me to change careers from Finance to Education was a layover in Dubai International Airport in 2013. I had planned a trip back home to Afghanistan after 20 plus years. Coming from the US, I had a 7 hour layover in Dubai during which I walked around the terminal with the peace of mind and confidence of a person that had control over the situation. I had the means and the knowledge of how to buy food when I walked out of the plane hungry. My mind was at rest knowing where my next destination was and how to get there, yet decades before this trip I had crossed that same terminal a very different person under some different circumstances. I was a refugee child on the way to the United States of America; filled with uncertainty of not knowing where home was going to be, fear of being rejected and a deep of sense of not belonging in that exact space and time. It was as if being a refugee was a disease that I had somehow inflicted upon myself and I had the moral responsibility to not contaminate others by taking a place next to them as an equal.

So, what made the difference for me to walk that same airport path years later feeling like a different person? It was, simply, having access to education. My trajectory from a war zone to HGSE was not a straight path. So, when I received the call, just after receiving my MEd, to work with Afghan refugee children in Greece, I jumped on the opportunity. I went to Greece with a group of Human Rights Lawyers to provide legal support to refugees stranded in the small Greek island of Chios. Upon landing in Chios, it immediately became clear that the majority of the refugees were children, a good portion of whom were unaccompanied minors in high risk situation with no educational facility or a plan in place to educate them. The United Nations High Commission for Refugees (UNHCR) and the Norwegian Refugees Council ran child friendly safe space programs for a limited number of days for children under twelve years of age. However, many of the unaccompanied minors were above that age and spent days upon days idle. Many of these kids had left home two years ago in the hope to reach a safe country and get access to education. Yet, they found themselves stranded in an unsafe and volatile situation. These kids came with many emotional and psychological burdens. Many of them were child soldiers, or had served time in prison in Iran and in Turkey for being Afghan refugees and had faced abuse in the hands of the smugglers on their way to Europe. They spoke of the explosions and kidnapping that befell their friends and family in Afghanistan, they showed me videos of Taliban executing people from their tribe and their fear for their families that were left behind. They told stories of seeing dead bodies that had rolled down the mountain as they were climbing to cross all the way from Afghanistan to Turkey's European border. Once there, they were put on dingy plastic boats to cross the waters into Europe. Some of the kids were so traumatized by seeing or experiencing sinking boats that they could not look at the ocean. Yet, here they were held prisoner in an island surrounded by water from all sides with no information on when they could get out. These kids came from different parts of Afghanistan, but two things they had in common were trauma and a strong desire to continue with their education. As a field coordinator, I used to interview the minors to match them with a lawyer to receive legal assistance. There was one seventeen-year old (who I will call 'Ali') from Afghanistan who despite being born in Iran had been deported to Afghanistan twice just because he was caught working in a city other than the one where he was registered. When I met him for the first time, he had tried to commit suicide a few days prior. He told me how back in Iran he went to another city to find work to support his younger brother and mother, who had been diagnosed with cancer. They had lost their dad years before. He single handedly supported his family, paid for his mother's medical expenses, and was studying at the same time until he was caught by the Iranian police and deported to Afghanistan on the sole charge of working in a city other than where he was registered. After this deportation, he decided to head towards Europe, but little did he imagine that he would be held prisoner on the island for years. He was so worried for his family and out of an extreme feeling of helplessness, he had tried to commit suicide. Every time after taking the minors' case histories, I would ask them one last question and that was, "What do you want to be when you grow up?" This question was meant to assess their emotional state and to give them a sense of

352

hope to look forward to a future over which they had control. That question always brought out shy smiles, sparkles in their eyes and a range of responses. Anything from football player to a doctor to a president. Yet Ali gave me a response that I had never heard before. He wanted to be an environmental scientist so he could save the planet and show to the world that Afghans can be scientists, too. His posture changed and his tone of voice became more resolute every time he explained to me his theory of how he wanted to control pollution by applying the laws of chemistry to lessen the carbon footprint. I was more excited for him than he had expected and that led him to think about different theories everyday so he could explain them to me. Ali was extremely talented and motivated, yet he was spending every hour of his day sitting in the dusty refugee camp and facing abuse at the hands of adult male refugees and Greek police. Towards the end of my four months of work, my team and I coordinated to get him a 9th and 10th grade chemistry book in Farsi, so he could continue to practice his theorems which he would then explain to me over WhatsApp once I had returned to the U.S.

Working with these child refugees in Greece, I realized one of the major pull factors to Europe was the opportunity to access quality education. On the other hand, one of the major push factors was the lack of educational opportunities in Afghanistan. That led me to work on a USAID-funded primary education initiative designed to improve equitable access to education in Afghanistan. The goal of the project (*Afghan Children Read*) is to build the capacity of the Ministry of Education to provide an early grade reading (EGR) program (in Dari and Pashto) for grades 1 to 3 students in both formal and Community Based Education (CBE) schools.

Impact

The goal is to strengthen systems, models and materials that will enable future development of additional local mother-tongue languages into the national reading program. With the MoE in the lead, the project team will launch an Afghan While I was in Greece, working with about 200 kids, the biggest impact was on the psychological well-being of the kids, knowing that they had someone to talk to and that there was an adult that checked on them daily. The days revolved around making sure the kids had access to legal help, shelter at night and stayed out of trouble during the day. Other than the ad hoc book distribution and advocating with the UNHCR, Save the Children, and other NGOs to provide educational opportunities for the minors, there was very limited scope to achieve any educational impact.

It is too early to speak about substantial impact since the *Afghan Children Read* project just completed its first full year of implementation. The overall goal of the project is to build the capacity of the Government of Islamic Republic of Afghanistan Ministry of Education's capacity to expand early grade reading to all the provinces. As a Program Associate, I provide operational and technical support to ensure the project activities, such as training of master trainers, training of teachers, coaching and mentoring of school staff in EGR techniques and social emotional learning, goes smoothly. Also, the project is in the process of book distribution and tracking, EGRA and many other activities that will expand beyond the three pilot provinces to national level coverage. According to Afghanistan National Education For All 2015 report, the total number of school age children will increase from 11.9 million to 13.8 million by 2020. If the project is successful in its implementation goals and in building the capacity of the MoE in Early Grade Reading, the project can impact all the 13.8 million children with the assumption that insecurity will not impede access. I will have contributed to that impact.

Challenges

One of the most difficult challenges I faced while working in Greece was the lack of motivation from well-known organizations to engage in providing a safe learning environment for the minors. While there were many reasons behind this lack of motivation; lack of funds, limited mandate, lack of technical expertise, and legal constraints were among the major ones. The other challenge was to have the staff in the large NGOs whether in the field or in the HQ change their perspective and view refugees as humans. For some of the people employed in aiding/providing assistance to refugees, it was just a means to earn money and make the next step to a dream career. They lacked the will to learn about the countries the refugees came from in order to understand their challenges and the reasons behind their suffering.

The other problem is most of the NGOs had difficult relationships with the minors and there was mutual lack of respect and trust on both sides. Minors emotional and psychological well-being were not prioritized; thus, education was seen as a privilege rather than a need. My personal goal was to make sure education was viewed as a necessary component of aid for the refugees. Education gives hope, provides a sense of normalcy and enables the person to gain a sense of control over his/her situation. For this message to get across, I had to speak up in cluster meetings held in Save the Children office every week and in UNHCR weekly meetings. But coming from a very dysfunctional education background as a child refugee, I had to first give myself the permission to feel that I belonged in that room with the rest of the people and that my voice mattered, and I had to abandon my concept of self vs. others that was so strongly engraved in me by my childhood experiences.

On the other hand, one of the major struggles with which to cope while working with USAID was to manage the bureaucracy and politics of the organizations. The most prominent challenge which was a common thread in both contexts was facing prejudice due to my gender and my cultural background. As an Afghan woman, I had to constantly fight to break away from the single story that is used to define this complex identity. It is painted with shades of pity and presented as someone that needs saving. Whereas, the strength of this identity is not acknowledged and mostly undermined.

Lessons Learned

The most significant lesson I have learned in the past year and a half is that I need to step outside of myself and my pre-conceived concept of self vs. others; refugee vs. host community. For this to happen, I need to undo years of work that a dysfunctional education system instilled in me. Education should enable students to bring out their best self and give them the inner strength to carry on with the many challenges as adults rather than an education system that instills a sense of inferiority whether it is based on sex, religion, cast, disability, country nationals vs. refugees, or any other concept that creates divide and breaks down the inner strength of the child. The traditional way of education that takes place inside a school might not work for all children. It is important to acknowledge that and foster an enabling environment where the student feels safe and continue their education.

Working with the refugee kids in a very unfair system gave me the opportunity to see how the unjust system limited and hindered the growth of the child. Since I am a product of the similar system, it helped me to realize the need to own my ground and celebrate my refugee identity as a source of strength rather than a weakness. Individuals are the sum of their experiences and I need to use my education and my career goals to add a story of strength to the narrative that defines this complex identity – female Afghan refugee.

Bio

Zohal Atif graduated from the International Education Policy Program at the Harvard Graduate School of Education in 2016. She is passionate about making quality education accessible to all Afghan Children. Currently she supports an education project in Afghanistan to build the capacity of the Ministry of Education.

Leading Collaborations to Addressing Educational Inequity

By Shajia Sarfraz

Goals and Work

I find the best part about a career in international development is the ability to learn from new challenges and bring together the expertise of several knowledgeable and devoted people who rarely have the opportunity to communicate with each other. My most recent role has been as a Fellow with the Varkey Foundation in the United Kingdom. I worked as a fellow for the Global Education and Skills Forum Alliances - groups of experts brought together by the Varkey Foundation to think about how education can change the world. Currently, I am consulting for education reform programs in Pakistan, as well exploring the option of relocating to a different country to learn and grow from addressing a different challenge in a new context.

In my role at the Varkey Foundation, I helped create sustainable and meaningful partnerships between various organizations operating in the education development sector including various experts, ministers, grassroots workers, donors, and international development organizations. Through these alliances, I helped build a network of individuals who are committed to addressing the deep and complex problem of educational inequity with the central goal of shaping public policy, stimulating new dialogue, influencing political agendas, and driving new initiatives.

From my personal experience in the development sector, I have found that there is too much work that takes place in silos and there is a dearth of avenues to share best practices, learn from each other's mistakes, and most importantly, build a national, united movement that is serious, systematic and transparent about how access to quality education is being met for the most marginalized groups in developing countries..
Different actors within the education sector face scrutiny from each other. Large international development organizations are critiqued for their bureaucracy. Non-governmental organizations (NGOs) are criticized for their policy deficit with respect to developing best practices. In light of a flourishing network of private schools, citizens

have become disengaged from their civic responsibilities of raising their voices to improve public education. Governments and the public sector lack trust from local people because of corruption, poor or underutilization of funds, and inertia to change. In the constant struggle between these different groups, we end up creating a world where it seems that the goals of international development agencies, NGOs, donors, policy makers, and researchers are somehow divergent from each other. In order to engage meaningfully in a global movement that makes quality education for all everyone's business, we need to create platforms that encourage open and honest dialogue across multiple sectors of a society.

Impact

The dynamics of shaping public policy on education are complex. What is perhaps even more difficult is the ability to capture the impact of this work in traditional log frames and theories of change. In advocacy work in education development, it is difficult to quantify the direct influence one has on learners. Since most of my work involves interactions with different stakeholders such as policy makers and private sector organizations, it would be erroneous to quote the number of the students who have been influenced by my work.

Having said that, I evaluate the difference I have made in the lives of others by the number of different people and sectors I have managed to engage in solving problems that need sustained global attention. For example, during my work with the Varkey Foundation I helped put together global education alliances to address complex issues on education topics. These included alliances in: girls' education, global citizenship education, education in conflict, public-private partnerships in education development, and assessment for impact (an alliance I continue to serve on in order to identify innovative ways of measuring what matters in education for sustainable development). One of the most important aspects of this work is being able to engage various private sector organizations and the business community whose presence has been traditionally lacking from the development world.

Challenges

I have faced three types of challenges in my work. The first, and perhaps biggest challenge I have found, is to identify and scale ideas that emerge organically from local communities and disaggregate a donor-funded narrative from the true and authentic needs of a nation. For example, Pakistan, and its dismal federal education budget, is an oft harped about issue in terms of identifying what needs to be done to improve the number of out of school children here. When not realizing that when one re-evaluates the data on education spending from the public and private sector as well as provincial funds, Pakistan's budgets are at par with the global average of 15%, the same as the US and the UK. Instead of shaping the public narrative around increased accountability and better utilization of education budgets, at large, the major focus of education organizations has been an unashamed cry for more money without sufficient monitoring of where it goes.

Moreover, I have also found it challenging to dissuade the idea that English-speaking-foreign-educated graduates are the bastions of truth and knowledge and will be the "magic bullets" that solve the long withstanding problems of education development in low-income countries. It is so important to understand that any kind of sustainable effort will come from home and that is where we need to invest. We need to trust local communities and understand that it is they who will be able to decide how best to fix their schooling systems. Only by shifting funding and the locus of control away from the center to communities in villages and districts, will we be able to empower them to truly participate in sustainable education sector reform.

Finally, it has not been easy to be a part of a work culture that supports entrepreneurial decision-making. One of the best things I learned in Harvard's International Education Policy Program was the importance of taking initiative to solve a problem. By seeing so many of my peers in the IEP program practice proactive behavior by looking to themselves for the answers to problems they had identified, I became convinced that solutions that challenge the status quo require innovation, initiative, and a sense of security with the idea that it is OK to fail for the sake of attempting to solve difficult challenges.

Bio

Shajia Sarfraz is an education development professional specializing in creating and sustaining strategic partnerships in international development. She is interested in using evidence-based research to inform educational reform policies and strategic interventions to address issues of educational inequity, diversity, access and quality in developing countries. She has previously worked with the Varkey Foundation (United Kingdom), where she led and managed the planning of the Global Education and Skills Forum Alliances - a network of experts who collaborate around key education related subjects with the central purpose of stimulating new dialogue, shaping agendas and driving initiatives. She graduated from the International Education Policy Program at the Harvard Graduate School of Education in 2016.

GLOBAL

NON-PROFITS

Leading Teacher Organizations to Professionalize Education Practice

By David Edwards

Goals and Work

I am the Deputy General Secretary of Education International (EI). EI is the world federation of more than four hundred teachers' organizations, associations, and unions in 172 countries - together those organizations represent approximately 32.5 million educators. I am responsible for the areas of education policy, research, dialogue, employment conditions, and advocacy.

Specifically with regards to expanding educational opportunities my work at EI can be characterized in the following manner:

- Holding governments accountable for full implementation of the Education 2030 agenda that provides the roadmap for achieving Sustainable Development Goal 4
- Working to ensure that every student is taught by a highly qualified, professionally trained, motivated, and empowered teacher
- Informing national, regional, and global policy dialogues with the first-hand knowledge and experiences of rank- and- file teachers
- Advocating for and monitoring sustainable and predictable long-term financing of public education based on progressive and equitable domestic resource mobilization and taxation
- Defending every person's right to inclusive and equitable public education in the face of corporate attempts to commoditize that right and make profit off of students

We do that by running campaigns such as the Unite for Quality Education that mobilized hundreds of thousands of teachers, parents, and students to push for and achieve a broad and bold standalone education goal in the SDGs. We also run campaigns calling for tax justice and adequate public investment in public education and global response campaigns that expose the ways private companies seek to commercialize education and water down the legal frameworks that protect students' rights.

We do that by constructing policy dialogue platforms in countries that are members of the Organization for Economic Cooperation and Development (OECD) and countries which participate in the Global Partnership for Education (GPE). In the OECD we annually bring ministers of education and the elected leaders of teacher organizations together through the International Summits of the Teaching Profession (ISTP) to discuss sometimes seemingly intractable problems with the benefit of research evidence and mutual accountability. Now in its eighth year, the ISTP uniquely focuses on developing good teacher policy to benefit the most marginalized and underserved populations. In GPE countries, we have partnered with UNESCO to elevate and institutionalize policy dialogue with teachers as part of the development of national education plans funded by the GPE.

We also carry out research on topics ranging from global learning metrics to school-based gender related violence and then use the results of that research to build capacity within teachers' organizations so that they can negotiate and bargain more effectively. We also use it to raise awareness and collaborate more deeply across the spectrum of organizational partners. One of my achievements in this regard was to form a global network of academic critical friends who publish weekly blogs and articles on our Worlds of Education blog.

Impact

Assuming that our influence is spread evenly across our members' organizations and their individual members, one might approximate that on average each member teaches around forty students per year (this could vary between 20-150) – 32 million multiplied by 40 equals 1.28 billion students. Clearly this is indirect influence as we do not reach students directly, but via the teachers who are in turn influenced by the leaders of the teacher organizations we do influence directly. Our goal is to ensure that every member has the professional knowledge, tools, opportunities for development and working conditions to deliver quality, inclusive, and relevant education to their students from early childhood to higher education.

Challenges

Constructing a global vision for the future of the teaching profession that allows for national variation and local context across sectors and categories is a huge leadership challenge. Layered upon that are the different political visions, languages, cultures, and histories that each member organization brings to the multiplicity of democratic governance structures which decide the direction, scope, and scale of my work. Building that vision depends on a common commitment to our core values of human rights and democracy. The challenge is to strategically and consciously braid the strands consisting of our values strand with our professional strand and our industrial strand in ways that strengthen our collective resolve and move us to action. The way we do this in each context and country varies by degree and may require prioritizing one strand over the others at a particular moment in time. The challenge for me is to keep listening and reflecting to get the balance right between supporting and pushing. That is our internal leadership challenge.

Connected to that is the challenge to maintain an informed, pluralistic, and solutions-focused dialogue with governments, international organizations, and partners when and where we can, but simultaneously reserving the right to criticize, contest, speak out, and dial up the pressure. There will always be those with political litmus tests who seek to simplify the decisions we must make and characterize our actions or words in ways that benefit them and their agendas. When I joined EI I was determined to push back on what I perceived to be a growing narrative advanced by a handful of conservative policy wonks who claimed that learning did not require teaching and highly trained professional teachers. We spent a great deal of time organizing events, carrying out and pulling together research, lobbying and increasing the visibility of the centrality of the teaching profession. I remember when we were doing this within the EFA movement and SDG process and I started hearing the narrative change. However, it moved/slid to the other extreme. The new policy fad was to say that teachers are the *only* thing that matters – not poverty, family characteristics, time, tools, nor a supportive environment. My challenge at that moment was to help move us to a systems approach within a world that sees education as a simplistic result of a few inputs, and to build partnerships across sectors with a view to a whole-child, whole-school approach. We asserted our responsibilities for leading our profession and continued to demand our rights and the rights of our students.

Another major leadership challenge was recognizing that the demands for our engagement were not always well matched to our capacity to dedicate ourselves across those demands. I spent my first year arguing for increased representative teacher voice across OECD and GPE countries alike. I fought for and won seats on every major global and regional education body where education related decisions were being taken. But I quickly realized that the specialized knowledge one needed to navigate those spaces coupled with the time it would take for national teacher leaders to prepare and effectively execute their role was in limited supply. At the national level we succeeded in getting EI affiliate leaders on local education groups where they could bring firsthand knowledge about their students' and colleagues needs into policy dialogues with serious resources. Real coordination, I learned, was not simply fighting for spaces and hoping for the best. It meant we had to help members see the opportunity to organize towards their goals and then build the needed technical capacity to sustain their engagement in an incredibly complex process. Becoming real meant communicating effectively at key moments with the right people about how our democratic structures could be mobilized more effectively and what their role might be towards that end. It meant that we were going to have to apply our pedagogical aspirations internally and get serious about teacher learning and leader development.

Lessons Learned

Get past the spin, skip the fad, attend to the conditions. – There are people who wake up every morning thinking about how best to pitch the next big thing in education. Some continue to pitch and cherry-pick evidence well past an idea's 'sell by' date. Their persistence eventually breaks down donors' defenses but the fact that their innovations never take root or get taken up should make education equity activists cautious. They may have found something that does work for a certain population at a certain time but my experience has taught me to look at the conditions as much, if not more than, the edupreneur. The organization Bridge Academies, for example, which offers low cost for profit education to poor children in Africa, will never be Escuela Nueva, an organization that for over six decades has offered public schools professional development to change the culture of schools to make them more effective.

Innovation does not mean private sector involvement. – In education policy wonk speak there is a tendency to equate the public sector and public investment as old- fashioned and inefficient. New private equity firms and consultancies in education use slick marketing strategies to propose numerous solutions where risks are passed to the very citizens for whom they purport to expand educational opportunities. Yet, the truly remarkable and promising work in expanding educational opportunities in democracies has come through innovative arrangements and interventions precisely within that public sector. Countries whose students perform at high levels in the OECD Programme of International Students Assessment (PISA), that are democratic, inclusive, and multiethnic have healthy private sectors who benefit from highly skilled and prepared graduates, but they also know the limitations of markets. There is nothing innovative in turning over the running of schools to companies who must yield returns for shareholders. Ask the Swedes if they now wished their public education system had emulated Finland more than Chile.

Teaching is a profession. - Teaching is not charity and cannot be done by "smart people" without developing their craft in a collective manner with the benefit of research and expert practitioners. Yet, expensive programs continue to proliferate that overpromise and underperform. They have bought their own rhetoric and are blind to the hypocrisy and myopia that accept a revolving professional door as a given. Most disturbingly these groups, when pushed, state that they know they will not put a dent in teacher recruitment or attrition because they are about forming leaders, not teachers, and certainly not communities. From what I have seen in working around the world, too much money and oxygen has already been wasted on luring the best and brightest into teaching the poorest, instead of mentoring and developing future teachers who show promise at an early age. High performing countries and jurisdictions that reach the most marginalized invest in teaching as a profession and treat their teachers as professionals.

Talk to people, ask lots of questions and advice. – I will always be grateful to a colleague who encouraged me to form EIs Critical Friends Network. Having a sounding board of some of the world's best educational researchers, activists, and leaders makes it possible for me to sharpen my thinking and be more reflective as a leader. I am constantly amazed by the openness and candor I encounter with people who are working in education. I have had the luck to count as mentors some of the greatest teachers and thinkers in our field, and have experienced them to be as thoughtful, generous, curious and engaged with people across ages, cultures, languages as they were with their fellow luminaries. Whenever I get stuck in a challenging political situation or technical dead end, I reflect on who might have a view, and I drop what I am doing and seek them out. I have many mentors in their late seventies and eighties, by the way.

Lastly, I **recognize how lucky I am to even get to consider this question**. Leading an organization, a change process, a school, a classroom, a team, whatever, means we have the privilege of being a change agent and more importantly part of a collective of people working to realize the right to education. That recognition makes us vulnerable to a certain critique in some circles, but it is not weakness. I have seen too many colleagues try and hide their doubts and project confidence in an effort to gain more responsibility and credibility. Maybe they opt for a narrative of self-made men and women, who struggle and excel within a meritocratic sea of individual resilience. My advice, for what it is worth, is that there will be many difficult challenges and many opportunities to take credit for success, share those. There will be myriad ways in which you can build a system to carry out a given strategy and manage teams of people too. I have found authentic collaboration around shared goals, trusting people, and good process and communicating, honestly and openly, has served me well even in the midst of the most difficult crises.

Jacques Delors, the former chair of the European Commission, who led the preparation of a report on education for the 21sttwenty first century for UNESCO, reminded us that learning to know and do are certainly important but we should never forget the other two, learning to be and learning to live together. In the end, I do not believe that the economic argument nor the security argument for expanding educational opportunities and achieving greater equity are the right drivers. I say this because the great challenges that face us today cannot be "hacked" or solved with Big Data any more than we can harness our greed for the common good. Education is a human right that transforms lives. To this end the best way to ensure the right to education is translated into the appropriate regulatory frameworks with predictable and sustainable financing is by educating globally- minded and locally-focused citizens who demand their rights and hold their governments to account.

Bio

David Edwards PhD is Deputy General Secretary of Education International where he is responsible for EI's work in the areas of Education Policy, Employment and Research. Prior to joining EI in 2011, David was Associate Director of Governance and Policy and head of International Relations, at the National Education Association (NEA) of the United States. Before NEA, David worked as an Education Specialist at the Organization of American States (OAS) and), a project coordinator and activist in Bolivia, and began his career as a public, high school foreign language teacher. David graduated from the International Education Policy Program at the Harvard Graduate School of Education in 2001.

Promoting Literacy and Education for Girls in Africa and Asia

By Peter Cooper

Goals and Work

Since graduating from college, I have devoted my entire professional career to making a difference in the lives of others. This began with six years as a classroom teacher in Africa, the US, and Japan, and continued with nearly two years as a Research Associate for WestEd, a non-profit focused on K-12 education research in the US. For the past 10 years, I have been with Room to Read (www.roomtoread.org), an international education non-profit that promotes reading and girls' education in Africa and Asia. Room to Read is focused on increasing the access to and quality of educational opportunities for children globally. As Manager, Senior Manager, and now Associate Director of the Research, Monitoring, and Evaluation team, I have played an instrumental role in shaping the organization's monitoring and evaluation agenda. I have designed and managed numerous small- and large-scale research studies, including several multi-country studies funded by the Bill and Melinda Gates Foundation. I help oversee the organization's global monitoring system, through which data are collected from all active projects (more than 3,000 school-based projects in 2016) on an annual basis. I have led several mobile technology pilots that sought ways to increase the efficiency and cost-effectiveness of routine data collection. I also provide ongoing coaching and capacity to country office staff on topics such as research design, data analysis, results sharing and project management. Since joining Room to Read, I have helped the organization reach nearly 1 million children with its programming, including more than 900,000 children in 2016.[72]

---

[72] Room to Read. 2016. *Room to Read's Global Monitoring Report 2015: Focusing on Outcomes.* Available at: https://www.roomtoread.org/impact-reach/tracking-results/global-monitoring-report-focusing-on-outcomes/.

Challenges

As a research and evaluation professional in the international education sector, the biggest challenge I have faced is the failure to use data for decision-making. We live in a world with increasingly large amounts of data at our disposal, yet many decisions are not made based on evidence. This is a two-sided issue. On one side, those who are analyzing data often struggle with presenting evidence to key decision makers in a simple, easy-to-understand way with a clear message or call to action. On the other side, some decision-makers are only willing to listen to evidence that supports their pre-held position or belief. If the evidence runs to the contrary, decision-makers mute or discard it. I have found that overcoming this challenge requires skill (in presenting data), patience (in allowing decision-making audiences to absorb what the data mean), and persistence (in emphasizing how the data can inform the work).

Lessons Learned

During my time in the international education sector, I have learned several key lessons that have been critical to the success of my work. One is the importance of seeking input from those who are closest to the work. At Room to Read, we have country-based teams that implement and execute our work on the ground with schools and children. Unlike some other organizations, all our country-based staff are professionals from that country. The rationale for this is simple: people from that country are the ones who are most familiar with the language, culture, and context, and are therefore best positioned to successfully implement the work. When helping to design programmatic or research activities, I have relied heavily on country-based colleagues for input and ideas. Often, these colleagues have identified challenges or nuances that my headquarters-based colleagues and I had never even thought of. Moreover, many of the most innovative ideas I have seen over the past ten years at Room to Read have originated from our country-based teams, where necessity is often the mother of invention. One prime example is the library rating system, a system through which our staff collect data on a prioritized list of indicators from the school libraries we establish. The data serve two purposes: (1) they enable our staff to provide immediate and targeted feedback to schools and (2) they enable our country teams to strategically allocate support to those libraries that need it most. Before this became a global system that Room to Read implements across countries, our teams in Cambodia, Nepal, and South Africa developed it independently. After seeing the effectiveness of this system in action, we standardized it and rolled it out to our other country-based teams.

Another lesson I have learned is the importance of presenting data in easy-to-understand and compelling ways so that they lead to action. A critical component of my work at Room to Read has been sharing results with audiences in a way that leads to strategic action. I have regular meetings with country staff, programmatic team leads and members of the Management Team to discuss how monitoring and evaluation findings can inform program implementation, program design or strategic organizational decisions. Findings from the monitoring and evaluation activities I have led have directly influenced how the organization does its work, from moving forward with and/or scaling some initiatives to discontinuing others. I have found that the keys to ensuring that data are used for decision-making are understanding one's audience, identifying the "story" that the numbers are telling, and conveying that story in a way that is easy to digest. Some examples of how we have done this at Room to Read can be found in our Global Monitoring Report.

A third lesson is recognizing when it is okay to move on from an intervention that may not be working. When I first joined Room to Read in 2007, I managed our Computer Room Program, an intervention that sought to build children's 21st century skills by establishing computer labs in government secondary schools. Though well intentioned, the intervention faced several challenges. Nearly all the schools where the program was implemented lacked Internet connectivity because the schools were too remote or the cost of securing Internet access was too high for the schools to maintain over time. Sustainability of the equipment was also an issue. Room to Read provided computers at the initial stage of the project, but schools were responsible for maintaining and replacing the equipment over the long term. Few schools had the means to do this. A final issue was impact, as the intervention was unable to demonstrate consistent and meaningful effects on children's learning outcomes. Faced with these challenges and a push towards narrowing the focus of our work to literacy and girls' education, Room to Read (under my "watch" and with input from external stakeholders) made the decision to discontinue the program in 2009. Although this decision was difficult for me personally, I know it was the right one, as Room to Read could reallocate resources to its Literacy and Girls' Education Programs, which have since emerged as among the most impactful means of building children's reading skills and habits and empowering young women, respectively, in Asia and Africa.

Bio

Peter Cooper graduated from the International Education Policy Program at the Harvard Graduate School of Education in 2005. He currently serves as the Associate Director for Research, Monitoring and Evaluation at Room to Read. Prior to joining Room to Read, Peter served as a Peace Corps Volunteer in Cameroon (1998-2000), taught social studies at a public school in Somerville, MA, participated in the Japanese Exchange and Teaching (JET) Program, and worked as a Research Associate at WestEd.

The Importance of Promoting Global Citizenship in Schools in India

By Soujanya Ganig

Goals and Work

I currently work as the National Program Coordinator for the Mission Possible program in India with the World Federation of United Nations (WFUNA). WFUNA is a global non-profit organization which works to strengthen and improve the United Nations by engaging people who share a global mindset and support international cooperation – global citizens.

In its quest to engage global citizens, WFUNA launched 'Mission Possible,' a global citizenship education program for high school students. Over the course of a semester, students participating in Mission Possible acquire global competencies and 21st century skills, learn about the United Nations and the Sustainable Development Goals (SDGs), receive training in project management skills, and most importantly, apply their learning through student-led projects on topics that are important to them and to their communities.

Mission Possible was launched in two cities in India in 2015 and in Armenia in 2016. This July, we are launching the program across three cities in India with the aim of reaching 400 students and are likely to expand the program to Singapore later this year. Moving forward, we hope to expand the program to other cities and reach a wider demographic in India while also launching the program in other countries.

As the National Program Coordinator of the Mission Possible program, I am responsible for the implementation and expansion of the program in India. More specifically, I am involved in the recruitment of schools, curriculum development, teacher and student training, and monitoring student projects and progress.

Global Citizenship Education and 21st Century Skills

Along with providing global citizenship education and training in 21st century skills, the trademark of Mission Possible is the community projects undertaken by students. Students identify a problem they want to address in their community related to one of the 17 SDGs and work on it for 6 months. Through this practice of linking their project to a SDG, students understand that every problem at the local level has global relevance. Developing this worldview among our youth is crucial, especially today, when more and more countries are looking inwards and are propagating the "us versus them" mentality.

Another integral aspect of the program is project management training. While students lead and manage their community projects in their groups, they receive practical tools and techniques which enable them to improve the quality of their project and enhance the impact of their intervention. Students are trained to conduct a community-needs assessment, manage budgets and raise funds, develop a monitoring and evaluation system, and quantify and measure impact among other valuable skills. These project management skills, while highly crucial in the development sector, are also transferable and relevant in any other job.

Impact

In this cycle of Mission Possible we will be directly reaching about 200 students, 15 teachers and 5 school leaders and about 10,000 lives indirectly (through students' community projects) across three cities in India. We are also likely to launch in Singapore later this year. In the next cycle we hope to reach students and teachers across more cities in India and expand to more countries. In the next decade, we are likely to impact at least 10,000 students directly and about 500,000 indirectly.

Challenges and Lessons

My education journey started with the Teach for India fellowship where I taught in an under-resourced public school for two years. Hence, this is the demographic I have always wanted to impact with my work. One of the biggest challenges in my role has been taking Mission Possible to public schools. Since the program is in the pilot phase, we charge schools a fee to run the program which means we cannot take it to under-resourced schools yet.

In an attempt to work around these restrictions, we are exploring various models which would ensure that we can launch in public schools this cycle. One such approach is to try a Robin Hood model which essentially means that if we have enough participants from fee-paying schools, we will be sustainable enough to launch the program at no fee or a subsidized fee for public schools. Working in the education space I have understood that such challenges are everyday realities in the development sector and it is crucial to work around them to do impactful work. One of the early beliefs I held was that numeracy and literacy should be the sole priority of a struggling education system in a developing country. This belief largely emerged from my experience of teaching in a public school with poor learning outcomes, the exposure to a larger discourse within the country about students failing at basic numeracy and literacy tests, and India's poor performance on the assessments administered by the Programme for International Student Assessment of the Organization for Economic Cooperation and Development. When learning outcomes were so abysmal, focusing on 21st century skills or global citizenship education (GCED) seemed indulgent.

My opinion on this matter shifted when I studied International Education and understood the importance of GCED and 21st century skills. And now, working on the curriculum for Mission Possible and preparing to educate students, I am a strong proponent of GCED and 21st century skills being integrated into the mainstream. When I interact with school leaders and teachers about the program, some of them have the skepticism I once had. We work with students between 8th and 12th grade and students in India are expected to take 'Board examinations' in 10th and 12th grade which are high-stakes public exams that decide the future education and career paths of students. As a result, schools are apprehensive about including their 10th and 12th grade students in the program because they want students to focus solely on academics. This mindset is hard to fight as it is emerging more from how the system is designed rather than personal beliefs. We still have a long way to go to integrate GCED into the mainstream. Programs like Mission Possible are crucial in achieving this gradual shift.

Bio

Soujanya Ganig graduated from the International Education Policy Program at the Harvard Graduate School of Education in 2016. She currently works as the National Program Coordinator with the World Federation of United Nations Associations. Previously she has taught at a public school in Delhi as a Teach for India Fellow and has worked with a Member of Parliament in India.

Promoting University Innovation in Latin America and the Caribbean

By Colleen Silva-Hayden

There is immense opportunity for higher education in Latin America and the Caribbean (LAC) to facilitate the advancement of prosperous, democratic, and knowledge-based societies. In the midst of the most economically unequal region in the world, where the most affluent 10% of the population owns 71% of the region's wealth,[73] there is a vibrant generation of youth with new hopes and expectations, including that of a quality college education that will prepare them for a future in which they can thrive as innovators, entrepreneurs, and problem solvers.

While access to higher education has been steadily expanding over the past several decades, quality lags far behind. Even though international university rankings are a poor yard stick for comparison purposes, there is much to glean from the fact that even the most notable universities in the LAC region, such as the University of São Paulo in Brazil or the Pontifical Catholic University of Chile, are not listed among the top 200 higher education institutions (HEIs) in the world. According to a recent report by the World Bank Group, less than 50% of individuals who had started college have completed their studies by the time they are 25-29 years of age.[74] This is staggering loss of human capital and financial resources for families and societies.

---

[73] Bárcena Ibarra, Alicia and Winnie Byanyima. "Latin America Is the World's Most Unequal Region. Here's How to Fix It." 17 Jan, 2016. https://www.weforum.org/agenda/2016/01/inequality-is-getting-worse-in-latin-america-here-s-how-to-fix-it/. Accessed May 25, 2017.

[74] Ferreyra, María Marta, Ciro Avitabile, Javier Botero Álvarez, Francisco Haimovich Paz, and Sergio Urzúa. 2017. *At a Crossroads: Higher Education in Latin America and the Caribbean.* Directions in Development. Washington, DC: World Bank. doi:10.1596/978-1-4648-0971-2.

I lead the University Innovation programs at the Latin American Scholarship Program for American Universities (Laspau), a non-profit affiliate of Harvard University that focuses on improving access, quality and relevance of higher education throughout the LAC region. Every program I manage is deeply enriched by the input of my colleagues and our network of collaborators from universities across the globe. Thus far, I've worked with universities and colleges in fifteen countries across the LAC region to innovate and improve the quality of higher education. Over the course of the past year, the scope of my work has reached over 1,000 higher education professionals from 131 universities across the LAC region, thereby indirectly extending to an estimated 30,000 learners (when making a conservative estimate of thirty students per higher education professional). We operate at this scale by building consortia at the national level.

In Brazil, we have partnered with the Salesian University of São Paulo to develop a consortium of 47 public and private universities focused on innovating STEM and Humanities education. Thus far, professors in the consortium have redesigned over 500 courses to incorporate active learning methodologies. In Panama, my colleagues and I collaborated with Panama's National Council of Rectors to create The STEM Project of Panama through which we brought together a consortium of eleven public and private universities. This year, we are working with Costa Rica's National System for Accreditation of Higher Education to build a consortium of over twenty HEIs that will serve as a national network for scaling innovative practices in higher education.

In addition to constructing consortia and networks of innovation, my colleagues and I work closely with individual institutions. Most recently, we have had the honor of working with one of the oldest universities in the Americas, Universidad Nacional Mayor de San Marcos (UNMSM), whose history began in 1551, long before Harvard. We help to support its goal of re-envisioning its future and how it can better serve the needs of Peru. Twenty-three deans along with the vice presidents came to Cambridge, MA for a three-day university leadership program, during which they learned about best practices and trends for research and institutional transformation.

As a result of this program, the UNMSM is in the process of implementing a general curriculum across all its undergraduate fields of study, numerous deans are pursuing international research collaborations, and the university is cultivating 144 student leaders to grow as innovators, researchers, and potential junior faculty for the future. All of these students are working together on interdisciplinary teams to develop prototypes and solutions to Sustainable Development Goals within their local communities.

These experiences have taught me that it is vital to identify individual change agents within the universities and support them to as leaders that inspire their colleagues and jointly carry out the institutional changes in culture and practice. It might feel great as a practitioner to try to inspire a group of faculty members, but ultimately, the impetus for change has to be championed by internal leaders or else nothing will flourish in the long-run.

I have also learned how essential and easy it is to reach out to leaders and experts in higher education, industry, and government for their assistance. I used to feel that I was being brash or presumptuous by seeking out their help, but looking back, I see that they have been some of the most reliable resources and eager mentors. I will never forget how, without any hesitation, the former Minister of Education of Panama flew to Guatemala and got me a meeting with the Vice President to discuss national goals for STEM education. I had vastly underestimated how responsive leaders from the private sector would be. Collaborating with Microsoft Education and U-Planner, an Ed Tech company, has been one of the most rewarding experiences this year.

Over the next decade, I want to contribute to three key goals. First, I will focus on establishing a regional, annual conference that showcases best practices and trends of innovation in HEIs throughout the LAC region. It will bring together leaders of higher education, alongside key figures from government and industry, to discuss areas of shared interest, common goals and opportunities for collaboration. Moreover, the conference will serve as a platform for building communities of practice across institutions and countries, and for developing the innovation ecosystems throughout the region.

Second, international rankings systems for higher education provide some useful information but, unfortunately, many governments and universities misuse the rankings and place undue importance on them. Some higher education leaders are, in essence, leading to international standardized tests in the absence of their own set of metrics. I plan to work more closely with higher education leaders from universities, ministries, and secretaries of education to develop better metrics for evaluating quality and providing valuable feedback for continuous quality improvement. Even more importantly, I would like to bring together higher education leaders on a regular basis, in select groups, to envision and commit to ambitious and commonly shared societal development goals and joint initiatives that will strengthen them as research institutions. When these same leaders start with the impact they desire to achieve, a more authentic measure of success emerges.

Third, the narrow focus of most undergraduate education in the LAC region simply has to change. It fails to prepare students for the reality of knowledge and innovation based economies. I want to work with as many HEIs as possible to facilitate a transition to curricula that provide depth alongside the breadth of a solid foundation in 21st century skills and competencies that will be relevant throughout students' academic and professional careers.

Bio

Colleen is a Program Manager at the Latin American Scholarship Programs for American Universities (Laspau), a non-profit affiliate of Harvard University. Before returning to Cambridge, Colleen was an Associate Professor in Bogotá, Colombia at the Universidad de Jorge Tadeo Lozano. She holds a M.Ed. in International Education Policy from Harvard University and a B.A. in Sociology from Boston College.

FOUNDATIONS

Introducing a Sense of Possibility in Students and Educators

By Janhvi Maheshwari-Kanoria

Goals and Work

My purpose in education has been to expand access to thoughtfully designed learning experiences and empower other educators to be agents of change. There are no magic wands in education – no patents to protect, no best sellers to win, no diseases to cure. Instead, there are people to motivate – lessons plans to develop, homework to be completed, and assignments to grade. Relentlessly infusing sparkle into the mundane activities of every day, of every classroom, for every child is the only way to transform. We need to help every educator reconnect with his or her calling, empower them to work on something that truly motivates them and gives them small victories.

I started my career with a difficult two-year stint as a high-school teacher. I struggled with, and often succumbed to, the usual failings including following standardized lesson plans, testing for memorization, and poor classroom management. The job and routine of teaching somehow became bigger than the purpose of teaching, and I stopped trusting my instinct on what my students needed.

A defining moment for me was when I realized that my 17-year old students were hopelessly unaware of any current affairs, had absolutely no critical thinking skills, and lacked basic empathy. These were the high-performing students that I had helped score in the high-stakes exams, but these were also students that would be voting citizens in a year and were completely unprepared for that responsibility. I began to have extensive debates on pressing global challenges with my students in order to open their perspectives and generate empathy. The small changes that this had in my students as their awareness and ability to reason developed had a profound impact on me.

I did not know back then that my role was to immerse students in learning experiences that would help them grow as people and my single-minded focus was on academics. I realized that real learning happens in the most unexpected of places and it is easy, even as a committed teacher, to forget your cause. I pledged to spend my career helping other educators rediscover that sense of purpose and through my career I have always designed solutions, keeping in mind what it was like to be a new teacher.

I moved from the classroom to a senior role in the Ministry of Education. After my work on the national strategic review, the pieces of the failing system became clearer and the core underlying issue that I wanted to solve was the insidious challenge of motivation that comes from being born to privilege. We had to think of projects that would reinvigorate the schools, without relying exclusively on the internally jaded resources of the ministry. It was important to bring in international partners, evidence tested projects, and other elements of the civic system together in a practical way to help play their role in changing the system.

The first project was to launch the 32nd branch of the Teach for All Global Network as the first and flagship model in the region. Conventionally, the model focuses on low-income students and bringing talented youth into the teaching profession; we wanted to focus on breaking the deep-rooted family and community boundaries.

Due to the small overall population, our mission was not necessarily to retain people in the teaching profession, but to create an opportunity for the civically conscious youth to develop a deep understanding of the alternate contexts in their country. The project saw a 70% satisfaction rate from the approximately 500 students reached in the pilot year. It is in its fourth year and is growing to mentor all other chapters in the region and expand the number of schools reached. The power of youth's idealism is changing interactions in the classrooms and having unintended consequences across the school as leadership and teachers are getting more confidence to try their own mini-projects of improvement.

For our primary students, we decided to make the controversial decisions to reintroduce the classes of art and library into the timetable. With the student grades decreasing, policy-makers had decided to remove the "extra classes" from the system and focus more on literacy and numeracy. We fought the internal resistance by building a coalition of parties with vested interest and expertise from the outside with support from the thriving Museums Authority, Art Colleges, National Library and Publishing Houses in tandem with the disenfranchised art teachers and school librarians. We introduced revived curricula, which were a lot more practice-based and interesting for students, and within a semester the chronic absenteeism of students which stood at over 24% fell to 12% on the days of art and library classes. The initial success of the program is now being driven by teachers and school leaders to all primary government schools reaching approximately 30,000 children.

Empowered by the success of the initial offerings, my small team of eight began to develop interventions around some of the core challenges regarding school readiness and learning. The data showed that 68%of students were below minimum benchmarks in literacy, Numeracy, and science in international tests and approximately 33% fell below standards in national exams. We realized that failure was cumulative and increasing to about 40% by secondary school, so we decided to focus on primary school and early childhood, this also had the least resistance due to reduced test pressures.

We began with a premise of learning from our stronger schools to support the almost 50% of schools that required urgent attention. Our primary school improvement program focused on literacy (in the local language and English) and numeracy in grades 1-3 in 20 of the lowest performing schools (20% of the total cohort) that encompassed 6,000 students and 460 teachers. We determined that there would be low political appetite for structural changes such as timetable, selection of teachers and curriculum so we decided to focus on initiatives that would improve the current schools, such as coaching and development for teachers and school-leaders, data driven performance culture and resources for teachers. Our project was designed pulling together a predominantly local team that included school and Ministry-based educators with external specialized and consultancy support. The criteria were to find team members that were relatable, open minded, and had a willingness to learn, then coach them with external experts.

There were many internal debates around whether the solution, including the lesson plans developed and coaching support, were perfect or the right answer. We realized that there was never going to be any such perfect solution because ultimately the problem was a multi-faceted one determined by human interaction. We decided to validate our instincts by feedback from implementation and creative thinking. As an example, we initiated a school based performance management team that was quickly replaced by an inter-school principal's support group that continues to operate.

Impact

Over the course of my career, my projects and teaching have reached over 50,000 students, but the most exhilarating work is creating a sense of possibility that helps the weakest of students learn and the most exhausted of educators reinvest.

In the literacy and numeracy project, our initial baselines showed us that only 6% of target students met initial targets, but the determined and persistent support from the team resulted in students improving 10% more than in control schools meaning an additional 1,078 students were either literate, numerate, or both by the end of the year. The bottom quintile students improved the most and there was an over 80% satisfaction rating from teachers and school-leaders. More importantly, the program began building an important bridge over the loss of trust and chasm between the schools and the Ministry. Riding this optimism, we presented the project to the Prime Minister of the country and the program now continues expanding to grades 4 and 5, and is expanding to 10 additional schools.

In other cases, the impact was often around developing purpose and elevating educators. Through my multiple projects, I have worked to support over a 100 educators closely. A centralized and failing system often steals educators of their confidence and lowers the prestige of their career. A large part of my role has been to raise self-esteem and pride and make these educators believe that they can do better. In some cases it is harnessing the motivation of people new to the education field. I once told a team that was really dependent on me, that I would only solve three problems a day so they had to deeply consider what they needed my validation and support for, and what they could do themselves. This had a profound impact on the individuals as they began to trust themselves and began independently solving challenges. Just like the students, adults too needed a champion to believe that they could do more and better!

Challenges

The last seven years have had moments of euphoric inspiration where I believe in my ability to positively impact a child's future and crushing disappointment when faced with political egos and bureaucracy. The two challenges I continue to grapple with are the following.

- Managing the balance between people and impact: Education is about raising and developing individuals and is hinged on personal interactions. While all educators are committed humanitarians, for many of them this calling has gotten masked under many years of corporatized commitments. My continuous strife is that I still naively believe that my focus should be on impact and often working in a bureaucratic system requires managing leadership to make the required change.

- Giving people (including myself) a cause worth fighting for: Early in my career, I had taken on a role of research, strategy and policy translation for the government, as I believed that would have the most structural impact. I realized that I was too far removed from the classroom impact that motivated me to fight for change. Similarly, I noticed the same issue with relation to other leadership positions and educators. In order to ensure longevity to make change "stick," it is important to have people invested in a cause that they deeply care about.

Lessons Learned

As I continue to hone my toolkit some of my lessons have been:

- The most impact we can have is by being razor-focused on improving the school experience, by raising a sense of purpose and by being a champion to educators. The most exhausted of school staff can be bought over by empathy to their context, reducing their administrative burden and enhancing their everyday experience with students

- The only way to bring system change is to demonstrate it and infuse a sense of optimism and ability in all parts of the system, including senior leaders. A good report card is rare for leadership and is often what they desperately need.

- Significant relationships underpin all our work, but they aren't easy to build. Educators are used to being right and not being questioned and the value and prestige associated with education is low. People have disliked me for being ruthlessly focused on impact and making their lives difficult; it is the collateral damage of bringing change.

- Finally, trust your instinct and be creative with solutions – if you care about student learning it will not fail to be a compass to success.

Next Steps:

Improving systems is about sheer hard work but it is grossly inadequate when thinking about the multiple challenges facing our world. We need to go beyond improvement around academics to rethink the broader value of education by taking leaps that are incremental and built of simple core beliefs. I moved to a large foundation to help spearhead this research and development function for innovation in education, expanding my reach to millions of students. My work today includes developing a new action-research driven progressive lab school that hopes to be a beacon for curricular, structural, and pedagogical changes for other schools; working with universities to think about relevant 21st century multi-disciplinary degrees; and developing a comprehensive digital solution to bring low-cost and high-quality education to our students.

Bio

Janhvi-Maheshwari-Kanoria serves as the Education Portfolio Manager to the CEO of the Qatar Foundation, leading the innovation and future-thinking mandate. She previously headed the Vice-Chairperson's Office in the Ministry of Education, leading policy reform and school improvement. She graduated from the International Education Policy program at the Harvard Graduate School of Education in 2010. She also supports NGOs, such as Education Above All, Ektara, and Mantra for Change (where she serves on the Advisory Board).

Empowering Leaders to Advance Educational Opportunity for All Students

By Sandra Licón

Goals and Work

I began my career as a teacher in South Central Los Angeles, where I learned first-hand about the challenges facing some of our most underserved students. What I learned inspired, motivated, and at times angered me and continues to serve as my motivation to advance educational opportunity. Teaching was the best, and hardest, job I will ever have, but after five years in the classroom, I wanted to address systemic barriers and expand opportunity for larger numbers of students through policy.

A couple of years after completing the International Education Policy Program (IEP), I found myself working on US education policy issues at the Bill & Melinda Gates Foundation. While philanthropy can feel very far removed from students and classrooms, working at a foundation provides a unique opportunity to learn with, and from, some of the most innovative leaders working to create better opportunities for students at scale. For eleven years, I have held several roles making grants to partners to expand access for black, Latino, and low-income students to effective teaching, high standards, and innovation. In my last role, I was excited to leverage what I had learned as part of the IEP program, creating partnerships with global funders and educational leaders to accelerate the work of schools in the US. Research shows that high-performing systems and leaders benchmark themselves against successful system practices and purposefully adapt these to fit their own cultural and political contexts. In our work, we supported communities of practice (COPs) that paired innovative US district and state leaders with leaders in high-performing and fast accelerating systems such as Australia, Britain, Columbia, Singapore, Hong Kong, Finland, and Brazil. Participants exchanged lessons about their respective models of teacher preparation and building a professional culture of feedback and continuous improvement amongst teachers. The COPs demonstrated the power of bringing together leaders at

393

various stages in their reform trajectory to learn from each other and from experts. These learning and collaboration opportunities ultimately helped participants reflect on their respective strategies and successfully adopt new practices to improve the quality of teaching and learning.

Impact

Because my work involves empowering leaders of systems in the US and abroad, it is hard to estimate the number of students impacted. For example, one of the COPs involved several US teacher preparation institutions, which collectively train 7,500 teachers annually. In one year those teachers could reach 225,000 to 750,000 students. By contrast, the team from Brazil designed a new teacher induction for 150 teachers in 2016 in the city of Jacarei. This year, the program will serve all beginning teachers, which could impact more than 40,000 students per year.

Challenges

As they reflected on their work, many of the leaders we worked with remarked that one of the most significant challenges to creating meaningful, long-term change is that education systems are built to reinforce the status quo. Unless innovations or policy changes are purposefully designed to affect the important work that happens in classrooms between teachers and students, there will not be meaningful improvement in achievement. It is difficult for even the most ambitious, capable system leaders to adopt evidenced-based innovations that improve teaching and learning at scale. They face a myriad of barriers including a lack of capacity at the local level (whether it be talent or resources) to adopt new practices or garner political capital and trust. Even when leaders can overcome these barriers, they find it difficult to scale innovation system-wide, and in many cases inertia or resistance to change forces systems to revert to old practices.

One surprising challenge I encountered through the global learning work was skepticism among some US leaders to learn from best practice in international systems. While this is changing, there can be a perspective that the US is too unique/complex/large to be able to adapt practices of systems such as Singapore or Finland, which are smaller and have different governance structures. Part of the challenge is a lack of quality opportunities, such as communities of practice, for willing leaders and their teams to learn not just about how other systems approached change, but to understand at a granular level how the changes came about and to get feedback and support to apply those innovations in their context.

We also need to address the lack of diversity and representation of people of color and from underserved communities within leadership levels in philanthropy and parts of the education reform organizations. Innovations are more likely to dramatically improve learning in the most underserved communities when there are leaders who have a real understanding of not just the challenges involved, but also the strengths that could be leveraged and who have credibility to engage stakeholders such as parents, community leaders, or students themselves.

Lessons Learned

One of the most powerful roles for philanthropy is helping system leaders connect with other global leaders and provide high-quality opportunities for learning, reflection and feedback. We were very pleased that a majority of participants in the COPs made tangible changes to their strategies for teacher preparation, based on what they learned. We learned that effective learning opportunities require some key design principles: designing the learning sessions with significant participant input; selecting global leaders able to synthesize and translate their work effectively; active facilitation and support from researchers versed in practice and policy; and support for participants to identify clear problems of practice that get to an instructive level of granularity about similarities in their systems and potential adaptations.

I also believe foundations and reform organizations have a responsibility to commit to directly addressing racial and socioeconomic inequity and to increase the diversity of their leadership and programmatic teams. There are several foundations, such as Atlantic Philanthropies and Ford, who have made ambitious commitments and are moving in this direction and from whom others could learn. Organizations like Hispanics in Philanthropy are working to help foundations connect with more diverse candidates, as well as with local organizations directed by leaders of color who have deep roots and credibility in their communities. Ultimately, I think each of us working to address educational inequity has a responsibility to be purposeful about empowering the voices of those we seek to serve in our work.

Bio

Sandra Licón graduated from the International Education Policy Program at the Harvard Graduate School of Education in 2003. Sandra's career has been focused on improving educational outcomes for the most vulnerable students. In her current role at the Bill & Melinda Gates Foundation, Sandra builds global partnerships with funders and educational leaders to identify best practices in teaching and learning to accelerate the work of school networks, districts, and states in the US. Prior to working at the foundation, Sandra worked with a variety of non-profits, system leaders, and social entrepreneurs to address educational inequity in their countries and around the world. Sandra started her career as an elementary school teacher in South Central Los Angeles and Long Beach, California.

Facing our Failure to Promote Pluralism

By Zahra Kassam

About 12 years ago, during a workshop for community mobilizers in Mozambique, I had a conversation with a young woman named Angela. At 22, Angela was among the most educated in her village. She had finished primary school and earned a two-year health certificate. I had been working closely with Angela and her colleagues for a year on community-driven education and health programs in Qissanga and Ibo, remote districts in the coastal province of Cabo Delgado, Mozambique. The Aga Khan Foundation (AKF) had recently initiated the Coastal Rural Support Program (CRSP) in what, by most accounts, was one of the most destitute regions of the country, which itself was among the lowest-ranking countries for human development. At the dawn of the 21st century, most villages in Qissanga had no running water, no electricity and no paved roads. One in four children died before their fifth birthday; more than half of all children were malnourished; over 80% of youth and adults were illiterate; and average life expectancy was under 40 years. In the rainy season, it could take an entire day to travel a few kilometers from one village to another. What education and health infrastructure existed was dilapidated and under-resourced at best. Despite these distressing conditions, Angela and her colleagues, in collaboration with the government and village elders, were making great strides to improve the quality of life of the people in their communities.

While Angela celebrated the project's demonstrable early progress and shared in her team's excitement about the potential longer-term impact on local communities, she was wrestling with what seemed to be much more personal matters – ones which posed significant hurdles to her life and work. During our brief but important conversation, Angela shared with me her struggles with racial discrimination, the barriers she faced as a second-language learner, her difficulties navigating tribal conflict and pressure, and the abuse she faced at home for earning more than her husband. Our conversation echoed of issues faced by people, not only in rural Mozambique, but also in many other communities around the world. I realized that while I was addressing programmatic challenges (ones that I could manage for the bottom line numbers), the

397

challenges on the ground were profoundly more personal for Angela and were silently undermining development and progress. Between the lines of my conversation with Angela were layers of complexity that spoke of difference and human dignity, and ultimately, of our collective failure as a society to understand and embrace one another.

Throughout my career, I have been fortunate to work with, and learn from people—students, teachers, parents, government leaders, activists, and artists who, like Angela, are deeply invested in the progress of their communities and countries. Together, we have supported efforts that have reached over 100,000 direct beneficiaries and worked on policies and initiatives that have indirectly touched many more. Over the years, I have gleaned much about leadership from my colleagues–particularly, how we move people and complex organizations towards progress. However, there is one gross leadership challenge – personal, institutional, and systemic – which threatens peace and progress around the world: namely, our *ongoing failure to advance pluralism through our education systems and the communities and organizations that support them*. It's an area that I have focused on for the last ten years – initially through efforts with the Aga Khan Development Network, which does critical work to promote pluralism, and more recently through various endeavors which seek to bring youth together across difference to experience lived pluralism, and support them to be agents of change in their home communities.

Around the world, going to school no longer means getting an education. One only has to look at the daily headlines to realize that our collective gains in educational access are vacuous and inadequate, without a focus on quality and pluralism. Our children are growing up in a world that is characterized by deep ignorance, anger and intolerance. Changing demographics coupled with globalization, vulnerable economies, growing populism and political rancor continue to polarize our communities and exacerbate our differences—seeding conflict and giving rise to extremism. How we educate our young people in today's fragile and contentious global environment has considerable implications for future generations. In order for them to become fully active citizens with well-grounded ethics, we must ensure that our children receive a broad and inclusive education in the arts, sciences, technology and the humanities—an education that provides them with the knowledge, skills and values that enable them to thrive, embrace diversity, negotiate ambiguity and complexity, adapt to change and champion the principles that support progress and peace.

Education for pluralism requires us to take measures both small and grand. While much has been written of leadership, a few relevant lessons resonate for me:

1. *Be clear about both purpose and values.* The work of education is value-laden. It requires personal conviction, determination and clarity of vision. A clearly articulated purpose—that higher call to action that forces us to think and act beyond ourselves for the greater good—is essential. When everyone in an organization has commitment to a common vision, they are driven and empowered to make decisions that actualize it.

2. *Lead by example.* As leaders, we have an obligation to acknowledge that we are learners ourselves and that we too must examine our own prejudice, bias and assumptions that influence the way in which we govern our institutions. This awareness and ownership sets a tone and example, and can help to create a culture that is inclusive and respectful, while promoting reflective practice and continuous improvement and growth.

3. *People matter.* People matter in the most fundamental sense, from the authentic engagement of individuals and communities (parents, teachers, heads, community leaders) in the work of reform, to the mobilization and empowerment of staff to execute goals. Recruiting a diverse base of staff and volunteers—people who complement each other in background, perspective and skill—investing in their development, and ensuring that they have the space, agency and voice to innovate and actualize goals is critical.

4. *Invest in the development of strong institutions.* How we advance pluralism and quality educational opportunities over the long term is complex. It requires the building of institutional infrastructures that are dynamic and resilient – ones that are governed transparently, are sustainable over time, and which allow for innovation and adaptation.

5. *Build strong partnerships.* The systems that many of us work in tend to be in poor communities constrained for resources (people, funds and time). Despite seemingly grim conditions, however, we find inspired communities around the world that are passionate about the futures of their children; dedicated and driven staff who are willing to go to great lengths to ensure children are given opportunities; and partners who are keen to advance shared goals. Stitching together the support of multiple stakeholders – communities, government, civil society, and the private sector – that are deeply invested in the mission can help protect against fickle funders, changes in political priorities and evolving socio-economic conditions.

I walked out of graduate school having learned much more than I remembered to use. In my own journey, I am often reminded of the passage from Deuteronomy, "*We drink from wells we did not dig; we are warmed by fires we did not kindle.*" We benefit from the work of those who have come before us in ways that we do not always know or foresee. If we are lucky, perhaps we too can each contribute to advancing worthy, inclusive and compassionate values, ones that will underpin the futures of our children and contribute towards progress, development, peace and democracy around the world.

Bio

Zahra Kassam graduated from Harvard's International Education Policy master's program in 2000. Zahra works with organizations to advance pluralism and access to high quality education opportunities. She is co-founder and Executive Director of Common Ground Youth Collaborative and previously worked at the Aga Khan Foundation and the Ford Foundation.

Honesty and Transparency are Necessary in the Education Sector

By Anne Elizabeth Hand

Goals and Work

When I think about my career in education, and where I have come in the past ten years, I admit that my initial professional goals were to simply to keep learning and stay engaged as much as I possibly could, with as many projects as I could. Education is a world of possibility, and I felt as though I would be doing a disservice to others to limit what those possibilities could be in my own work, whether they were policy-based, operational, research, or directly teaching.

Now, my goals are to use this sector-level experience to work on projects that can directly inform public policy related to equity and inclusion. I work on projects that try and change people's habits, so they can better use the opportunities that targeted, culturally appropriate, education strategies will give them. This ranges from school-based literacy projects for teachers, children, and youth, to non-school-based financial education for adults. I am fortunate to have challenging and interesting projects with colleagues I learn from every day. I still choose projects that make me think, *"That's a different idea. Will it work?"*

Impact

All the projects I have worked on have been different, and the impact of these kinds of interventions is hard to predict. I have a broad idea how many learners have been directly and indirectly influenced by my work, but not specific numbers: maybe ten thousand learners in the last year directly? Tens of thousands in the past few years? A ballpark total of a hundred thousand over the course of the past ten years? Some projects are short-lived, and some last for many years after my participation ends. It is almost impossible to know which projects will be able to grow, flourish, and continue doing good work that many people can significantly benefit from.

401

Challenges

Challenges I face are centered around a lack of vision and focus for organization-based projects. An organization with a mission statement that is too broad, for example, will have trouble prioritizing its projects in a strategic way with limited resources. An organization with competing priorities will quickly lose focus and its staff will lose motivation. At their core, however, I have learned that both a lack of vision and focus are symptomatic of a leadership void from those at the top.

Lessons Learned

This brings me to some concrete lessons I have learned along the way, that center around the importance of professional transparency and honesty. For example, I used to have a boss. He was charismatic, well-regarded in his sector, and considered a leader. He was supposed to take a socially relevant nonprofit, and grow it to scale. After a few months on the job, he asked me in private, one day when we were stuck in traffic coming or going from a meeting, if I would be interested in working with him on a side project.

At the time, he did not give me all the details. It was taking clients from our nonprofit and offering them complementary services from his own business, to encourage their continued relationship with the nonprofit.

I didn't say 'no,' which he took as a 'yes.' Soon, the two projects bled together in an uncomfortable way; it was clear I was not the right person to participate in this kind of double dipping. There were other people at work who could, and did, which was fine. Nobody had signed a non-compete or similar agreement, and if everything got done what did it matter? Then my boss's boss found out, and my boss did not last much longer after that. One thing is what you *can* do, and another thing is what you *should* do.

This is not a cautionary tale, since everyone has their own version of it. It is one example of the reality we face in our working lives – gray areas that are difficult to navigate professionally and ethically. I had been working for quite a few years before any job gave me a mandatory ethics protocol to follow. I was shocked, because it would have served me well so many years before.

In the education and social sectors, we are scrutinized and held to a higher standard than in most sectors. We need to take a finely-tuned ethical compass with us everywhere we go. It is essential for our relationships with all project stakeholders, from the learners who are our ultimate beneficiaries, to our funders who deserve accountability. If we do not use this compass, we will not last long. It is imperative to take our most ethical selves with us to work every day.

The principles that have served me best in the long term are honesty and transparency. Honesty, because personal reputation and work ethic are what keep you employed in this sector. Transparency, because most people in our globalized work environments appreciate someone who works with confidence, and takes responsibility, if things do not go according to the plan.

Now, this is easy. To work in a way that is aligned with my values, to try to leave the world a little better than the way I found it, is a luxury. Most people are not able to determine their professional future in such a congruent way. It is no sacrifice to keep my ethical and moral compass pointed in the right direction.

My experience now allows me to say 'no,' with confidence. I can gauge situations and people better, and be sure when something is not right in a way that could jeopardize the integrity of our project. In not immediately saying 'no' to my former boss's offer, I was exposed to a full cycle of the "what-could-have-beens," and most definitely the "what-not-to-dos."

We need to be honest and transparent in our work, every day, to continue working in a way that is fun, exciting, challenging, and, hopefully, leaves people in a better place than where they began.

Bio

Anne Hand specializes in education and skills-related program design, implementation, and evaluation for the public and private sectors in the Americas. She has consulted with a variety of public and private organizations including the Inter-American Development Bank, TetraTech ARD, and Hispanics in Philanthropy. She graduated from the International Education Policy Program at the Harvard Graduate School of Education in 2011.

Shaping policy through research in the United Arab Emirates

By Susan Kippels

Goals and Work

Being a part of the 2013 International Education Policy (IEP) class at the Harvard Graduate School of Education (HGSE) helped to shape who I am as a person as well as where I am professionally. Prior to the IEP program, my work in education had predominately been in the classroom. While I had taught in multiple countries, my knowledge about international education policy and research was limited. A master's from HGSE not only provided me with the necessary skills and network to enter the education policy field, but also the confidence to address new challenges and the ability to share what I have learned with others.

At HGSE, I took many courses, worked in internships, gave presentations and participated in research projects that provided me with the qualifications to enter the education policy and research sector where I currently work. In addition to the practical skillset, IEP provided me with the network to both learn about and connect to relevant international organizations. It was following a conversation with Professor Fernando Reimers about my hope to return to work in the Middle East that he connected me to the Sheikh Saud bin Saqr Al Qasimi Foundation for Policy Research, the organization where I am working today.

I have worked at the Al Qasimi Foundation for the past four years, and I am currently the Acting Research Manager. At the Foundation, I have been able to work on a variety of education projects, receive a wide range of professional development opportunities, and take on greater responsibility and new roles. While the Al Qasimi Foundation is based in Ras Al Khaimah, the northernmost emirate of the United Arab Emirates (UAE), much of our work relates to, or has implications for, education quality in the wider Middle East region. There are approximately 30 people working fulltime at the Foundation, and three of those individuals fall under my direct supervision, as well as a number of interns and research assistants.

In addition to programmatic work, some of the research areas that I have been able to focus on include gender in education, private education, Arab migrant teachers, and philanthropy in education. As the Al Qasimi Foundation falls under the patronage of the Ruler of Ras Al Khaimah, our research findings are often communicated directly to the local and national government, including to the Ministry of Education. I have also presented our research at regional and international conferences, such as a regional International Labor Organization (ILO) conference in Doha, Qatar and at a Gulf Research Meeting (GRM) workshop in Cambridge, England. All of our research is made available for free in English and Arabic on our website in the form of policy or working papers, many of which I have been able to contribute to.

In my application to the IEP program, I wrote about my desire to support females in education in the Middle East. Contrary to the stereotype I had before enrolling in IEP of girls globally falling behind in education, much of our research on gender at the Al Qasimi Foundation focuses on the underachievement of males (as an extension of research conducted by the Foundation's Executive Director). Across the Gulf region, boys underperform girls on national and international assessments, such as the Program for International Student Assessment (PISA). Research also shows that boys have lower enrollment rates than girls in higher education. One of my favorite things about my work at the Foundation is that we also actively seek to bridge the often talked about gap between research and programmatic work and policy. For example, following the Al Qasimi Foundation's research into boys' lower education attainment and achievement in the UAE, the research department piloted a program specifically to help at-risk boys in public schools, adapted from a successful program run in Australia.

As well as supporting at-risk youth males, we also run a professional development program for local educators. The Al Qasimi Foundation has been running a demand-driven teacher and principal professional development program since 2010. Courses are free for public and private school teachers in the emirate. I have co-taught some of these courses and, so far, over 500 teachers have participated. While external experts developed and ran the first semester-long courses, the program is self-sustaining as participating educators from the local community are trained to be instructors and then train the next instructors, with the support of the Foundation. The teachers and principals who participate in our professional development classes return to their schools and make positive changes to improve the lessons delivered to students, both in the UAE and internationally as many educators are expatriates who eventually return to teach in their home countries.

Impact

Overall, the Al Qasimi Foundation's capacity development programs and policy research work has directly affected thousands of individuals from all over the world, as well as tens of thousands more indirectly. The Al Qasimi Foundation's policy research has a wide-reaching impact, particularly in the UAE K-12 education system, which serves approximately a million students (2014-15 academic year figure). Our work not only creates public records of educational policy in a country that is less than 50 years old, but also influences policy decisions through establishing platforms to discuss issues and ensuring research findings are widely shared.

Challenges

While the work is rewarding, there are leadership challenges associated with being a professional expatriate in the UAE, including the hierarchical structures. There have been challenges for me moving into a very hierarchical system where titles and positions may, at times, provide individuals with complete authority; this is in contrast to countries like the United States where, in general, workplaces are more horizontal. This sometimes makes it not only more difficult for me to have my voice heard, but also to encourage team members to speak up and share their opinions. Secondly, while I have a multicultural background and had studied Arabic before moving to the UAE, I still encounter unique cultural differences that can challenge my work in the education sector.

Lessons Learned

To mitigate some leadership challenges, I have learned a number of things, particularly about the importance of fostering relationships. For those working in education leadership anywhere in the world, relationships are vital as education is inherently about people. Whether you are asking a principal for access a school to distribute a survey, requesting that upper management listen to your idea, scheduling a meeting with a policymaker, asking a coworker to write a report, or teaching a class, the interactions you have leave a lasting impression. In addition to this, within a team setting, I have found that it is important to be open to learning from others and to foster an environment where ideas can be shared.

Once relationships are shaped, it is important to continue to take the time to hear and learn from others, especially when exploring areas of research, addressing issues or learning more about the local context. Problems and their solutions cannot be "cut and paste" from different countries, and the people you work with have unique insight and perspectives about causes and solutions. I have learned that communicating and encouraging brainstorming with team members can lead to innovative solutions that otherwise might not have been considered. People who know the local context can also alert you to the best way to proceed in line with specific cultural contexts.

Another lesson I have learned throughout my time in the UAE is that it is important to support anyone who is working to better education, whether they are part of your team or not, and to encourage others to do the same. At the Al Qasimi Foundation, the research team responds to all inquiries and will provide any support possible to those who are looking to support education, even if we have never met them or have no affiliation.

There were some internal conflicts between individuals and groups of people in my cohort at HGSE, and I believe some of this was because people became focused on advancing themselves and may have lost sight of the bigger goal. At the time, I did not know how to articulate this or what to do besides feel frustrated. In retrospect, I wish I had taken more of a leadership role and tried to encourage the group to focus on what was important. It is not about who receives credit, but about what impact actions make in the educational achievement of others. Today, in the UAE, I continue to use what I learned while studying in Massachusetts to support access to quality education, and I am incredibly proud to be a part of a much larger network of IEP alumni working around the world to achieve the same goal.

Bio

Susan Kippels graduated from the International Education Policy Program at the Harvard Graduate School of Education in 2013. She is the Acting Research Manager at the Sheikh Saud bin Saqr Al Qasimi Foundation for Policy Research in Ras Al Khaimah, United Arab Emirates. Prior to this, Susan conducted education research for UNICEF, worked with an international non-governmental organization in Uganda and managed a private sector business in Lebanon.

Made in the USA
Middletown, DE
05 September 2017